BRADDOCK'S COMPLETE GUIDE TO
HORSE-RACE SELECTION AND BETTING

BRADDOCK'S COMPLETE GUIDE TO HORSE-RACE SELECTION AND BETTING

WITH STATISTICAL INFORMATION BY 'TRAINERS RECORD'

PETER BRADDOCK

LONGMAN   LONDON AND NEW YORK

Longman Group Limited,
Longman House, Burnt Mill, Harlow,
Essex CM20 2JE, England
Associated Companies throughout the World

*Published in the United States of America
by Longman Inc., New York*

© Longman Group Limited 1983

First published 1983

British Library Cataloguing in Publication Data
Braddock, Peter
   Braddock's complete guide to horse race selection
and betting.
   1. Horse race betting – Handbooks, manuals, etc.
   I. Title
   798.4'01   SF331

   ISBN 0-582-50305-1

Library of Congress Cataloging in Publication Data
Braddock, Peter, 1930–
   Braddock's complete guide to horse race selection
and betting.

   Bibliography: p.
   Includes index.
   1. Horse race betting. 2. Horse-racing. I. Title.
II. Title: Complete guide to horse race selection and
betting.   III. Title: Horse race selection and betting.
SF331.B73 1983   798.4'01   82-17922
ISBN 0-582-50305-1

Printed in Singapore by
Kyodo Shing Loong Printing Industries Pte Ltd

Betting, Backers and Bookmakers

'Never in the field of human endeavour
has so much been given
by so many
to so few'

CONTENTS

FOREWORD

The millions of racing fans who either daily or weekly invest their pounds on the horses come in many shapes and sizes as do their bets. As someone who has lived with the betting ideal for two decades, it is easy to identify the born winners and born losers.

The racetrack and the betting shop are a minefield through which the backer must move in order to survive. Either painful lessons are acted upon or the result is certain penury.

The borderline between the poorhouse and prosperity where gambling is concerned is a thin one. But the serious backer needs to discipline himself to avoid the obvious pitfalls.

I believe that over the years, as the wounds have healed, I have managed an ad-hoc safety system. Peter Braddock, by contrast, in his *Guide to Horse-Race Selection and Betting*, has systematically laid down rules which he has found helpful in his own considerable success as a selector of horses.

The size of the work should not scare the reader. Logic is the thread which runs through these pages; common sense and analytical care the criteria for employing his thoughts.

Only the serious person should apply. Racing success only comes to those willing to work at it. As Fred Hooper, breeder of the year for 1982 in the United States said at the Eclipse Awards in San Francisco in February 1983, 'People say I'm lucky, it's true, I'm very lucky. In fact, the harder I work, the luckier I get'.

I think that speech is the most appropriate sentence or two I could use to apply to Peter Braddock's magnum opus. Luck comes to those prepared to work for it. I can guarantee that from the minute I changed my own approach from that of the lazy guesser to the keen form student, the winners began to roll in.

While it might be inappropriate to add my own private coda to someone else's work, I feel I must.

Two rules I always follow. Never bet odds-on, though I realise that a 5–4 on chance with nothing to beat on the Braddock system could for others be a betting proposition par excellence.

Second, never be afraid to win too much. I have found that when a horse is a better price than your research tells you it should be, the appropriate action is to increase your bet. If much shorter than you think, either drastically reduce or even abandon it. You will find that even a winner below the expected odds causes little irritation to the disciplined backer.

But now I leave you in the capable hands of Peter Braddock, and also the superb statistical tables of Peter Jones of *Trainer's Record*. They will give you plenty of food for thought, and just the right mixture of awareness and dexterity to win the battle with the bookies.

Good luck, work hard and accept the rewards which will follow.

Tony Stafford
Racing Editor
Daily Telegraph
1983

BIOGRAPHY OF PETER BRADDOCK

Peter Braddock, born 1931 in Northamptonshire, England, was educated at Wellington Public School and later Sandhurst. He began an association with horses at an early age, learning to ride when he was 5 years old, and maintained this contact throughout his formative years, being drawn into the sphere of race riding by the end of his late teens. He rode under both codes of racing as an amateur from 1949 to 1956 when a serious motor accident caused him to be invalided from military service and also abruptly end his race-riding career. After quite a long period of convalescence Peter returned to his family's country home where he began taking part in the management of his father's farming interests. The gradual recovery to health brought with it the desire to renew an active interest in racing that he fulfilled by gaining a permit licence to train a few horses.

This Peter Braddock did until 1961 when the opportunity arose for him to move to South Africa and manage the famous Stellenbosch Stud of H. P. Templeman. He quickly applied his abilities to this new task and the stud flourished even more successfully under his management. During this time he was writing articles on and about racing in the *South African Breeders Journal* and also served as a freelance racing correspondent contributing weekly articles in the *Cape Town Herald*.

In 1972, owing to the death of his father, Peter Braddock returned to England to take full control of his family's agricultural interests. The lure of racing, however, remained a magnetic influence in his life, and he was encouraged to reforge his links with English racing by entering into the ownership of a number of horses under both rules of racing. This involvement reawakened his interests in the selection and betting aspects of racing, and during this period of ownership Peter supplemented his income with many successful betting ventures.

While most people are content merely to rest on the laurels of their success, Peter Braddock has an enquiring mind which does not allow him such easy options. He therefore decided to write this book, analysing and documenting the approaches that were constantly responsible for producing successful selection/betting results, and hoping the reader may benefit in all aspects by applying the methods carefully outlined.

INTRODUCTION

The writing of this book has arisen in response to bitter-sweet experiences that have resulted from betting-selection decisions made with regard to horse-racing.

Its aim is simple – to promote the rational process of picking winners against the ever present temptation to gamble wildly, thus abandoning the principles of logical thought.

It begins by posing the essential question 'To bet or not to bet', vividly portraying the intrinsic possibilities facing anyone who accepts the challenge of betting before resolving to its main function of being a comprehensive betting selection manual. This manual identifies and analyses the factors responsible for producing successful selection results encapsulating these elements in an original and easy-to-apply **selection formula**. The selection formula stands as the foundation-stone of the manual, defining positively the practical principles upon which to base a selection.

The principles of selection are simple, encompassing four basic issues: **Form, Fitness, Class, Conditions,** with these carefully separated and refined elements serving consistently and continuously as a reliable framework to which each selectors may subject their personal race assessment for an objective scrutiny. The formula is application rather than seeking to limit the ability and individuality of each selector in a subservience to dogma, promotes the questioning of assumptions, the establishing of facts and encourages a development in the powers of logical reasoning.

The book makes no claim to hold the key to obtaining an easy or instant fortune from betting; rather it seeks to make perfectly clear that in the prediction of future events the only certainty is the existence of uncertainty.

It does, however, provide a reliable framework for the thorough understanding of horse-racing. By this means and by the backer's own application to the task can the bookmakers' advantage be nullified. Then, and only then, will a regular profit from horse-racing become a reality.

ACKNOWLEDGEMENTS

We are indebted to the following for permission to use copyright material:

The Jockey Club and Daily Mail for our Figs. 5.1, 5.2 and the race-cards featured in Chapter 10; The Jockey Club and The Sporting Life for our Figs 5.3 and 5.4; Sporting Chronicle Publications Limited and Raceform Limited for our Fig. 5.5; Timeform and Portway Press for our Fig. 5.6; and Ed Byrne for all the photographs.

Cover photograph by Ed Byrne

1 TO BET OR NOT TO BET

'To bet or not to bet', that is the question forever facing the backer. It is the challenge constantly present before every betting decision, for which the resolved course of action will reveal the two opposing influences vying for dominance within the personality of the backer. One promotes an attitude that demands calculated acts of judgement reign supreme, this shall be defined as *betting*. It is represented by the character to be called the *bettor* who symbolizes harmony between action and decision. The opposing attitude promotes irrational uncalculated emotion as its standard response to each betting situations and will be defined as *gambling*. It is represented by the character to be called the *punter* whose inept blunderings and dissarray is the role most frequently associated with all who bet money on horse-races.

It may unequivocally be said that risking money on the prediction of horse-races provides a most formidable test of the backer's courage and judgement, unmercilessly scrutinizing their quality by subjecting them to the irrefutable reality of results. Successfully executed, betting serves as the finest demonstration of co-ordination between action and decision personifying the ease of winning money. In contrast, unsuccessful acts of betting usually display a marked lack of such co-ordination and instead portray all the weaknesses of the gambling approach, emphasizing only the uncertainty in horse-race prediction and the ease of losing money.

The question 'To bet or not to bet' while presenting the backer with a continual dilemma contains within it, a vital factor – *choice* – which basically distinguishes the attitude of the bettor from that of the punter. A choice exists in every calculation and act throughout the selection and betting process. Correct choices pass unnoticed, unrecognized, they are taken for granted and only the uncomfortable experience of being incorrect brings the realization that an alternative existed. The bettor however, always remains aware of choice, for it establishes free will, judgement and self-control as the seat of his power, he alone decides whether or not to bet, and what, when and how to bet. The punter, conversely, is oblivious of having a choice to gamble, for without self-control the 'punters' choice' is but a compunction to bet that has become an insatiable desire in pursuit of an untenable goal.

Having outlined the two opposite poles of influence vying for supremacy within the personality, a detailed description of each represented by the characters of the bettor and the punter will illustrate the potential paths of strength and weakness that lie open to the backer.

THE BETTOR

WHAT OR WHO IS THE BETTOR?

The bettor is the character to which to aspire and who presides in the realm of betting by the nature of his confident precise actions that are the sequel to his reasoned concise decisions. The bettor is flexible in action yet unyielding in judgement, able to adapt to circumstance because he remains emotionally unattached to any viewpoint. The bettor therefore remains calm and aloof, unaffected by the confusion, panic and rumour that generally prevail among the betting fraternity where the common prevading fear is that 'someone knows something more than I know'. The bettor is unmoved by such speculation, assured in his well-considered judgement he is able to 'let go', abandoning himself to his fate, unsurprised at whatever the outcome and fully prepared to accept the consequences of his actions.

WHY THE BETTOR BETS

The bettor bets always with the sole purpose of winning money. Betting exists for the bettor as an activity with a clearly defined and limited aim, a concern only for the results obtained from betting rather than any strong attraction to being involved in the activity itself. Betting is considered as a financial investment of the highest risk money with the possibility of most lucrative returns. The bettor understands that having made a decision and placed a bet his involvement is complete, it is the irreversible step with nothing to be gained from hearing or watching the race except as an impartial objective observer gaining information for future reference.

WHEN THE BETTOR BETS

The bettor bets only when in his judgement making a bet is most favourable. It is always then an act of free will solely in response to the merits of the situation as he attempts to face the reality of the moment rather than escape from it. The bettor, therefore, never bets with a desire to suddenly change or escape from his immediate circumstances, i.e.: (i) to get rich quick, risking all on one race to win a fortune or end bankrupt; (ii) as a reaction to a disappointing result or series of results with a desperate bet in the next race or 'getting out' stakes.

HOW THE BETTOR BETS

The bettor bets with complete self-honesty, taking sole responsibility for all his actions and decisions. He does not make excuses for his errors in judgement by blaming others (i.e. the jockey, the horse or the trainer) but seeks to improve upon it, accepting that before the result was known this was his best considered decision. The bettor bets impassively, intent on dwelling only in the present, 'the now', not influenced to chase past losses or fantasize over 'might have beens' or hoped-for future winnings. The bettor is freed of the hopes, doubts and fears which straddle each betting act and then dulls and perverts judgement. He acts in the wisdom of insecurity, aware of the uncertainty that exists in betting and so remains attached to nothing whether it be money, pride or ego. There is nothing left for the bettor to lose and so he has the flexibility to adapt to changes of circumstances, changing opinion or maintaining a loyalty only to the dictate of his judgement.

The bettor bets expecting to win but prepared to lose (he does not bet above his limit), and so winning comes as a gratefully accepted bonus while losing is not unforeseen or a financial tragedy. Unbowed in defeat yet humble in victory neither bring the bettor intense sorrow nor lasting pleasure because he realizes that both are but opposite sides of the same coin with neither potentially more dominant than the other. The bettor bets resolute in the purpose of winning money, with betting being an activity that plays an important role in his life without ever ruling his entire existence.

THE PUNTER

WHAT OR WHO IS THE PUNTER?

The punter is the character to avoid becoming, appearing as he does a victim in the world of gambling on horse-races. The punter, allured by and initially attracted to the prospect of winning money, is therefore quite easily depressed, disheartened and disappointed at the actuality of losing, but nevertheless retains such a fascination for the involvement in gambling that he becomes mesmerized within its spell. The punter of such unbounding commitment quickly becomes entangled in illogical reckless acts that are always the reflex response to his tentative decisions. Gambling is the self-indulgence of the punter and serves to portray a person lacking in judgement and uncontrolled in action, who is a convinced and convicted loser striving desperately to be a constant winner.

The predicament of the punter is found most markedly in the person afraid or unaware of their lack of judgement yet who paradoxically seeks to subject it to the sternest possible test as is provided by betting on the result of horse-races. In such circumstances it is not surprising to observe the punter exemplifying an attitude of confusion and irrationality, unbalanced contrasts of rash boldness, and diffident timidity, languid flexibility fluctuating with adamant obstinacy as he appears like a leaf being tossed in the wind of events. The punter may then be seen as capricious and indecisive because his feelings and reasoning are always in conflict, and he is confident only in the self-deception that all his immense efforts are directed towards winning. This misguided belief stands as solace for the punter and the justification for his continuous acts of self-indulgence in betting enterprises.

WHEN THE PUNTER GAMBLES

The punter gambles whenever he can no longer resist the temptation. It is never an impassive act, but always as a response to retrieve past losses or fulfil a dream of having a big win. The punter gambles always in an attempt and with a desire to avoid rather than confront his predicament or the reality of the moment.

The punter usually presumes to gamble with the object of winning money, yet any close examination of his actions and approach quite belie this assertion. Initially, perhaps, and also after a serious bout of losing when monetary pressures become acute, it is that winning becomes the punter's immediate only aim – for essentially the punter gambles for thrills. The magnetizing attraction is the excitement, the emotional involvement in the action which sets the adrenalin flowing as the punter listens to the commentary in the betting office or else witnesses the race live, shouting home the finishers at the racecourse. The punter rejoices in taking part in acts of gambling, whether rushing frantically to the betting-office counter or scurrying between bookmakers in 'the ring' at the racecourse to get the best odds. Winning for the punter is only the infrequent happening whose future promise keeps him hooked to gambling, often coming at just the right moment to avoid financial disaster and then providing the vital encouragement to continue gambling. However, personal participation in gambling is the essential quality which the punter savours for it allows him to see the physical unfolding of judgement, with his viewpoint upheld or denied by the result. A victory signals a fleeting reassurance, even elation, yet only to be followed by the anti-climax of facing the same test in the next race with the fearful prospect of familiar defeat. The punter from this level of involvement obtains the intensity of experience for which he yearns as he is thrown between peaks of euphoria and troughs of accustomed depression.

HOW THE PUNTER GAMBLES

The punter gambles devoid of any degree of self-honesty, willing to take the credit for being correct but unwilling to accept the responsibility for being incorrect. The punter's typical response after winning is to tell everyone what a 'certainty' the horse was, while after losing he lies to himself and everyone else saying how he did not really fancy the horse anyway, but someone twisted his arm to make him back it. The punter then continues to bemoan his luck, and seeking someone to blame accuses the jockey, trainer or owner of being crooked and not wanting to win as an excuse or justification for his original decision. The punter is never satisfied: even if he wins he wishes he had staked more on the horse and if he loses, well, he wishes he had not staked so much and then begins indulging, seemingly with delight, in masochistic recrimination for his actions. The punter gambles by placing at risk – whether it be his money, pride or reputation – the things most dear to him and that which he is least prepared to lose. When he gambles the punter demands emotional intensity that can only be gained by backing at the maximum level of stakes, getting a tremendous exciting charge from this daring but remaining unprepared for the consequences of failure and instead blithely hoping for success. Gambling with this level of commitment is a precarious activity, the realization of which causes the punter to suddenly become fearful and seek the most incongruous element within the scope of prediction – certainty. Gambling – if not before this, definitely now with this desire hoisted upon it – contrives to become an exceedingly complicated activity for the punter. He loses all faith in his own ability and judgement but instead turns to blindly follow the views of others. He either accepts the most widely held opinion (i.e. typified by the short odds-on chance) or else decides to seek inspiration by delving into the obscure and follow the most tenuously based assumptions (i.e. usually outsiders at long odds who have only the remotest chances of winning). The punter having once sunk to this level is completely at the mercy of fortune or luck, having abandoned his judgement yet wanting to take part in an activity requiring the most precise use of judgement. The punter then gambles expecting and fearing to lose and only vaguely hoping to win, with losing in fact coming almost as a relief for it is a familiar reassurance compatible with his accepted role as a loser.

The punter, however, despite the constant rebuffs of losing and only infrequent encouragement from rare wins retains a compelling itch to gamble. This becomes an obsessive habit that rules his life, sentencing him to an endless, fruitless quest of trying to be a winner.

These are the graphic descriptions of the developed potential of each character. In practice the backer, rather than permanently residing in one role or maintaining unswervingly one attitude, is likely to fluctuate between the two approaches, more easily being drawn into the weak acts of the punter rather than aspiring to the strong posture of the bettor. The backer faced with the daunting challenge from these competing forces either grows in stature from the encounter or else shrinks from its intractability as awareness, courage and judgement are placed on trial. Betting viewed in this light displays the predispositions of the backer which determine whether he plays the role of the bettor or the punter. The bettor's task being both arduous and awesome demands that *whoever* fills the role be acute in awareness and judgement. The punter's part makes no such demands and attracts the backer who is deficient in both. The bettor is confident and relaxed, certain in his own judgement, unafraid of being wrong because he knows equally he can be right and therefore is always able to acknowledge the times when he is unsure. The punter is never confident or relaxed because his uncertainty in judgement makes him afraid of being wrong, never knowing if or when he will be right and so unable to admit he does not know because to do so would confirm his state of indecision.

The bettor approaches betting with a clear understanding of what it encompasses and treats it seriously and with respect by neither demanding nor expecting automatically a reward from the encounter. The punter, meanwhile, approaches betting without understanding what it involves and so treats it as fun, enticed by its apparent kindly face that belies its truly fierce nature. The punter on experiencing the reality of betting starts to put greater effort into the activity until he begins equating this endeavour with work, demanding and expecting financial reward from a pursuit he has treated principally as fun.

The backer faced by these competing forces from opposite fields of influence can only become successful by remaining loyal to the strong independent stance practised by the bettor. The backer failing to follow this example and instead succumbing to the habits of the punter surely will face a sentence on the frantic treadmill of gambling. It is an experience of turmoil and confusion with the punter's thoughts directed entirely to gambling, as he chases past losses, always afraid of missing a winner and searching for the elusive big coup that will turn him into a winner.

Betting can be seen as a hard relentless struggle in which only the most able survive, and so with this stern warning it must be left finally to the backer's own counsel in accepting the challenge and deciding whether
'To bet or not to bet'.

2 SELECTION FORMULA

Having made the decision to bet, accepting the responsibility for such an action and with ambition to win money by betting, it will be essential for the backer attempting to fulfil this aim to establish a mode of selection which will consistently produce a high degree of successful results. While there may be various methods of non-independently achieving successful selection results (ranging from 'informed tips' to a computerized evaluation of selection), it is intended here to provide the backer with an *independent selection method* that produces successful results.

This selection method is encapsulated in a *selection formula*, which incorporates four cardinal principles – *Form, Fitness, Class, Conditions* – which collectively and individually have almost total effect on the results of horse-races. The formula has been devised to allow for objective identification, evaluation and comparison of these principles which dominate horse-racing. It enables the selector to develop confidence in the power of a reasoning mind and maintain a consistency in selection despite the constant unpredictable factors in racing which may at any time cast their shadow on events.

Although rigid in structure and demanding of content, the formula allows for the individual expression of interpretation that each selector's experience and knowledge will bring to bear in the formula's application. It constantly provides a sound reasoned basis for selection, founded as it is on the four principles mentioned above: form; fitness; class; conditions.

FORM

Of the four principles guiding selection, form is the foremost and dominant constituent of the formula, acting as the major consideration in selection with the other factors serving only as modifying agents. Form is the undisputable record of performance, being a record of what a horse has or has not achieved, it is the objective recording of racing performances which is the sole means of reliably assessing and comparing *ability*. *Top-class form* is extremely reliable and evokes the statement: 'Form beats everything.' Form is the factor in selection which should never be underestimated.

FITNESS

This is the second principle in the formula, it is the constituent that is always likely to have the major influence on form.

Fitness as a term for consideration in selection means 'peak race fitness' and is a physical condition of a horse which must never be assumed readily without some proof. Although there is never absolutely conclusive proof (until after the race), the most reliable evidence that a horse is 'fit' will be indicated from a race performance within the previous 7 days.

SEVEN-DAY RACE FITNESS

This can be attributed to a horse finishing and/or figuring prominently in a race (of similar class – possibly higher – and conditions) suggesting that the horse is at the peak of form and fitness or about to reach peak fitness. A horse should, however, not be automatically considered 'fit' because it has run within the previous 7 days if the quality of that performance is not up to the prescribed standard.

Seven-day race fitness is a positive indication of fitness for all types of horses (Flat and National Hunt), but especially in races involving inexperienced or moderate horses (i.e. 2 y.o., 3 y.o. mdn novice hurdlers, novice chasers) and at all times of year but especially early and late season (Flat and National Hunt) when fitness will beat the ill-prepared and sometimes jaded horses. Inclement weather, winter or summer, which disrupts training schedules and racing programmes gives the opportunity for recent race fitness to have a deciding affect on the day.

Fitness is the balancing factor which can invalidate form.

CLASS

This is the third principle of the formula, and can have a most powerful modifying influence on selection. In terms of horse-racing, class

9

can be defined as the quality of competition a horse races against. Class in these terms ranges from top class (the very best horses) to low/poor class (the very worst horses). A horse will be assessed from its performances and be adjudged on its level in class.

For selection purposes:

- A horse when raised in class has to improve upon its known ability and form.
- A horse in the same class has to reproduce form equivalent at least to what it has shown in that class.
- A horse lowered in class has merely to repeat its normal level of ability as shown in the higher class to have a winning chance.

Class, therefore, in selection assumes a negative, neutral or positive character; lowering a horse in class is the most favourable aspect for selection for it gives a horse a winning opportunity simply by repeating its known form.

CONDITIONS

This is the fourth and final principle of the selection formula. Conditions will act as the important balancing mechanism in the selection decision when other factors in the formula appear almost inseparably equal. The conditions covered by the formula for consideration are: distance; going; weight (penalties); course/draw; jockeyship; sundry factors.

DISTANCE

A horse's ability to stay a distance cannot be accepted until proven by the test of a race. Most horses have only one distance at which they can produce their best form and are classified as:
Flat – sprinters; stayers; middle-distance horses.
National Hunt – 2m hurdlers/chasers; staying hurdlers/chasers needing 3m+.
In some special cases horses have a limited range of distances (i.e. 5–6f; 7f–1m; 1¼m–1½m, etc.) and National Hunt equivalent. A change of distance is often responsible for reversals of form and horses being unable to reproduce their true form.

GOING

This is the term referring to ground conditions of the racetrack. Most horses have a preference for a certain type of going and may be unable to produce their true form on other going. Even the best horses have going preferences. For example, BRIGADIER GERARD could never show his best form on soft going and he came close to defeat by inferior animals when ground conditions were against him. On fast ground BRIGADIER GERARD was a real champion, while on the soft he was merely a good-class performer. It should be carefully noted the type of going a horse has shown its best form on. Extremes of going (e.g. hard–heavy) usually suit horses that can only act on these extremes of going. Sudden and extreme changes of going will often be responsible for reversals of form.

WEIGHT

This refers to the weight carried by a horse. The more weight a horse carries the slower it will run – it is the leveller of ability. In handicap races horses have been allotted weight according to their ability (in the opinion of the handicapper) with the best horse given the most weight and the worst horse least, each theoretically handicapped by weight to have an equal chance of winning. The handicap weights of horses are constantly being reassessed and changed to correspond to their performances remaining the same or being raised or lowered. Horses are allotted weight by the handicap or through the conditions of entry of a race.

Penalties

Penalties of weight are given to horses after they have won a race (i.e. if they have not been rehandicapped since their win, or if they are competing in non-handicap races). Weight penalties are a handicap which require that a winner will have to improve upon its last performance to overcome. Penalties range from 3 lb upwards and apply to all types (Flat and National Hunt) and most classes except the very highest (e.g. Classic and National Hunt equivalent).

Weight conditions and penalties in a race must always be very seriously considered for weight is a factor that will defeat even the best horses.

COURSES

These are the different racecourses in the British Isles, which vary as much in size, shape, sharpness and stiffness in undulation as they do in location. This applies equally to Flat and National Hunt courses, and on National Hunt courses the fences that will be encountered also vary in size and stiffness. The peculiarity of courses produces course-specialists; whether a track suits a horse's style of racing and action may be an important consideration in certain instances.

DRAW

The draw is the position across the racecourse from where a horse must be placed to start a race – whether a flag banner or stalls start ('stalls start' applying only to Flat racing).

The draw is mainly of significance in sprint races (5–6f) when there are large fields, and one side of the course gives a particular advantage to a horse. *The draw in these instances will be a distinct advantage* to a horse, often to the extent of completely nullifying the chances of a badly drawn horse. Chester is a prime example of a course where the draw frequently influences results. On the 5f course a low draw is a major advantage worth a couple of lengths at least. The significance of the draw will vary from course to course and may change or reverse in response to abnormal or extreme weather conditions. The draw is a crucial factor which may be of overriding importance, especially in all sprint races where there are large fields (above seven or eight runners) and always demands careful consideration in the final selection decision.

JOCKEYSHIP

The quality of jockeyship essentially resolves to the selector's individual opinion of a particular jockey. However, the performance of a quality jockey, experienced and currently in good form, can be the difference between wining a race that he had no right to win and losing a race he had no right to lose. Jockeyship at all levels (and types of racing) is often the margin between victory and defeat.

SUNDRY FACTORS

The fitting of blinkers can have a devastating or detrimental effect on a horse's performance (a horse fitted with blinkers for the first time always demands, initially, an added consideration by the backer). A trainer's record and the stable's current form, etc. are also factors to be carefully noted.

This selection formula has been designed to make the process of selecting winners a more exact and less hazardous operation. It identifies the constantly important elements which affect the results of races, and demands that they always receive the fullest consideration, thereby endeavouring to place the approach to selection on a truly scientific basis. By careful formulation of the relevant factors, the often forgotten or unrealized material and physical elements which are responsible for producing the results of races are revealed. The orderly presentation of this vital information will enable the bettor to make logical selection decisions.

Throughout the British Isles there are two major different types of horse-racing: Flat racing and National Hunt racing. Flat racing principally concerns younger horses, and is ostensibly oriented to improve the speed qualities in the thoroughbred horse. National Hunt racing concerns older horses with an emphasis on qualities of strength and endurance as well as speed.

There are separate racing seasons for each type of racing. The Flat race season in the United Kingdom lasts approximately 8 months, beginning in late March and finishing in the early part of November. Meanwhile, the National Hunt season lasts approximately 10 months, starting in the first week in August and ending in the last week of May of the following year. The Flat race season coincides with the natural order of the seasons throughout the year (nature's awakening in spring, the height of activity in summer, fruiting and slowing down in autumn). It allows for the younger horses (colts and fillies still in a process of growth and development) and much affected by climatic conditions, to reach their natural physical peak during the more clement weather of late spring, summer and early autumn. The National Hunt season in contrast, encounters the extremes of climatic conditions; meetings in midwinter may be cancelled due to the harshness of frost, snow or rain, while early in the National Hunt compaign, meetings may be cancelled due to the hard ground and equally dangerous conditions for racing.

FLAT RACING – THE SEASON

There are good-class (valuable) Flat races throughout the season, commencing with the competitive 1m Lincoln Handicap at Doncaster in March in the first week of the season and culminating with the equally competitive 1½m November Handicap in the last week. In between there is a carefully planned programme of racing, highlighted by the three Classic meetings of: the Guineas (at Newmarket in early May); the Derby (at Epsom in June); and the St Leger (at Doncaster in September). Similar competitive prestigious and valuable race meetings are held at: Ascot (in June) the Royal Meetings; at Good-wood (in July); and the York Festival in August. Many of the leading Flat-race stables focus their training schedule on these events, and are aided in a balanced programme of other races which serve as, and are often recognized as, trials for the major events. Throughout the Flat-race season, there will be opportunities for horses of all classes and preferences to find a race particular to their needs where they should be able to display their true ability.

THE FLAT-RACE HORSE

Flat racing and flat-race horses are essentially concerned with *speed* – speed in races, and a demand for swift physical development, so a horse's abilities at racing may be quickly exploited resulting in many horses being quickly 'burnt' out after a few races and ensuring a short and sharp Flat-race career.

A Flat-race horse's racing life usually begins as a 2 y.o. All thoroughbred racehorses are given an official birthday of 1st January irrespective of what date in the year they are actually foaled – a horse foaled in February and a horse foaled in June will both be officially considered a year old on the 1st January of the following year when one is approximately 10 months old and the other 6 months old.

This can lead to considerable physical disparity in horses in the early part of their lives, especially as 2-year-olds and this imbalance may not be properly resolved until the middle part of their 3-year season at racing. Most horses that begin racing as 2-year-olds end their Flat racing lives by the time they are 5-year-olds. This is either due to injury, complete lack of ability, because they have been retired for breeding purposes (this happens to most fillies, and the best colts will stand as stallions), or more generally because their waning powers of speed means a generation of younger horses supersedes them.

- As a 2 y.o a horse is physically immature (comparable to a child in human terms).
- As a 3 y.o its maturity begins (ossification will begin to occur) and it is like a teenager becoming a young adult.
- At 4 years of age a horse is reaching its physical peak – and is usually considered to be at its prime for Flat racing.
- As a 5 y.o a horse is fully mature – a colt is considered a horse and a filly is considered a mare – there will unlikely be further physical development which would aid a horses Flat race career.

Flat racing has a rapidly and constantly changing population in horses as a new crop of 2-year-olds appear every season and replace other and older horses. The fortunes of most Flat-race stables revolve around their yearly intake of new fresh young horses from the sales and private studs. These horses arrive as unbroken yearlings, and each trainer has the often unenviable task of attempting to turn these raw recruits into efficient racing machines. The pressures on a trainer are likely to be high, many of these horses may represent a high financial investment by their owners who will get little or no return on their outlay unless these horses become winners. The risks, therefore, are great, but similarly the rewards to the successful will be enormous for top/good-class Flat-race horses have a considerable value at stud as potential brood mares and stallions.

It will be only the comparative few who are successful and whose future may seem pleasantly assured; the remainder are likely to encounter varying fates. Some will be sold to race abroad in racing of lower standard. Some will be sold out of racing altogether and some will enter a new career as novice National Hunt horses.

NATIONAL HUNT RACING – THE SEASON

The National Hunt Season is long and protracted lasting 10 months and encountering the best and worst extremes of weather conditions. Beginning at the height of summer in the first week of August, it slowly unfolds throughout the autumn, reaching a zenith of activity during the winter months of December, January and February (weather permitting).

The climax to the season comes in March with the 3-day Cheltenham Festival meeting which serves as a championship decider for horses of all types (hurdlers/chasers, novices and experienced horses) over varying distances. Competition is extremely fierce, for not only are the best English horses contesting these most valuable and prestigious races but also the best of Irish horses as well. Irish-bred and trained National Hunt horses for many years have held sway over the British National Hunt scene, and each year they continue to display their influence by capturing a high proportion of races at the Festival meetings. The Aintree (Liverpool) meeting follows a few weeks later and includes the running of the Grand National. This meeting held similarly over 3 days signals the progressive slowing down of the National Hunt season during April and its culmination at the end of May.

Throughout the season there should have been opportunities and conditions to suit every type and class of horse, i.e. early and late season provides chances for the more moderate horses and those specializing on firm ground, while the bog-like conditions of winter should allow the heavy-going specialist chances to excel.

The better-class and champion horses will usually not be risked on anything but the best going, and this will certainly be found at some stage during the season. Good-class and valuable races are programmed throughout most of the season, but they tend not to commence until November, when public attention will be focused fully on National Hunt racing, as by this time the Flat season has ended. Many races will serve as trials in the build-up to the Cheltenham Festival, giving the public and trainers ample information upon which to assess ability.

THE NATIONAL HUNT HORSE

National hunt racing is an extreme test of basic physical qualities in a horse – soundness, endurance and durability. Although speed and jumping ability are essential requirements of any winning performance, these talents will never be fully realized unless a horse is able to withstand the constant rigours inherent in this code of racing. The ever-present unpredictable element posed in a race by obstacles and injury conspires to make National Hunt racing a powerful leveller of horses and men. This ensures it retains its original sporting flavour, attracting its supporters (owners, etc.) from farming and hunting communities where there is an appreciation of the difficulties, uncertainties and patience required to bring a National Hunt horse to full racing maturity. Many successful National Hunt horses have been bred and reared by their owners whose sympathetic interest and involvement has made certain the horse be given unhurried consideration to establish a racing career. Success emanating from such an approach cannot be simply bought, and therefore this aspect of the National Hunt horse has no attraction for the business-orientated Flat-race entrepreneur of bloodstock who seeks a fast and assured return on investment.

While the racing life of a Flat-horse is likely to be short by contrast the National Hunt horse avoiding serious injury may expect five or six seasons, involving a two-part career, first as a hurdler then as a chaser. The length of time a horse spends as a hurdler or chaser will be determined by the age at which it embarked on a National Hunt career and what was considered initially as its possible forte. A hurdler is considered to be at its peak at 6 or 7 years and a chaser is thought normally to be at the height of its powers at 9 or 10 years. Horses taking part in National Hunt races have come into this type

17

of racing from two different sources: ex-Flat-race horses and those horses bred primarily for National Hunt racing (often called 'store' horses) Ex-Flat horses with any ability at all are usually quickly able to learn the requirements of their new career and develop into efficient hurdlers. However, they tend to lack the physical scope and resilience that is necessary to become top-class chasers. The 'store-type horses' bred on more stoic lines whose long-term objective is to 'make up' into chasers develop more slowly, sometimes being unable to win a hurdle race before they achieve success as chasers. A horse's ability as a chaser may bear no resemblance to its ability as a hurdler (for better or worse) and it is therefore necessary to consider objectively the progress of a novice chaser.

All horses when first entering either mode of National Hunt racing are considered novices, novice hurdlers/novice chasers – and initially for their first season compete in novice events against similar horses. If a horse wins in its first season of National Hunt racing, it will no longer be considered a novice, and will graduate to handicap class in its second season. A horse that does not win can seasonally remain in the novice class until it achieves a success. Similarly, a horse – whether an unsuccessful novice hurdler or an experienced handicap hurdler or a previously unraced National Hunt horse – when tried as a chaser will compete in the novice chase class.

A horse cannot compete in a National Hunt race until the August of its 3-year season, so officially it will be at least $3\frac{1}{2}$ years old (and ossification will have taken place, or will be taking place in its development).

A 3 y.o. can then only compete in juvenile hurdles against horses of the same age until it reaches its official fourth birthday at the turn of the year, midway through its first season. A horse may also not compete in chases until it is 4 years 8 months old (officially). This will occur in the August of its second season of racing.

Horses will vary in capacity and rate of development as National Hunt performers – learning how to jump quickly and accurately and gaining the physical strength necessary to endure the stress of National Hunt racing will be factors comparable with speed in the make-up of a successful National Hunt horse. (This is why horses of moderate Flat-race ability can become stars at the winter race game for it requires different qualities.) National Hunt horses are generally geldings, because entire horses are usually less than inclined to maintain an interest in racing if certain sensitive parts of their anatomy are endangered – this means that a horse's future and value outside racing is limited. (Unsuccessful National Hunt horses will be sold out of racing altogether, as hunters or as potential point-to-point hunter–chasers.)

It is therefore necessary for a National Hunt horse to maintain and/or increase its value entirely from its participation in racing (this will be closely associated with its earning potential as a racehorse) and is best served by the consideration on its long-term rather than short-term future. National Hunt horses will normally be raced on this basis, and it is a factor that should always be carefully considered when making a selection.

4 TYPES OF RACES

(Those most favoured for the purpose of selection).
To achieve consistent successful results it is necessary that selection is limited only to the most easily discernible type of races.

This fundamental consideration places all races into two distinct categories:

1. *Level weight contests*. Races where horses carry (basically) the *same* weights.

   These are the more easily discernible and therefore the more favourable type of race for selection.

2. *Handicaps*. Races where horses carry different weights.

   These type of races are usually indiscernible and should not be contemplated for the purpose of serious selection.

THE TYPES OF 'LEVEL WEIGHT' CONTESTS

Races where horses carry level weight exist for horses of all ages, class and distances in both codes of racing (Flat/National Hunt).

There are acceptable variations in the strictest literal interpretation of the term 'level weights' where every horse should carry exactly the same weight. These are:

1. *Sex allowance* (Flat racing). Colts are expected to give fillies (and sometimes geldings) a 3 lb weight allowance to offset their expected physical superiority. Sex allowances have been extended to National Hunt racing from 1983–4. Colts, horses and geldings giving a weight concession of 5 lb to fillies and mares in all chases, hurdles and National Hunt Flat races.

2. *Weight-for-allowance* (applies to Flat and National Hunt). Horses of different ages racing against each other are apportioned varying weights according to the time of year and distance of the race to take account of the maturity advantage.

3. *Condition races* (Flat/National Hunt). Races where horses *may* be

carrying weights according to their qualifications in respect of the entry conditions of the race.

The 'level weight' type of race most favoured for purposes of selection are, in order of preference and reliability:

Flat races
  (i) 2 y.o. races – maiden and condition races
  (ii) 3 y.o. races – maiden and condition races

National Hunt
  (i)   Novice hurdles – condition hurdles
  (ii) Condition chases
  (iii) Novice chases

FLAT RACES

TWO-YEAR-OLD RACES

These are and have always been the most reliable type of races in which to make selections, for 2 y.o. horses usually run consistently, and there are few discrepancies in the evolution of form. Races from 5f to 7f are the best 2 y.o. races in which to consider selection (see Table 4.1).

TABLE 4.1   Winning favourites in races for 2 y.o. during 1981 Flat season

Distance	Condition WFA* races Winners – Races	Maiden races Winners – Races	Total Winners – Races
5f	55 – 123	57 – 160	112 – 283 = 39.5%
6f	44 – 101	32 – 100	76 – 201 = 37.8%
7f	29 – 64	27 – 65	56 – 129 = 43.4%

* WFA = weight for age.

TABLE 4.2

Distance	Condition WFA races Winners – Races	Maiden races Winners – Races	Total Winners – Races
8f	5 – 22 ⎫	9 – 32 ⎫	
9f+	1 – 2 ⎭	1 – 2 ⎭	16 – 56 = 28.5%

5f races – contested all season are races demanding pure speed.
6f races – are contested from mid–May onwards and are similarly focused towards the speed element.

7f races – are contested from July onwards and while requiring a strong element of speed allow an opportunity for the horse bred to stay middle distances (1m 2f).

Races for 2-year-olds of 1m and 1m + **are not** reliable mediums for making selection (see Table 4.2). The 1m races are staged from September onwards – 1m can be an extreme distance for a 2 y.o. even those bred to be stayers (1½m+). They are notoriously difficult races to assess as most horses competing have unproven form and are un-proven over the distance, and many are horses which are proven too slow over shorter distances but are being run in the final hope that their lack of speed was the strength of stamina in disguise.

THREE-YEAR OLD MAIDEN RACES

'Maiden' is the term used to describe a horse that has not yet won a race.

Maiden races are the next most reliable type of races for selection consideration. They are races designed for horses that did not win a race during their 2 y.o. season. The better-class maiden 3 y.o. prob-ably up until the end of July or August are good mediums for selection (a horse still a maiden after this time, except in special circumstances, is likely to be at best moderate).

These races can involve well-bred and potentially good horses that were backward as 2-year-olds and unable to be given serious race opportunities, but who are likely to develop and display their ability over longer distances as 3-year-olds.

There are two types of 3 y.o. maiden races:

(a) *Maiden races* – limited strictly to horses that have not won a race.

(b) *Stakes races* – (formerly referred to as maidens at closing) which allow any horse to run providing it has not won up to a month before the date of the race. These races, therefore, are contested by both maidens and previous winners, allowing winners to con-tinue in maiden company for a short time after winning before graduating to more competitive handicap company.

Overall, 3 y.o. maidens are second only to 2 y.o. races as reliable mediums for selection. However, some races according to distance are better than others and the selector is advised to become aquainted with and identify their characteristics (see Table 4.3).

5f, 6f, 7f

The basic quality necessary to win races over these distances is speed and this is an attribute that is usually readily discernible.

TABLE 4.3   Winning favourites in races for 3 y.o. during 1981 Flat season

Distance	Condition WFA races Winners – races	Maiden races Winners – races	Total Winners – races
5f	6 – 13	8 – 17	
6f	9 – 20	10 – 20	61 – 126 = 48.4%
7f	18 – 29	10 – 26	
8f (1m)	18 – 64	22 – 70	
9f (1m 1f)	5 – 12	6 – 15	87 – 274 = 31.75%
10f (1m 2f)	14 – 46	15 – 46	
11f (1m 3f)	3 – 12	4 – 9	
12f (1m 4f)	29 – 65	15 – 50	
13f (1m 5f)	3 – 3	4 – 6	
14f (1m 6f)	2 – 4	5 – 12	72 – 173 = 41.6%
15f (1m 7f)	3 – 6	1 – 2	
16f (2m)	7 – 10	3 – 15	

1m–1m 3f

The attributes necessary to win races between 1m and 1m 3f (usually referred to as middle distances) are not so readily definable for they are neither a test of pure speed nor a true test of stamina. Although some horses successful at these distances are specialist bred, many more are horses that have failed at other distances (i.e. horses bred for sprinting that have stayed longer distances and potential stayers that have won over shorter distances). As a result these events often prove less predictable and provide some unexpected outcomes.

1m 4f +

These are staying races and require that a horse has stamina to last out the longer distances. This is usually an easily discernible quality, making these reliable mediums for selection.

Three-year-old maiden races can therefore be approached on this broad basis of characteristic requirements according to distance. It should be noted that the longer a 3 y.o. remains a maiden competing at sprint distances (5f–7f) the more moderate it is likely to be. For most horses numerous opportunities occur to win as 2 y.o. over these distances, but to no avail. Similarly, the extreme distances (1m 7f) are likely to attract moderate horses who finally it is hoped a test of stamina will prove their forte, thus compensating for their proven slowness over shorter trips.

Races for 3 y.o. maiden fillies, are definitely to be approached with caution because fillies with promising 2 y.o. form often fail to 'train on' in the transition to becoming 3-year-olds. Unfortunately, they remain in training only continuously to disappoint in race performances. Meanwhile many fillies train at differential speed and consequently their form is not always consistent, resulting in unlikely and unexpected results.

THREE-YEAR-OLD CONDITION RACES – OVER ALL DISTANCES

These are similarly suitable type races for selection. They will include Classic races, their trials and some group races which can all be competitive events – however, established form of good class is reliable and is a fair test for selection.

All age condition races over all distances are equally fair and attractive mediums for selection.

NATIONAL HUNT RACES

NOVICE HURDLES

The best and most reliable type of races are novice hurdles which are for horses in their first season of National Hunt racing (see Table 4.4). All National Hunt races (except National Hunt Flat races*) require the jumping of obstacles – hurdles are smaller obstacles, are the least incumbent and produce few fallers.

(a) The minimum and best distance for selection is 2m. A horse will need speed to win over this distance and this quality will be clearly discernible from examination of form.

(b) *Age*: 3 y.o. (juvenile) and 4 y.o. hurdlers in their first season racing against their peers are usually the most reliable – form will be recent and not subject to the complexities of studying the value of previous season('s) form which is sometimes necessary when considering the chances of older horses.

Older horses (4 y.o. and upwards) are an almost equally attractive selection proposition – the only minor consideration is the possible existence of good older form which has to be reconciled with recent form.

* Races run on National Hunt courses with the hurdles removed – limited to claiming jockeys and amateur riders

TABLE 4.4 Novice hurdles during the 1980–1 National Hunt season

| | Novice hurdle (all age except juvenile) | | | | Juvenile novice hurdle (first season – 3–4 y.o. – all distances) |
	2m to 2m 2f	2m 3f to 2m 5½f	2m 6f to 3m+	Total	
Fav.	206	36	13	255 = 39.9%	67 *38.7%
2nd fav.	108	18	5	131 = 20.5%	35 20.2%
3rd fav.	60	15	3	78 = 12.2%	18 10.4%
Non-fav.	151	20	4	175 = 27.4%	53 30.7%
Total	525	89	25	639	173

N.B. Novice hurdles up to 2½m are an acceptably reliable medium. For 4-year-olds 2½m races and over can often prove to be unreliable mediums for selection – it is an extreme distance for these younger horses who often lack the strength and stamina to last this distance.

2m 6f novice hurdles. This is a specialized distance (for any class of horse) and is not a satisfactory distance for most horses – most require a distance of 2m 4f or 3m.

3m novice hurdles. These are likely to be difficult races for selection. There are not many such races in the calendar and the form in those that exist tends to be moderate or unreliable. These races are contested primarily by horses of slow maturing or decidedly moderate ability. It is hoped that the slow maturing types may 'make up' into chasers, but they often lack the technique or speed to be successful as hurdlers. Others, meanwhile, are entered in the vain hope they may have the strength of stamina to compensate for their proven non-ability over shorter distances. Results can therefore be unpredictable and this type of race *must not* be contemplated for the purpose of selection. (It should, however, be noted that horses with ability in these contests are likely to so easily overshadow their rivals that they may win a number or sequence of long-distance hurdles, but usually at increasingly unrewarding odds.)

CONDITION HURDLE RACES UP TO 2½m (4 Y.O. AND UPWARDS)

These type of races for selection purposes are on a par of reliability with novice hurdles. They will include the Champion Hurdle and Champion trials.

Form is consistent, although top-class hurdle races may be competitive and provide a searching test for skilful selection.

N.B. All novice hurdles of distances in excess of 2½m tend to be unrewarding mediums for selection.

CONDITION CHASES

All chases require a horse to jump the larger obstacles provided in National Hunt racing. The size and concentration of fences can act as formidable hazards and may prevent horses who are jumping at racing speed from completing the course. This has therefore given rise to the assumption that all chases are hazardous ventures which should be avoided for selection purposes. However, this is *not* a fair assessment and experienced good-class horses are extremely reliable jumpers.

N.B. Condition chases may be considered a good medium for selection.

Horses of unequal ability, over all distances up to 3½m, will race against each other on a basis of level weights (condition of entry providing for readjustments) providing a basis for the test of selection to be a clear assessment of comparative ability.

The very top-class condition races will include the non-handicap races at the Cheltenham Festival and other races which will serve as trials for these, all of which are likely to be competitive. These races involve top-class experienced horses which are reliable and provide a fair test of the selector's skills (see Table 4.5.)

TABLE 4.5

	2m to 2m 2f	2m 3f to 2m 5½f	2m 6f to 3m+	Total
Fav.	6	13	10	29 = 52.7%
2nd fav.	1	5	7	13 = 23.6%
3rd fav.	—	1	2	3 = 5.5%
Non-fav.	4	3	3	10 = 18.2%
Total	11	22	22	55

NOVICE CHASES

In certain instances these are acceptable races in which to make a selection.

Proficient jumping is an essential quality which wins novice chases – a horse that does not complete the course has no possibility of winning the race. The fear of horses falling (which has to be strongly considered) has dissuaded many astute judges from selection in novice chases. This view gains support from the fact that all novice chasers by their nature will be inexperienced jumpers of the larger obstacles and that some will have been put to chasing after their failure in other aspects of racing (Flat racing and hurdling). This type of horse can be clearly identified and *must be avoided*. However, accepting that novice chases are often principally contested by slow and indifferent jumpers, it then becomes obvious that these type of race often take very little ability to win. Therefore a horse of proven hurdling ability (i.e. a good-class handicap hurdler) if 'put to' chasing (providing it has been properly schooled and can adapt its jumping technique to fencing) will have too much speed and ability for the average slow-moving novice chasers.

Handicap hurdlers (of ability) set to chasing are horses that must always be strongly considered in selection of novice chasers.

2m–2½m novice chases

These are usually the more attractive type of novice chase for the purpose of selection. They are contested frequently by horses with proven abilities in other spheres of racing (i.e. a previously successful hurdle or Flat race record) who from the speed aspect are therefore likely to outclass their rivals.

2m 5f+ novice chases

Described as long-distance novice chases, these may be seen as less desirable mediums for selection because they are contested principally by horses of moderate or unproven ability who lack this aspect of speed. The accent in long-distance novice chases is that of stamina, strength and steady, proficient jumping, especially as there are many obstacles to negotiate. These races attract contestants either specifically bred for this task and whose career is focused on their development to become staying chasers, or else horses of mediocre ability whose lack of speed render longer-distance chases as their last hope for redemption. It can therefore often take little ability to win these races, being contested as they are usually by inexperienced or moderate horses. With recent results showing an above-average record for the most favoured horses in long-distance novice chases this may suggest them to be attractive mediums. However, a closer examination and realization of the nature of these races (i.e. long-distance races, over many large obstacles, often contested in extremes of ground conditions by horses usually without sound credentials of form who are offered frequently at unattractive short odds) show these races in their truer perspective of holding many selection pitfalls and from a long-term betting viewpoint to be uneconomic (see Table 4.6).

TABLE 4.6 Novice chases during the 1980–1 National Hunt season

	2m to 2m 2f	2m 3f to 2m 5½f	2m 6f to 3m+	Total
Fav.	81	26	52	159 = 40.4%
2nd fav.	41	20	27	88 = 22.3%
3rd fav.	30	12	13	55 = 14.0%
Non-fav.	61	11	20	92 = 23.3%
Total	213	69	112	394

HANDICAPS

Handicap races are full of enigmas and are therefore always the most difficult races to predict the outcome.
They must not be considered for serious purposes of selection
   It is, however, advisable to examine some of their aspects to gain a wider understanding and realize their context in racing. Handicaps are designed to give horses of different abilities an equal chance of winning the same race carrying different amounts of weight. Weight is allotted to each horse in accordance with its abilities; the best horse(s) carrying most weight and the worst horse(s) least weight. Handicaps are compiled by an experienced handicapper appointed by the Jockey Club.
   Handicap races exist for horses of all types, ages, classes and for all distances.

TYPES OF HANDICAPS AND PRINCIPLES

For Flat races and for National Hunt – official handicappers tend to specialize in one or the other.

Age

Handicap races restricted to 2-year-olds are called nursery handicaps and are staged from July onwards. Older horses compete throughout the whole season in either all age handicaps or handicaps confined to horses of a certain age group (i.e. for 3-year-olds only; for 4-year-olds and upwards etc).

Class

From selling class to horses just below (group class).

Distance

From a minimum 5f to the marathon 4m 865 yd of the Grand National.

Horses become eligible for handicaps:
* Two-year-olds if they have been placed 1st, 2nd, 3rd, 4th in a race and run three times unless having won a race.
* Other horses – Flat and/or National Hunt – must have run in three races or have won one race. National Hunt horses wishing to run in handicaps, but who have not qualified, are given an automatic top weight.

29

Initially, a horse is handicapped on the best form which it has shown. To win from that allotted weight a horse must repeat and/or improve upon its best performance. A horse's form is constantly being reassessed by the handicapper, and where and when necessary the horse is rehandicapped, i.e. a horse that has improved on its best form and/or won a race since being originally handicapped is moved up the handicap and given increased weight.

Horses that no longer seem to be able to reproduce their best form from their current weight have their weight reduced and moved down the handicap.

If a horse wins a race and then runs again (in a race where it has been handicapped on its previous best form) it is usually required to carry a winner's weight penalty (appropriate to the value of the race won).

Weight is the greater leveller of the abilities of horses and this coupled with the change in abilities (improvement and deterioration) contrive to make handicap races the most difficult races to predict confidently. To be confident of winning a handicap requires that a horse is handicapped with a lower weight than is the true reflection of its ability. This situation occurs for a number of reasons:

1. A horse improving with and after every performance, yet can only be rehandicapped on what it has done; therefore it remains ahead of the handicapper.
2. A horse which has improved since its initial handicap assessment, and is better than its current handicap mark.
3. A horse that has been lowered in the handicap from its initial assessment, but has still retained the ability of its appropriate original handicap weight.

These occurrences, especially when a horse is considered remarkably leniently handicapped, are known as a 'blot in the handicap' – they occur very rarely as seldom does the handicapper make serious errors in judgement.

Deliberately losing a horse's form has long been a device used to gain a handicapped horse a winning opportunity. Before the horse is considered 'a good thing' it must be considered that similar conditions of legitimate improvement or malpractice apply equally to other horses in the race.

The consideration of these issues further complicates the difficulties and contrary elements which are present in handicaps.

Horses handicapped for Flat racing are rated by the official Jockey Club handicappers on a scale from 0 (the lowest) to 100 in steps of 1 lb. Thus, a horse rated 70 is thought to be 2 st better than a horse rated 42. Because the normal weight range in Flat handicaps is from 7 st 7 lb to 10 st, i.e. 35 lb, handicap races are graded to confine them to horses of broadly similar ability. A handicap of grade 0–40 would therefore not be open to horses rated above 40.

The scale of grades for handicaps covering all distances are: 0.35, 0.40, 0.45, 0.50, 0.55, 0.60, 0.65, 0.70 plus 30.75, 35+, 40+. As horses improve they may be raised in class in accordance with their rating and if they deteriorate are then lowered. The range of handicaps allows for a horse rated at 40 to be given top weight in a 0.40 handicap yet bottom weight in a top-class (40+) handicap. A guiding rule to handicaps is – *The best horse on proven form is the top weight.* (If in doubt select the top weight.) Although a horse will not be top weighted without having shown some performances of merit it is rather too sweeping a statement without consideration of other factors. These include:

1. Is the top weight clearly top weighted, i.e. having to give 7 lb, 14 lb, 21 lb to the second and third weight horses or is the difference merely 1 lb, 2 lb or 3 lb in which case the difference of ability is likely to be negligible? If the horse is clearly top weighted, are the conditions favourable to concede the weight (its current form, fitness, going, distance and jockey)? It must then be considered how has the horse achieved top weight in the particular handicap.
2. Has the horse been promoted to top weight on the evidence of its most recent performances (i.e. an automatic weight penalty for winning or recent regrading as top weight as the resulting assessment of recent performances)? To defy this newly incurred top weight a horse must be capable of further improvement – only the horse that is constantly improving and thereby keeping just ahead of the handicapper's rating can overcome the weight burden.
3. Has the horse top weight because it has been lowered in grade (i.e. a horse rated 55 – previously carrying low weights in 40+ handicaps, dropped in grade 0.55 and required to carry top weight)? The size and confirmation of the horse will be a factor, some horses running better with lighter burdens against good-class opponents while others perform better carrying heavy weights against inferior opponents. Recent form, fitness and ground conditions will similarly have great influence.
   It is more difficult for horses to carry big weights on soft or heavy ground because the weight has a more telling effect when conditions are testing. Conversely, when the ground is firm weight matters less and top weights are more likely to prevail.
4. The horse remains top weight (without being downgraded) yet has no recent winning form. The handicapper in this instance, then, still considers there is not enough evidence to constitute a lower rehandicapping of the horse.
   (a) It may be because the horse has had an absence from racing, but is handicapped on its very best old form and therefore has had no

31

recent opportunity to show whether its current ability still warrants its previously assessed handicap weight.

(b) The horse may be readily holding its form but not making the necessary improvement to better it. In these circumstances the top weight to gain a winning opportunity must have the horses below handicapped to the limit of their ability and capable of no further improvement.

A horse to win a handicap must be on a weight level that is most favourable to its current fitness, form and ability.

It may be necessary in comprehending the intricacy of handicap form to specialize in particular handicaps, e.g.

5f/6f – 3 y.o. – all age
7f/1m 1f – 3 y.o. – all age
1m 2f/1m 5f – 3 y.o. – all age
1m 6f+ 3 y.o. – all age

Similarly, National Hunt racing:

2m hurdle – 4 y.o – all age
2½m hurdle – 2m 7f – 4 y.o – all age
3m+ hurdle – all age

2m chase
2½m chase
3m+ chase

The selector will become familiar with the valve of form in particular, a task almost impossible to someone trying to understand any and/or every type of race.

NURSERY HANDICAPS

Nursery handicaps are handicaps exclusively for the 2 y.o. and are not staged until the middle of July. Form is always recent, the oldest form even by October will not be more than 6 months old. Form of the top weighted horses tends to work out consistently, although late-season (late October and November) horses that have had a hard season and reached the top of the handicap can become jaded. Opportunities then arise for lighter weight opponents who appreciate the softer ground conditions.

The success of top-weighted 2-year-olds in nursery and penalized 2-year-olds generally, has given credence to the assumption that all 2-year-olds must be good weight carriers. This has no particular truth, although 2-year-olds (in company with other horses) that win races and gain top weight in handicaps or penalties in stakes races are invariably the fastest, strongest and healthiest. They tend to have the best conformation, and are thus able to withstand the rigours of racing better than their peers and produce good consistent form.

The 5f–6f nurseries normally see a good display from the top-weighted horses. Races over these distances have been available for contention from the beginning or early season, giving an opportunity to most horses if good enough. The variances occur in races over 7f–1m, these races being staged for the first time later in the season.

Often, horses handicapped on their form over shorter distances are unable to reproduce it over longer distances while other horses improve considerably over longer distances.

HANDICAP CHASES

Like all chases, handicaps are won primarily due to jumping ability. They are seldom run at full racing pace from start to finish and place a pre-requisite on fast, accurate jumping, consequently weight is of less account.

The horses who have reached the top of the handicap possess this ability, while the horses lower down the handicap tend to be poor, slow and/or erratic jumpers. Dependable jumping ability always gives a horse a possibility of winning, because if a horse does not complete the course it has no possibility of winning (see Table 4.7).

TABLE 4.7   Handicap chases during the 1980–1 National Hunt season

	2m to 2m 2f	2m 3f to 2m 5½f	2m 6f to 3m+	Total
Fav.	86	54	111	251 = 40.0%
2nd fav.	56	27	65	148 = 23.5%
3rd fav.	31	26	42	99 = 15.7%
Non-fav.	41	27	63	131 = 20.8%
Total	214	134	281	629

The best horses are those at the top of the handicap, and in many instances they can be clearly seen to have a winning chance, the modifying factors being:

Current form (does it merit handicap weight?)
Fitness (is there proof of current fitness?)
Going (are conditions favourable — weight is a greater burden to concede on heavy or soft going?)

SUMMARY OF HANDICAPS

Handicaps are designed to be competitive. The handicapper has sought to nullify the different abilities of horses by allowing each a weight in accordance with its abilities. Horses are then considered to have an equal chance of winning, weight being the great leveller of ability. Sufficient weight will defeat any horse and this constant consideration places a fine balance of judgement in selection and assessment of any handicap.

It is therefore advised that making selections in handicaps be avoided. Handicaps on the Flat and National Hunt racing are popular spectacles, usually providing nail-biting finishes for excited punters, as frantic whip-waving jockeys are seen to drive their horses towards the winning post in a frenzy of action and colour.

Bookmakers often sponsor the more competitive type of handicaps quite substantially, gaining business prestige and publicity in the process. Races of such a competitive nature enable the bookmakers to make a 'nice round book' (this means they show a very good profit whoever wins) beguiling the naive punter with generous odds.

The willingness of bookmakers to involve themselves in the sponsorship of handicaps must confirm to the selector that 'Handicaps can't be all good'.

COMMENTS ON VARIOUS TYPES OF RACES

THE CLASSICS (FLAT – LEVEL WEIGHTS)

The Classics are the top races for 3 y.o colts and fillies. There are five Classic races programmed to take place throughout the season:

2,000★ and 1,000 Guineas, for colts and fillies respectively, run at Newmarket over a distance of 1m in the spring.

Derby★ and Oaks, for colts and fillies respectively, run at Epsom over a distance of 1½m in June.

St Leger, a race open to and regularly contested by both colts and fillies run over a distance of 1¾m at Doncaster in September.

The five Classic races are the Blue ribbon events of the Flat race season; they are a stern and true test of ability, the most prestigious and among the most valuable in prize money of any events in the racing calendar. Only the best horses compete in the Classics, they are usually trained by the best trainers and ridden by the best jockeys and are therefore always fiercely competitive races. The challenge to selection in these events is to select the very best from the best – a daunting task – when

★It is worth noting that although fillies are eligible they rarely take part.

- the size of the field may be large;
- most of the runners will have at least a semblance of a chance of winning;
- each horse will be at peak fitness,
  (time in preparation will not be spared).

The main point in favour of selection in such circumstances is that it will be made of top-class horses who reliably hold their form and can consistently reproduce their best performances. A note of caution, however, must be exercised in the consideration of form especially for the first two Classics (1,000 and 2,000 Guineas).

Form for the two early Classics will be based on two sources, the previous seasons 2 y.o. form (which will normally be over distances short of a mile) and the early season Classic trials; both require careful examination because their face value often proves deceptive and unreliable.

2 y.o. form in the consideration of Classic contenders

Some horses vastly improve from their 2 y.o days as they gain strength and maturity, while other more precocious individuals fail to develop further. This seems particularly to apply to fillies who were 'flying machines' as 2-year-olds over distances of 5f, 6f or 7f but fail to 'train on' as 3-year-olds and truly stay the distance of 1m.

EARLY SEASON TRIALS

The early season trials in April often involve only partially fit horses on soft going and this form may be reversed as other horses obtain peak fitness and race on the normally fast dry ground of Newmarket Heath on Guineas days. Unless an unchallenged contender emerges with outstanding proven form – the first two Classics are likely to produce results which are difficult to forecast.

The Derby and Oaks pose other problems in selection. In June, Flat race form will have begun to be settled and the Classic trials will have produced a number of contenders for the premier Flat race crowns. The two major factors which consistently emerge as being responsible for a horse's failure at Epsom are: (i) its inability to stay the distance; (ii) the inability to act on the gradients and undulations of the course. Horses with the latter characteristic completely fail to negotiate the steep climbs, uphill and downhill gradients and the bends, while horses of speed with unproven stamina (i) tire quickly in the last 2½–3f of the race. Another factor which only to a slightly lesser extent spoils a horse's chances is temperament – a horse becoming upset and overwrought before the race in the preliminaries in response to the noise and size of the 100,000 people thronging the course and downs.

The Derby and Oaks normally produce winners from among those horses which are considered the leading challengers of form and rarely provides shock outsiders. The winner of these premier Classics will normally be bred in the purple (by a British Classic winner or foreign equivalent) and will need the priceless ability to be able to accelerate almost instantly when asked in the last 2f of the race.

The St Leger can be considered the Classic race which is the most discernible for selection. It is staged in September, and by this time Flat race form at Classic level is well exposed and the abilities, stamina, limitation and requirements of the leading candidate is almost fully exposed. The only shadow to be cast on the consideration of a selection is that some horses who throughout the season may have proven their abilities in hard-fought races over shorter distances may have reached their peak and be unable to withstand the gruelling challenge over this extended distance. This is a factor that should be particularly noted, especially with the failure in recent St Legers of Shergar (1981), Ile de Bourbon (1978), Alleged (1977).

SELLING RACES (FLAT AND NATIONAL HUNT-LEVEL WEIGHTS AND HANDICAPS)

Selling races are contested by horses with the poorest racing ability. *They cannot be recommended* as satisfactory mediums for the purposes of selection. They were designed to give opportunities to horses of the most moderate ability, the winner being offered for sale at public auction after the race (hence 'selling' races) and so providing an owner with the chance to sell slow and unwanted horses for a reasonable price. The conditions of many selling races allows for any horse competing in the race to be claimed afterwards (sold to anyone) for a sum of fixed value in accord with the conditions of entry. These type of races therefore attract the worst type of horses who either have:

1. Little or no racing ability;
2. Are physically and/or temperamentally unsound and who cannot be depended upon to reproduce consistent performances.

In these circumstances there can never be any basis for confident selection and they are races that should normally be avoided.

The only positive factor in favour of selling races for selection or any other purpose is that they are races which require very little ability to win. This has led over the years for them to become a popular medium (especially by trainers and connections) for tilts at the betting ring and led to the adage 'follow the money in selling races'. Some of the less fashionable trainers who struggle to make a living from training alone subsidize their income with carefully planned and concealed coups in selling races. They retain in their stable a horse or two imperceptibly better than selling class who, when skilfully prepared and entered, can be guaranteed to collect the spoils. Such attitudes and approaches further undermine confidence in making selection in selling races, as sudden turnabouts in form can be incomprehensible. While stating that nefarious practices can occur in selling races, most often expectations fail to materialize because of the unreliability of bad horses. Although usually not a suggested medium for selection, the selector occasionally in very rare instances finds a horse of proven ability somehow inexplicably dropped into selling class and is presented with a golden opportunity to take advantage of such fortune.

APPRENTICE RACES (FLAT-LEVEL WEIGHTS AND HANDICAPS)/CONDITIONAL JOCKEYS OPPORTUNITY RACES (NATIONAL HUNT – LEVEL WEIGHTS AND HANDICAPS)

Apprentice/opportunity races are staged to give young riders experience competing against their peers rather than against the senior and more experienced jockeys. These races can be divided into different types:

1. Races limited to apprentices riding only for the stable they are apprenticed to. (This applies only to Flat racing and is designed to give the newest and youngest apprentices an early racecourse riding experience – many apprentices make their début in such races.)
2. Races limited to apprentices/opportunity riders who have not ridden more than a prescribed number of winners.
3. Non-conditioned apprentice/opportunity – open to all claiming jockeys. These races whatever type, class or distance tend to be won by the most experienced rider competing (especially when there are considerable differences in experience) who is likely to be offered the mount on the horse with the best winning chance.

All apprentice/opportunity races must be judged on their merits for selection purposes, but conforming strictly to the criteria suggested for race selection – level weights receiving first consideration.
N.B. Do not engage in selection in races where inexperienced horses (who may require strong and skilful handling) are ridden by young, equally inexperienced riders.

AMATEUR RACES (FLAT AND NATIONAL HUNT – LEVEL WEIGHTS AND HANDICAPS)

Amateur races, once the almost exclusive preserve of National Hunt racing, have with the introduction of lady riders into the sport become increasingly popular and grown in number in the Flat race calendar.

Amateur races initiating from the hunter chases in the National Hunt programme have spread to include handicap chases, hurdles and novice events, as well as now running the full gamut of distances and types of races in the Flat programme. Amateur races are largely supported by, and provided for, owners who wish to ride their horse(s) in public and by other dedicated and often more proficient enthusiasts who cannot or have no wish to enter the professional riding ranks in racing. Similarly to apprentice races, the most proficient and experienced riders gain the mounts on the best horses, and carefully noting the jockeys in these races often holds the key to selection. The top leading amateur riders (National Hunt) rank with many of their professional counterparts, and many leading professional riders have graduated from the amateur ranks.

Leading amateur riders during recent National Hunt seasons are:
Mr D. Browne (9st 7 lb) – Amateur Champion 1981–2, 1982–3
Mr T. Easterby (9st 7 lb)
Mr O. Sherwood (10 st 10 lb) – Amateur Champion 1979–80
Mr T. Thomson-Jones (10 st 2 lb)
Mr P. Webber (10 st 3 lb) – Amateur Champion 1980–1
Mr A. J. Wilson (10 st 7 lb)
Leading amateur riders during recent Flat race seasons are:
Mr R. Hutchinson (9 st 7 lb)
Mr J. Hills (9 st 10 lb)
Mr O. Sherwood (10 st 10 lb)
Mr T. Thomson-Jones (10 st 2 lb)
Mr A. J. Wilson (10 st 7 lb)
Elaine Mellor (7 st 7 lb)
Brooke Sanders (8 st 12 lb)
Franca Vittadini (8 st 3 lb)
Amateur races play a useful role and provide variety in racing – amateur races of level weights (Flat and National Hunt) can be an extremely reliable medium for selection.

HUNTER CHASES (NATIONAL HUNT – LEVEL WEIGHTS; DISTANCE 2½m+)

Hunter chases begin the National Hunt programme on 1st February, continuing for the remainder of the season. They are limited to horses

TABLE 4.8   Hunter chases during the 1980–1 National Hunt season

	2m 6f+	%
Fav.	42 =	40.8
2nd fav.	26 =	25.2
3rd fav.	8 =	7.8
Non-fav.	27 =	26.2
Total	103	

that have been certified as hunters during the hunting season and have not taken part in any National Hunt or Flat races after 1st November. These races are supported by the farming/hunting community who provide the backbone to National Hunt racing and are contested by point-to-point horses and ex-racehorses who have been sold out of racing.

(*N.B.* Some professional stables retain horses that have been hunted by their owners during the winter to compete in hunter chases.)

The form of hunter chases normally works out extremely well and they can be recommended as a reliable medium for selection.

5 TOOLS OF THE TRADE

The successful execution of any trade is subject to three factors – the workmanship, the materials and the use of the best and most appropriate tools.

The trades of selection and betting are no exception to the rule, these trades consisting of such skills as: (i) assessing information; (ii) formulating judgements; (iii) taking calculated action in response to these judgements. Good workmanship demands consistently practising the trade to the highest standard of personal ability and this is particularly aided if enthusiasm can be maintained in the approach to performing the selection/betting skills. The material of the selection/betting trade is the information upon which judgements will be made and actions taken, with the quality and reliance of this information having a fundamental affect in the formation of decisions. The *tools of the trade* are the sources from where the essential information is obtained and the facilities available where the results of this information may be put to the most effective use (i.e. in betting).

DEFINITIONS

WORKMANSHIP

These will be the reflection of the varying abilities according to the experience and intelligence of each selector/backer.

MATERIALS

These are the basic information requirements which makes a well-considered selection/bet possible; these will include:
1. Details of race – time, venue, value, distance and going. A list of the declared runners, riders, trainers, owners and weights.

2. Details of the form of each declared runner.
3. Details in a concise biographical account of each runner with particular reference to breeding and conformation.

TOOLS

These are the instruments/sources by which and from where the material information may be gleaned and can be found:

1. *Details of race.* Most national daily newspapers or a national daily racing newspaper.
2. *Details of form.* The official Jockey Club form books (supplied in weekly additions), and daily racing newspapers.
3. *Horse's biographies.* Weekly or annual specialized horse publications (i.e. Timeform Books).

With selection firmly dependent for success upon the quality of the information received it is essential that this information be derived from only the most dependable of sources – these sources if of quality may be considered as being the best tools of the trade.

DETAILS OF THE RACE AND DECLARED RUNNERS, ETC.

A DAILY NEWSPAPER

Although a list of the declared runners, riders, etc. can be found in most of the national daily newspapers it is a matter of personal choice as to which newspaper is preferred; the factors which have to be considered and offer considerable assistance in selection are: (i) the clarity of the print of the newspaper; (ii) the general layout and presentation of facts; (iii) any unique of features of the newspaper which provides vital information that is not otherwise readily obtainable without more involved investigation. The daily newspaper which is found consistently to fulfil the above requirements in respect of its horse-race coverage is the *Daily Mail.* This is a newspaper of tabloid size, excellently printed with clean, clear lettering thereby giving the reader immediate visual access to information (see Fig. 5.1). Its layout and presentation enables the selector to receive a direct yet comprehensive impression of the race-card at a glance; different race meetings are neatly separated, with races arranged in time order and sequence descending down the length of the page. This allows for relevant information (e.g. trainers' arrangements and jockey engagements) to

Epsom

ROBIN GOODFELLOW	GIMCRACK
2. 0 Brondesbury	2. 0 Brondesbury (n.b.)
2.35 Lafontaine (n.b.)	2.35 Lafontaine
3.35 1 : GOLDEN FLEECE (nap)	3.35 1 : PEACETIME (nap)
2 : Persopolis	2 : Super Sunrise
3 : Peacetime	3 : Silver Hawk
4.20 Johnny Nobody	4.20 Johnny Nobody
4.50 Tender King	4.50 Tender King
5.25 Spectral	5.25 Minmax

JIMMY LINDLEY'S TV TIPS.—2.0, Brondesbury. 2.35, Aperitivo. 3.35, Peacetime. 4.20, Johnny Nobody.

FIVE-YEAR RECORD

Jockeys : L. Piggott 34, Pat Eddery 25, W Carson 25, G. Starkey 20, S. Cauthen 19, P. Cook 12, J. Mercer 12,	Trainers : B. Hills 17, M. Stoute 14, B. Swift 12, P. Walwyn 11, R. Smyth 11, H. Price 10, C. Brittain 10, H. Cecil 10.

RADIO 2: 2.35 3.35

308 (21)   612610 RACEMAIL (B) 18 (C & D BF) A Tryin 3-8-7 L Piggott ●78

KEY to all-in-a-line card : Racecard number (with Jackpot prefix)—draw—six-figure form to ninth place, plus L for last, S—slipped up, R—refused, F—fell, P—pulled up, C—carried out. Horse's name. (B)—blinkers, H—hood.

Daytimer is the number of days since horse last ran. C—course winner (different distance), D—distance winner, C & D—course and distance winner, BF (beaten — favourite)—trainer—age and weight — Jockey — Formcast rating (Racemail's private handicap).

DRAW ADVANTAGE: Up to 1m 2f LOW, 1m 4f and over MIDDLE.
PRINCIPAL MEETING : L.-H. Course. Going : Good to Firm.
TOTE DOUBLE 3.35., 4.50. TREBLE : 2.35, 4.20, 5.25. TOTE JACKPOT—All Six Races.

2.0 — GREAT SURREY STAKES. (2-Y.-O.) £5,000 added. (£3,622·50). 5f (5) STALLS   ITV   Formcast

101	(2)	11211 BRONDESBURY 11 (D4) W O'Gorman 9-5 .... T Ives ●78
102	(1)	1133 BLACK GLAZEPTA 21 (D2) A Jarvis 9-3 ......Pat Eddery 64
103	(4)	121 DORSET EAGLE 9 (D2) K Brassey 9-3 ....W Newnes 64
104	(3)	4 TRY TROFFEL 39 D Kent 8-11 .... B Raymond —
105	(5)	4 ANTUM 26 A Ingham 8-8 .... G Ramshaw —

Probable S.P. : 8-13 Brondesbury, 9-2 Dorset Eagle, 7 Black Glazepta, 8 Try Troffel, 12 Antum.
FAVOURITES : 3 1 1 1 2 0 2.
1981 : Lucky Hunter 8-11 (W Carson) 5-2 Jt.-Fav. C Brittain, 7 ran.

2.35 — DAILY MIRROR HANDICAP STAKES. £12,000 (£8,332·80). 1m. 2f. (8) STALLS   ITV

201	(1)	444L-26 BUFFAVENTO 30 G P-Gordon 4-10-0 ....A Murray 71
202	(2)	7/133- NEAT 380 J Tree 4-9-11 ....Pat Eddery 60
204	(3)	01-L131 LAFONTAINE 30 (C & D C D3) C Brittain 5-9-8 G Starkey 76
207	(4)	0-01423 APERITIVO 13 (D2 BF) R Armstrong 4-9-0 ..... L Piggott 70
209	(7)	63/7-434 CANNON KING 15 J Dunlop 6-8-11 ....W Carson 70
211	(8)	5-03330 HERBIE QUAYLE 18 (BF) B Hills 4-8-8 ....S Cauthen 77
212	(6)	75-2261 GOLDEN BRIGADIER (5lb ex) 18 J Old 4-8-5 ...W Newnes ●78
213	(5)	0L-LL03 SILLEY'S KNIGHT (B) 11 J Hanson 6-8-1 .... E Johnson 77

Probable S.P. : 5-2 Aperitivo, 3 Lafontaine, 7-2 Golden Brigadier, 11-2 Cannon King, 8 Herbie Quayle, 10 Neat.
FAVOURITES : 0 3 3 0 0 0 0 1.
1981 : Easter Sun, 4-9-1 (B. Raymond), 5-1 Jt-fav., M. Jarvis. 12 ran.

3.35 — THE DERBY 1m. 4f. (18 runners)   ITV

Runners & Riders—Page 39

FIG. 5.1   Extract from a typical racecard as displayed in the *Daily Mail*.

3.35 THE DERBY, for three-year-old entire colts and fillies only (no fillies run this year). All carry nine stone. With £100,000 added to the stakes. First prize includes a golden trophy valued at £3,500. BBC RADIO 2

18 RUN ITV Formcast

301 (16) 3511-14 **COUNT PAHLEN** 21 (C) (Mrs A Villar) B Hobbs ....G BAXTER ●78
 gr c Hotfoot-Tanara *(Black, red cross-belts and hoop on cap)*

302 (14) 25-12 **FATHER ROONEY** 29 (D Schwartz) B Hills ....S CAUTHEN 70
 bc Val de l Orne-Royal Honoree. *(Black and red hoops; black cap, red diamonds)*

303 (2) 089-731 **FITZWARREN** 8 (D) (Hitchcock Enterprises) G Balding ....R WEAVER 45
 ch c Busted-Dove. *(Yellow, royal blue stars on body, striped cap)*

304 (1) LO1-L **FLORIDA SON** 21 (R Ogden) J Hanson ....E JOHNSON 40
 b c Busted-Peach Stone. *(Mauve and pink check, white sleeves)*

305 (9) 1-11 **GOLDEN FLEECE** 25 (R Sangster) M V O'Brien ....Pat EDDERY 70
 b c Nijinsky-Exotic Treat. *(Emerald green, royal blue sleeves; white cap, green spots)*

306 (3) 1113-31 **JALMOOD** 25 (D) (Sheikh Mohammed) J Dunlop ....W CARSON 77
 b c Blushing Groom-Fast Ride II. *(Maroon, white sleeves and star on cap)*

307 (7) 113-063 **LOBKOWIEZ** 29 (Mrs C Elliot-Lemoine) C Brittain ....B TAYLOR 70
 b c Radetzky-Fulcrum Miss. *(Purple, white chevron and cap)*

308 (5) 2124-85 **NORWICK** 14 (J Bodie) G Harwood ....G STARKEY 74
 b c Far North-Shay Sheerv. *(Emerald green, brown chevron, hoop, armlets and cap with green hoop)*

309 (10) 46-232 **PALACE GOLD** 21 (Mrs Poh-Lian Yong) W O'Gorman ....T IVES 71
 bl c Rheingold-Palace Rose. *(Yellow, red sash; check cap)*

310 (11) 3-11 **PEACETIME** 14 (D) (Beckhampton Ltd) J Tree ....J MERCER 72
 b c Nijinsky Peace. *(Pink, black and white striped sleeves; white cap)*

311 (17) 110-211 **PERSEPOLIS** 17 (S Niarchos) F Boutin ..,.......Y SAINT MARTIN 75
 gr c Kalamoun-Perlita. *(Dark blue, light blue cross-belts, striped sleeves; white cap)*

313 (12) 321 **REEF GLADE** 25 (Elisha Holding) P Haslam ....P WALDRON 40
 b c Mill Reef-Green Glade. *White emerald Cross of Lorraine)*

314 (15) 211-4 **ROCAMADOUR** 32 (R Buckley) A Pitt ....W R SWINBURN 76
 b c Royal Match-Blakeney Belle. *(Dark blue and yellow quartered, hooped sleeves and cap)*

315 (4) 1212-15 **SILVER HAWK** 32 (BF) (Mahmoud Fustok) M Albina ....A MURRAY 75
 b c Roberto-Gris Vitesse. *(Green, red armlets and cap)*

317 (6) 4115-51 **SUPER SUNRISE** 29 (J Maxwell) G Hunter ....E HIDE 73
 b c Sagaro-Lay Aboard. *(Black, white cross-belts and sleeves; yellow cap)*

318 (13) 250-046 **TIDWORTH TATTOO** 15 (Dr D Davis) D Elsworth ....B ROUSE 45
 ch c Native Charger-Beautiful World *(Dark green, orange chevron, white sleeves, dark green armlets; quartered cap)*

319 (8) 3-22 **TOUCHING WOOD** 14 (Maktoum Al Maktoum) Thomson Jones ......P COOK 63
 b c Roberto-Mandera. *(Royal blue, white chevron; light blue cap)*

320 (18) 244-20 **WONGCHOI** 32 (S Wong) E Eldin ....D BROSNAN 60
 b c Bustino-Lady of Chalon. *(Black and royal blue halved, gold sleeves; black cap)*

FAVOURITES : 1 2 2 2 2 2 2 1.

1981 : Shergar (W R Swinburn) 10-11 fav, M Stoute. 18 ran.

KEY TO CARD : From the left—Racecard number ; draw ; form in last six races (last second—this season) ; horse's name ; Daytimer (number of days since horse last ran) ; C = course winner ; D = distance winner ; BF = beaten favourite last time out ; owner : trainer ; jockey ; Formcast figure (Racemail's private handicap rating). Second line shows breeding (bc = bay colt, br = brown, ch = chestnut, gr = grey, bl = black) and colours the jockey will wear.

Betting forecast

5-2 Golden Fleece	20-1 Rocamadour	100-1 Reef Glade
9-2 Jalmood	25-1 Count Pahlen	100-1 Tidworth Tattoo
9-2 Peacetime	33-1 Father Rooney	100-1 Wongchoi
5-1 Persepolis	33-1 Norwick	200-1 Fitzwarren
12-1 Silver Hawk	33-1 Palace Gold	200-1 Lobkowiez
14-1 Super Sunrise	33-1 Touching Wood	500-1 Florida Son.

FIG. 5.2 Typical presentation of a more prestige race as displayed in the
Daily Mail.

be quickly recognized. Prestige races are usually given more detailed coverage. A typical example is given in Fig. 5.2. The special and unique feature of the *Racing Mail* is its daytimer information (the number of days since a horse last ran) which is represented by a figure after the horse's name. *This is vital information* (a recent race performance is the most positive indication of a horse's present fitness and well-being). Another unique feature of the *Racing Mail* is in its form figures preceding a horse's name, for here up to the first nine placings are recorded as and when a horse finished last, whether it be in a two-runner field or a multi-runner field. The fulfilment of the above qualities outlined unequivocably places the *Daily Mail* in the supreme position of being the only daily newspaper which can be recommended to have the most comprehensive racing coverage for the purpose of studied selection.

A DAILY RACING NEWSPAPER

While the basic needs for making a selection (i.e. the declared runners and riders) will be accommodated in the daily national newspaper of preference, the selector desiring a wider aquaintance with horse-racing is recommended to obtain a national daily racing newspaper i.e. *Sporting Life*. This newspaper contains comprehensive articles and information covering all aspects of racing, plus reports and a detailed results page of the previous day's racing and the 4-day declared runners with provisional riding arrangements of the next day's race programme. Naturally there is full coverage of the current day's racing programme, each meeting with declared runners and riders is usually featured on separate pages in a race time sequence and in columns down the page. This comprehensive coverage includes a full description and entry conditions of each race, the prize-money awarded to the first three of four finishers, the weight-for-age scale when appropriate, the complete long handicap and raising of weights if and when it applies, plus the position of the starting stalls and the considered draw advantage for flat races. An extract from the *Sporting Life* showing the typical layout of a race is given in Fig. 5.3. The layout in the newspaper of the declared runners and riders, etc. is clear and precise and includes the added information of ownership which may provide an important consideration for the experienced selector conversant with the training methods and influential connections of various stables. These features are finally complemented by the essential inclusion of each horse's recorded form in usually its last three races, an example of which is given in Fig. 5.4.

A national racing newspaper therefore serves as a comprehensive accessory to the basic needs of selection, providing the general news

On ITV: 2.0, 2.35, 3.35 and 4.20
On Radio 2 (330 and 433 metres): 2.35 and 3.35

JACKPOT PREFIX No. 3

3.35—DERBY STAKES (Group 1) one mile and a half; £100,000 added to stakes; distributed in accordance with Rule 194 (ii) (includes a fourth prize); for three-year-old entire colts and fillies; £400 to enter; £100 ex unless forfeit dec by April 20, £400 ex unless forfeit dec by May 18, £100 ex if dec to run; weights: colts 9st, fillies 8st 9lb. The Horserace Betting Levy Board Prize Money Scheme provides for the inclusion of £70,000 in the added money subscribed for this race; the prize to include a golden trophy value £350; There will be a parade for this race; The Stewards of the Jockey Club have modified Rule 121 (ii) (a) for the purpose of this race (Total ent 288, £400 ft dec for 141, £500 ft dec for 109 and £900 ft dec for 18).—Closed Nov 4, 1981.

Penalty value £146,720; 2nd £55,626; 3rd £27,313, 4th £12,541.
STALLS: Inside rail. DRAW: Middle numbers usually have advantage.

1	3011-14 COUNT PAHLEN—Cse Wnr 1m 110yds— (Mrs A Villar) ....B Hobbs *Black, red cross-belts and hoop on cap*	9 0	......	G Baxter	16
2	20-12 FATHER ROONEY (USA) (D Schwartz) B W Hills *Black and red hoops, black cap red diamond*	9 0	......	S Cauthen	14
3	000-031 FITZWARREN (Hitchcock Enterprises) G-B Balding *Yellow, royal blue stars on body, striped cap*	9 0	......	R Weaver	2
4	001-0 FLORIDA SON (R Ogden) ....J Hanson *Red, mauve and pink check, white sleeves*	9 0	......	E Johnson	1
5	1-11 GOLDEN FLEECE (USA) (R E Sangster) M V O'Brien, in Ireland *Emerald green, royal blue sleeves, white cap green spots*	9 0	......	P Eddery	9
6	1113-31 JALMOOD (USA) (Sheikh Mohammed) J L Dunlop *Maroon, white sleeves and star on cap*	9 0	......	W Carson	3
7	113-003 LODKOWIEZ (Mrs C M Elliott-Lemoine) C E Brittain *Purple, white chevron and cap*	9 0	......	B Taylor	7
8	2124-00 NORWICK (USA) (J E Bodie) ......G Harwood *Emerald green, brown chevron, hoop, armlets and cap with green hoop*	9 0	......	G Starkey	5
9	40-232 PALACE GOLD (Ire) (Mrs Poh-Lian Yong) W A O'Gorman *Yellow, red sash, check cap*	9 0	....	T Ives	10
10	3-11 PEACETIME (USA) (Beckhampton Ltd) A J Tree *Pink, black and white striped sleeves, white cap*	9 0	......	J Mercer	11
11	110-211 PERSEPOLIS (Fr) (S Niarchos) F Boutin, In France *Dark blue, light blue cross-belts, striped sleeves, white cap*	9 0		Y Saint Martin	17
13	-321 REEF GLADE (Elisha Holding) ...P C Haslam *White, emerald Cross of Lorraine*	9 0	......	P Waldron	12
14	211-4 ROCAMADOUR (R J Buckley) ....A J Pitt *Dark blue and yellow quartered, hooped sleeves and cap*	9 0		W R Swinburn	15
15	1212-10 SILVER HAWK (USA)—Btn fav— (Mahmoud Fustok) ....M Albina *Green, red armlets and cap*	9 0	......	A Murray	4
17	4110-01 SUPER SUNRISE (Jack Maxwell) G H Hunter *Black, white cross-belts and sleeves, yellow cap*	9 0	......	E Hide	6
18	200-040 TIDWORTH TATTOO (USA) (Dr D B Davis) D R C Elsworth *Dark green, orange chevron, quartered cap, white sleeves, dark green armlets*	9 0	....	B Rouse	13
19	3-22 TOUCHING WOOD (USA) (Maktoum Al Maktoum) ....H Thomson Jones *Royal blue, white chevron, light blue cap*	9 0	....	P Cook	8
20	244-20 WONGCHOI (S T Wong) ....E Eldin *Black and royal blue halved, gold sleeves, black cap*	9 0	......	D Brosnan	18

Eighteen runners.

FORECAST: 11-4 Golden Fleece, 4 Peacetime, 9-2 Jalmood, 5 Persepolis, 14 Silver Hawk, 16 Super Sunrise, 18 Rocamadour, 22 Palace Gold, 25 Count Pahlen, 28 Father Rooney, 33 Touching Wood, 40 Norwick, 100 Reef Glade, Wongchoi, 250 others.

Last Year.—SHERGAR, 9-0, W R Swinburn, 10/11 fav (M Stoute). 18 ran.

FIG. 5.3 Extract from a typical racecard as displayed in *Sporting Life*

May 1, Newmarket, 1½m (3-y-o) good, £3,376: 1 Rushbeds (9-0, 10); 2 Cashel Prince (USA) (9-7, 7); 3 Master Boatman (9-0, 5); 7 **FITZWARREN** (9-0, E Hide, 4), never a factor (25 to 1). 11 ran. 1½l, 2½l, 1½l, 3l, 6l. 2m 34.34s (a 2.34s).

Oct 30, Newmarket, 1m (2-y-o) good, £1,812: 1 Dudley Wood (USA) (8-9, bl, 15); 2 Corked (8-9, 24); 3 First Mint (NZ) (8-9, 29); 9 FITZWARREN (8-9, E Hide, 26), prominent over 5f (11 to 1 from 20 to 1). 27 ran. 2l, sht hd, 1½l, ¾l, sht hd. 1m 45.34s (a 6.34s).

Oct 10, **Ascot. See** TOUCHING **WOOD** (USA).

Sept **18, Newbury. See SUPER** SUNRISE.

001-6 FLORIDA SON (9-0) b c Busted—Peach Stone by Mourne. **1981, 1m soft (York). £2,826 (——).**

May 12, York. See **PALACE** GOLD (Ire).

Oct **7, York,** 1m (3-y-o) mdn., soft, £2,826: 1 **FLORIDA** SON (9-0, E Johnson, 5), led after two furlongs made rest, pushed out (25 to 1); 2 Bless 'Em All (9-0, 4); 3 Lucky Choice (9-0, bl, 1). 14 ran. 2l, 2½l, ¾l, sht hd, 1½l. 1m 49.63s (a 12.63s).

Sept 16, Ayr 1m (2-y-o) good, £1,633: 1 Outlaw (9-0, 7); 2 Orange Sorbet (8-11, 1); 3 Saxon Farm (9-0, 9); 0 FLORIDA SON (9-, E Johnson, 11) (33 to 1). 14 ran. 1½l, 2½l, ½l, sht hd, 1l. 1m 42.32s (a 5.32s).

1-11 GOLDEN FLEECE (USAY (9-0) b c Nijinsky — Exotic Treat. **1981, 7f good (Leopardstown); 1982, 1¼m firm (Leopardstown), 1¼m good to soft (Curragh). £18,860 (£17,618).**

May 8, Leopardstown, 1¼m firm, £8,356 (Group 2): 1 GOLDEN FLEECE (USA) (3-8-12, P Eddery) (3 to 1 on); 2 Assert (3-8-12); 3 Lords (USA) (3-8-5). 11 ran. 2½l, 1½l, 8l, 2½l, nk. 2m 6.8s.

April 17, Curragh, 1¼m, good to soft, £8,762 (Group 2): 1 GOLDEN FLEECE (USA) (3-8-4, inc 1lb ow, P Eddery) (5 to 4 on); 2 Future Spa (3-8-3); 3 Salutely (USA) (4-9-10). 15 ran. 3l, 1l, ½l, 2l. 2m 12.3s.

Sept 19, Leopardstown, 7f (2-y-o) mdn, good, £1,242: 1 GOLDEN FLEECE (USA) (9-0, P Eddery) (evens fav); 2 Assert (9-0); 3 Duke Of Dollis (9-0). 13 ran. 2½l, 6l, hd, 1½l, 2l. 1m 22.6s.

1113-31 JALMOOD (USA) (9-0) b c Blushing Groom—Fast Ride by Sicambre. **1981, 1m good (Goodwood), 1m soft (Goodwood), 7f 40yds good to firm (Haydok); 1982, 1½m good to firm (Lingfield). £26,856 (£18,048).**

May 8, Lingfield, 1½m (3-y-o), good to firm, £18,048 (Group 3): 1 JALMOOD (USA) (9-0, W Carson, 3), chased leaders, third straight, led well inside final 2f, ran on (11 to 8 from 7 to 4); 2 Mr Fluorocarbon (9-0, 7); 3 Electric (9-0, 2). 6 ran. 2½l, 2l, 10l, 7l, sht hd. 2m 33.51s (b 1.49s).

April 24, Sandown. See **PEACETIME** (USA).

Oct **24,** Doncaster. **See** COUNT PAHLEN.

Sept 28, Goodwood, 1m (2-y-o), soft, £3,325: 1 JALMOOD (USA) (9-2, L Piggott, 3), chased leaders till went on half-way, readily (5 to 4 on tchd 11 to 10); 2 Rockfest (USA) (9-2, 11); 3 The Nub (8-11, 7). 12 ran. 1½l, 1l, 1l, 6l, 1l. 1m 46.2s (a 6.9s).

Sept 14, Goodwood, 1m (2-y-o), good, £2,624: 1 JALMOOD (USA) (9-2, P Eddery, 2), chased leaders, switched stands' side shortly after entering straight, led 1f from home, quickened comfortably (4 to 1 from 6 to 1); 2 Vin St Benet (9-2, 1); 3 Padalco (9-5, 6). 6 ran. 4l, 4l, ¾l, ½l, 12l. 1m 43.23s (a 3.93s).

Sept 5, **Haydock, 7f** 40yds **(2-y-o)** mdn, good to firm, £2,859: 1 JALMOOD (USA) (9-0, G Duffield, 5), always well there, led inside last, ridden out (5 to 1 op 9 to 2 tchd 6 to 1); 2 Cordite Spear (USA) (9-0, 8); 3 Hill's Pageant (9-0, 11). 14 ran. 1l, 1½l, 1l, 2½l, 10l. 1m 31.94s (a 3.94s).

July 31, Newmarket, 7f (2-y-o) mdn, good, £3,552: 1 Oxslip (8-11, 10); 2 Beldale Fleet (USA) (9-0, 19); 3 Outlaw (9-0, 18); 5 JALMOOD (USA) (9-0, L Piggott, 6), with leaders, every chance final 2f, not quicken inside final furlong (5 to 4 tchd 13 to 3 from 6 to 4). 22 ran. Sht hd, 1l, hd, 1l, 2l. 1m 28.66s (a 3.46s).

July 18, Newbury, 7f (2-y-o), good £4,582: 1 Treboro (USA) (9-2, 4); 2 Diamond Shoal (8-11, 5); 3 Adonis Rex (USA) (8-7, 2); 5 JALMOOD (USA) (8-7, R Muddle, 6), outpaced to half-way, good headway final furlong, running on (20 to 1 from 10 to 1). 8 ran. 1l, 2½l, ¾l, 3l, 1½l. 1m 29.05s (a 3.65s)

113-063 LOBKOWIEZ (9-0) b c Radetzky—Fulcrum Miss by Fulcrum. **1981, 1m firm (York), 1m good to firm (Doncaster). £7,588 (——).**

May 4, Chester. See **SUPER SUNRISE.**

April 20, Epsom. **See** COUNT **PAHLEN.**

April 3, Salisbury, 7f 3-y-o, good to soft. £10,924: (Group 3) 1 Hays (9-1, 12); 2 Sabutai (USA) (8-10, 9); 3 Cornish Gem (8-10, 7); 11 LOBKOWIEZ (8-10, W R Swinburn, 11), speed 4f (11 to 2 op 4 to 1); 12 TIDWORTH TATTOO (USA) (8-10, B Raymond, 13), (33 to 1). 14 ran. 3l, hd, 1½l, nk, sh hd. 1m 31.02s (a 4.52s).

Sept 26, Ascot. See **NORWICK** (USA).

Sept 10, Doncaster, 1m (2-y-o) h'cap, good to firm, £3,407: 1 LOBKOWIEZ (8-7, inc 8lb ex, L Piggott, 8), soon close up, led three out, kept on close home (6 to 1 op 5 to 1 tchd 13 t o2); 2 Final Strike (8-9, 9); 3 Spanish Pool (8-6, 16). 16 ran. Nk, 3l, 3l, sht hd, 8l. 1m 39.11s (a 1.11s).

Sept 2, York, 1m (2-y-o) h'cap, firm, £4,181: 1 LOBKOWIEZ (8-3, inc 1lb ow, P Eddery, 8), always front rank, left 1f out, ridden out (9 to 2 tchd 6 to 1 from 4 to 1); 2 Lucky Choice (8-5, 2); 3 Santella Man (9-7, 6). 9 ran. ¾l, ½l, 4l, sht hd, hd. 1m 42.21s (a 5.21s).

Aug 6, Brighton, 7f (2-y-o) mdn, good to firm, £1,432: 1 Nunsruler (USA) (9-0, 8); 2 Saenredam (9-0, 5); 3 LOBKOWEIZ (8-11, B Crossley, 3*, 12), good headway final furlong, ran on close home (9 to 2 from 11 to 2). 11 ran. 2l, 4l, nk, 1½l, 1l. 1m 23.57s (a 2.57s).

July 24, Ascot, 7f (2-y-o) mdn, good to firm, £4,376: 1 Loyal Toast (USA) (9-0, 1); 2† Incandesce (9-0, 8); 2† Telephone Man (9-0, 7); 6 LOBKOWEIZ (9-0, B Taylor, 2), prominent until lost place quickly one and a half furlongs out (40 to 1). 8 ran. 6l, dd-ht, ½l, hd, 3l. 1m 31.64s (a 3.64s).

July 9, Newmarket, 6f (2-y-o) mdn, good, £3,426: 1 Tin Boy (9-0, 13); 2 Forest Ride (USA) (9-0, 20); 3 Blue Emmanuelle (9-0, 9); 0 LOBKOWEIZ (8-9, P Bradwell, 5*, 11). prominent 4f (33 to 1). 26 ran. ¾l, 2l, 1½l, ¾l, 2½l. 1m 16.55s (a 4.15s).

June 16, Ascot, 6f (2-y-o), good. £20,5527: (Group 2) 1 Red Sunset (8-11, 1); 2 Chris's Lad (8-11, 10); 3 Bronowski (USA) (8-11, 0 LOBKOWEIZ (8-11, P Cook, 4), (50 to 1). 16 ran. ¾l, 2½l, 2½l, nk. 4l. 1m 16.32s (a 1.32s).

FIG. 5.4 Extract of a horse's previous form as displayed in *Sporting Life*.

of racing which enables the selector to remain constantly abreast of events in the racing world.

FORM

In the assessment of form, the serious selector requires the fullest information of form and for this there can be no substitute of the Form Book.

THE FORM BOOK

This is the officially accepted Form Book printed annually in a bound volume, but received by subscribers throughout the season in weekly up-to-date editions. It is called *Raceform Up-to-Date* – there are separate volumes for Flat and National Hunt racing – one referred to as *Flat Racing Season 19–* and the other called *Chaseform*.

The Form Book is the selector's most important and indispensable tool; it is the only publication which has a record of every British racehorse's race performance(s) and is indexed and presented as a book. The Form Book contains the result of every race run and/or that was programmed in the British racing calendar. The results recorded always show the first four placed horses in each race and usually the first nine horses (the size of the field permitting, of course). The official distances between the first six finishers is also normally recorded, together with a commentary on their running and any other horse(s) who figured prominently during the race. A page from the Form Book is illustrated in Fig. 5.5. Altogether the Form Book records:

The meeting – the going, the time of the race (and time of the 'off').
The value of the race, and its distance.
The weights carried, including overweight and allowances.
The draw (where applicable – Flat), blinkers and hoods.
The winning owner, trainer and breeder.
The race time is also recorded with comparison to standard time and speed figures calculated on these times.
The betting market and starting prices are recorded plus the equivalent Tote prices including the daily double, treble and placepot, etc.
Such detailed coverage of races, which are so clearly marked make the Form Book a trusted asset in the sometimes involved process of form selection.

977 **Derby Stakes (Group 1) (3y colts & fillies) £146,720 (£55,626; £27,313; £12,541)—1m 4f** **3-35 (3-38)**

725*GOLDEN FLEECE (USA) (fav) 9-0 P Eddery (gd sort, lw, hdwy 3f out, led wl over 1f out, edged lft 1f out, drvn out) 1
708[2]TOUCHING WOOD (USA) 9-0 P Cook (4th st, ev ch fnl 2f, r.o wl) 3—2
436 SILVER HAWK (USA) 9-0 A Murray (hdwy 3f out, hard rdn 2f out, r.o) .... 1—3
895*aPERSEPOLIS (FR) 9-0 Y Saint Martin (gd sort, l.w, bhd 7f, gd hdwy 3f out, rdn 2f out, nt qckn) .... hd—4
708 NORWICK (USA) 9-0 G Starkey (l.w, 2nd st, led 3f out, onepcd fnl 2f) .... 1½—5
594[2]PALACE GOLD 9-0 T Ives (lw, hdwy 4f out, ev ch 2f out, wknd fnl f) .... 3—6
708*PEACETIME (USA) 9-0 J Mercer (hdwy 5f out, 5th st, ev ch when hung rt 2f out, wknd over 1f out) .... 4—7
436[4]ROCAMADOUR 9-0 W R Swinburn (nvr nr to chal) .... 4—8
594[4]COUNT PAHLEN 9-0 G Baxter (no hdwy fnl 4f) .... 1½—9
823*FITZWARREN 9-0 R Weaver (a bhd) .... 2—10
704 TIDWORTH TATTOO (USA) 9-0 B Rouse (a bhd) .... hd—11
510*SUPER SUNRISE 9-0 E Hide (l.w, hdwy 5f out, wknd over 2f out) .... hd—12
510[2]FATHER ROONEY (USA) 9-0 S Cautnen (hdwy 5f out, wknd over 2f out) .... sh—13
549*JALMOOD (USA) 9-0 W Carson (lw, rdn 7f out, no rspnse) .... 8—14
510[3]LOBKOWIEZ 9-0 B Taylor (3nd st, wknd 3f out) 15
559*REEF GLADE 9-0 P Waldron (6th st, wknd over 3f out) 16
436 WONGCHOI 9-0 D Brosnan (chsd ldr 7f) 17
594 FLORIDA SON 9-0 E Johnson (led 9f) 18

Page 331

3 GOLDEN FLEECE (9/4), 4 Jalmood (7/2), Persepolis (5's), 6 Peacetime, 14 S Hawk '16's), 20 Rocamadour, S Sunrise, 25 P Gold, 28 F Rooney (40's), 33 C Pahlen, Norwick (40's), 40 T Wood, 150 Wongchoi, 200 Lobkowiez, 250 Fitzwarren, F Son, R Glade, 300 T Tattoo.
M V O'Brien (R Sangster), Cashel, Co Tipperary, Ireland.
Breeder—Paul and Mrs Hexter In USA
Tote—52p Pl 24p, 37p, 33p D/f £6.96 CSF £11.70
Time—2/34.27 (b1.73) (0.96) SF—105/99/97/96/93/87/79/71/68

FIG. 5.5 Extract from the Form Book.

FORM SHEETS

These are the abbreviated version of the Form Book provided in the national daily racing newspaper, the *Sporting Life*. They are not a satisfactory substitute for the more complete information contained within the Form Book, but may in close co-operation serve in the role of an eliminating agent in the initial review of form. In this respect form sheets act as reference points, requiring that the selector undertake a more searching investigation with the aid of the Form Book.

Form sheets present the selector with a useful outline of form but cannot be confidently accepted as providing the complete picture as often they withhold as much information as they reveal.

A HORSE'S BIOGRAPHY (BACKGROUND)

This is the in-depth information which may finally confirm or deny the impression of a horse's ability that has been developing in the form

SHE

SHEDAR 3 b.f. Owen Anthony 102–Saratoga Maid (Saratoga Skiddy 113) – (1980 5.3fg 5g 6fg 5f 5g 1981 5d 7d 5v 6g) only poor form, including in sellers; blinkered last 2 starts. *R. Hoad.*

SHEER DELIGHT 3 ch.f. Gay Fandango 132–Sheer Joy (Major Portion 129) 92 (1980 5g 6s³ 6d 7g⁴ 1981 8s 8f* 7fg* 8f⁴ 8fg² 8f) well-made, robust filly; improved and in June won maiden race at York (ran on well under pressure and beat Majieda by ½ length) and minor event at Folkestone (by 7 lengths); gave impression she would have been suited by 1¼m; was well suited by firm ground; given plenty to do by her apprentice rider fourth start; retired to stud. *B. Hills.*

SHEER GRIT 3 b.c. Busted 134–Abettor 103 (Abernant 142) (1980 6g 7g* 8g* 104 8d³ 1981 7d 10fg⁴ 12g² 12d 12f² 14fg³ 11.1f) rangy, attractive colt; has rather a round action; smart and genuine as a 2-y-o, winning at Kempton and Doncaster and finishing excellent third behind Beldale Flutter and Shergar in William Hill Futurity, also at Doncaster; disappointing in 1981, although was second in Ladbrokes Derby Trial at Lingfield in May (held up, looked a difficult ride when going down by 1½ lengths to Riberetto) and 3-runner Churchill Stakes at Ascot in June (made running but couldn't quicken at all when challenged by Six Mile Bottom and was beaten ¾ length); never really on terms when about 20 lengths sixth of 18 behind runaway winner Shergar in Derby on fourth start, best of his other efforts; stays 1½m; best form with some give in the ground; probably suited by forcing tactics; said to have jarred a shoulder at Ascot. *C. Brittain.*

SHELL TOP 3 ch.f. Spitsbergen 103–Mis Tor (Little Cloud 113) (1980 NR – 1981 10.1fg 10.1g) third foal; dam placed over jumps; bought 850 gns Ascot March Sales; behind in minor event at Windsor in July and maiden race (last of 16) on same course in August; sold 675 gns Ascot November Sales. *J. Davies.*

SHENOULA 3 ch.f. Sheshoon 132–Yanoula 79 (Nosca) (1980 5d 5s 6d 1981 – 12g 12.2g 12f 13.8f) lengthy filly; soundly beaten in varied company, including selling; blinkered final start. *W. Haigh.*

SHERE BEAUTY 4 b.f. Mummy's Pet 125–Mossgo 106 (Vigo 130) (1980 §§ 7.2fg 8fg 1981 6d 6s) tall, sparely-made filly; moderate (rated 83) at 2 yrs but has gone the wrong way temperamentally and is best left severely alone; has worn blinkers. *W. Stubbs.*

SHERELCO 3 ro.c. Relko 136–Mary D 99 (Vigo 130) (1980 5g 6g 6fg 6g 1981 – 10d) leggy, lengthy, lightly-made colt; little worthwhile form in maiden and minor events; blinkered fourth outing in 1980; dead. *S. Matthews.*

SHERGAR 3 b.c. Great Nephew 126–Sharmeen (Val de Loir 133) (1980 8fg* 140 8d⁷ 1981 10fg* 12.3g* 12d* 12fg* 12fg* 14.6g⁴)
Who but Shergar could be Europe's 'Horse of the Year' in 1981? There wasn't a middle-distance performer to stand comparison with him and he built up an imposing record in some of the most important events for a horse of his type. Shergar's Derby win was one of the most prodigious in the long history of the race: he demolished the field by ten lengths, the widest margin of victory officially recorded in an Epsom Derby. Shergar won the Derby in the manner of a great racehorse and his exhibition will remain an abiding memory of the racing year. Until his unexpected defeat in the St Leger, Shergar was unbeaten as a three-year-old. He won the Guardian Newspaper Classic Trial and the Chester Vase before Epsom and then took the Irish Sweeps Derby and the King George VI and Queen Elizabeth Diamond Stakes; in none of these events did he win by less than four lengths. Alas, Shergar did not contest Europe's most prestigious and most competitive mile-and-a-half race, the Prix de l'Arc de Triomphe in October. Although he reportedly worked well at home after the St Leger—and tests carried out in the interim showed him to be in excellent health—his connections apparently felt there was too much at stake to risk a repeat of his below-par run at Doncaster. There was never much hope that the racing public would have the chance to see Shergar as a four-year-old. Such was the clamour for his services as a stallion that thirty-four shares in him offered before the King George were quickly taken up at £250,000 each, representing a valuation of £10,000,000, a record syndication for a stallion to stand in Europe. Shergar has been retired to his owner's Ballymany Stud in the Irish Republic.
Shergar was lightly raced as a two-year-old, having only two outings, in the Kris Plate at Newbury in September—when he won impressively—and in the William Hill Futurity at Doncaster in October. He was well fancied for

---

FIG. 5.6   Extract of a typical page from *Timeform Annual.*

evalution process. It will be found most easily and reliably in the specialist racing publications of Timeform – namely the weekly *Black books* and the more detailed *Annuals* (Flat and National Hunt).

The Timeform book contains a brief or detailed account of every horse that has raced, plus some as yet unraced (see Fig 5.6). There is a brief biography of a horse's breeding, its foaling date and cost if bought at public auction (in the cases of 2-year-olds), a description of its conformation – plus an analysis and rating of performance(s) by their experts. The Timeform publications have rightly gained a high reputation for their consistently sound analysis and judgement and will prove extremely useful in providing important background detail for the selector who has little or no visual contact with horse-racing.

TOOLS FOR BETTING

The Backer, having made a confident well-chosen selection seeks access to the best facilities to make betting an easy and profitable practice. There are two possible ways to bet, cash or credit – credit is normally the better and more convenient way to bet, especially for the serious backer who bets in higher stakes. The inconvenience of having the necessary amount of cash always readily at hand is removed and therefore allows the backer more flexibility in financial transactions. The instructions for credit betting (except in person at the racecourse) are made by telephone and this removes the troublesome rush to the betting office to place the bet in time.

The choice of a credit bookmaker is entirely a personal matter, with all the leading bookmakers offering credit facilities in two kinds of services; *deposit* accounts and *personal credit* accounts. Deposit accounts are usually easily obtained as they only require the backer to deposit a sum of money with a bookmaker who will provide credit facilities until this amount has been used up.

Personal credit accounts are, however, not so easily made available; the bookmaker will require proof of the applicant's credit-worthiness by way of a reference from a bank or from another credit bookmaker. An account will only normally be granted after these references have been successfully taken up, and then with a strictly imposed credit limit. This limit may later be reviewd and adjusted in accord with how the account has been conducted by the client.

Each account holder has their own personal account number which serves as vital proof of identity when betting instructions are conveyed by telephone. These instructions are accepted by the bookmaker's courteous and efficient staff who seldom make an error in their dealings and who will always obligingly relay a show of board prices and give earlier results as part of their service. Accounts are rendered for settlement either weekly or fortnightly, and may be used as regularly or as infrequently as the backer desires.

Credit facilities may be most efficiently used by the backer obtaining two or more accounts which are used as complements to each other. Once a profit has been shown on one account, the backer refrains from betting on this account until after settlement day, ensuring that a cheque from this source will be arriving in the post. Meanwhile the backer, if the situation requires, continues to bet on another account, fully aware that the stakes now in use are not euphorically confused with the recently won 'bookies money'. *Credit betting* is undoubtedly the superior facility for betting, it reduces the stress and strain from the activity by requiring no more than access to a telephone and eliminates the need to visit the casino-like atmosphere of betting office.

The factual aspect of losses or winnings being acknowledged in a written account places credit betting activity on a professional level which is normally disguised by the flow of cash in hand.

6 METHODS OF SELECTIONS

The selector having gained access to the relevant and most reliable sources of information through the use of the finest selection tools is suitably poised to begin the task of producing a selection.

Achieving consistently successful selection results will be dependent upon a specific and thorough approach being adopted and maintained throughout the process of selection. This requires:

1. The selector studiously to examine and consider all aspects of information that may have bearing in the shaping of the selection decision;
2. The elimination of speculative views unsupported by fact from any position of influence in the decision-making process;
3. The establishment of *reasoned probability* as the dominant feature of all selection judgements.

THE SELECTION OF THE RACE

The first practical step in the actual selection process is the choice of the race for *selection analysis*. At this initial stage of the decision-making process it is essential that a correct decision be taken which will then place the remainder of the process on a solid foundation. Such a proposition therefore demands that selection must be contemplated only in the most easily discernible and favourable type of races where the competition will not be fierce and there will be a limited size of field (i.e. no more than 12 runners) and therefore numerically a restricted possible result. Once these conditions are fully recognized and complied with, the analysis of the race may commence in earnest.

The studied approach prescribed as being essential to achieve successful selection results is aided and supported by the application of the *selection formula*.

This is structured systematically to examine, separate and evaluate information within its well-ordered boundaries of *Form, Fitness, Class,* and *Conditions,* allowing logical reasoned argument to be the commanding influence in the formation of the selection decision. The formula is designed with its first constituent – form – assuming the role as the main factor to be always principally considered and with the other constituents serving as modifying elements. This means that the success of the formula is constantly dependent upon the skilful interpretation and evaluation of form. Form must therefore receive the greatest consideration when comparing and assessing all the factors of the selection formula. The value of proven form can never be underestimated for it almost constantly withstands the pressures exerted by the other factors in the formula which often ply to receive equal consideration.

In the approach to, and the examination of, form, it is essential for the selector to accept three basic principles:

1. Horse-races are being honestly run, and that horse-racing is controlled by a fair and honest administration.
2. The facts of form can only reliably be accepted as fact if they have been obtained by unprejudiced analysis.
3. The interpretation of form must always be conducted in a logical, uncomplicated manner with attention focused on the immediate issue.

The selector must consider horseraces to be honestly run otherwise there can be no confident basis upon which to make a neutral assessment of form. Proven cases of flagrant malpractices in racing, although well publicized are few in actual number, and these should not be allowed to place a slur on the intergrity of British racing which is deservedly held in high esteem. Any undue emphasis on supposed malpractices can be of no positive benefit, but serve only to dissipate a selector's energies by planting an inherent mistrust in the power of a logical reasoning ability to produce successful selection results.

The suspected dishonest practices epidemic in horse-racing have been for a long time the regularly lame excuse made for inept selections by incompetent selectors. The selector in gaining an understanding of horse-racing is often confounded by situations where fact appears stranger than fiction, but soon realizes that most of the unexpected occurrences are due to equine and human fallibility rather than to any nefarious design.

The real facts of form can only be obtained by form being subjected to objective, unbiased analysis. This will require each situation to be judged strictly upon its merits, demanding that the selector becomes aware of the prejudices that he may bring to each situation and thereby seek to control them. The facts of form gleaned from a truly objective analysis rightly assume a position of paramount importance because they dependably present an accurate view of a situation and therefore may be relied on as a basis for selection.

A direct and simple interpretation of objectively analysed facts of form is an essential part of all consistently successful selection. The selector adopting this mode of interpretation remains in close contact with the immediate relevant issues and is forced to make a factual translation which rationally corresponds to the pertinent issues. In precise terms this will evoke an evaluation specifically concerned with the *what, when, where* and *how* of form:

What has the horse achieved in race performance (who has it defeated or been defeated by)?

When was the performance(s)?

Where was this performance (at what course, i.e. denoting class)?

How did it achieve its accomplishments (with ease, with difficulty)?

What was its manner of racing (always prominent – late challenge)?

What was the time of the race: (fast or slow)?

What was the going, who was the jockey?

An intricate explanation of form will usually fail to recognize and/or satisfactorily answer these specific and relevant questions. The obscure interpretation emanates from misunderstanding and exists where the selector has allowed nebulous intrigue to become a substitute for the more uncompromising and less attractive predictable realities of racing. Selection by such means descends from an eminent role of passive interpretation of facts to the position of subversive creation which can only undermine the power of reasoning probability.

Interpretation of form in the best interest of selection should always be clear, direct and concise.

The selector having been introduced to the basic principles which govern successful selection is ready to consider the possible methods of selection.

SELECTION METHODS

Although there may appear to be numerous possible selection methods, the process of selection is in fact limited to three fundamental approaches:

1. *Elimination*;
2. *Verification*;
3. *Predetermined selection.*

ELIMINATION

This is the only true objective method of selection. It is the most involved approach that requires painstaking and studious application.

The selector must examine the facts and accordingly eliminate improbabilities. The elimination method of selection demands that:

(a) Each runner (competitor) in a race must receive initially equal consideration;

(b) A runner must not be eliminated as an improbable unless there are facts to support this conclusion;

(c) The runners who after examination are not eliminated must be considered possible(s) or probable(s) and the distinction made between them – only the probables qualify for final consideration in the selection process.

(d) The runner(s) identified as probable(s) are compared and the one(s) with the most negative qualities are eliminated until there is only one remaining probable who is adopted as the selection.

Elimination is the strictly factual method of selection. It is the most comprehensive and discriminating method which, if carefully practised, will produce consistently successful results. It requires always a calm, studied approach that may become involved and time-consuming because of the need for a constant thoroughness.

The elimination process in operation requires that each runner receives equal consideration initially, until contrary evidence deems its elimination as an improbable. The conclusions arrived at during this examination are without prejudice and enable a selection judgement to be reached which is free from unsubstantial assumptions.

The elimination method applied strictly in this manner promotes a clarity of thought and an ensuing development of judgement. Selection becomes a process that is objective and decisive, allowing the final selection judgement to be reasoned yet detatched.

The elimination process as a method of selection appropriately fulfils the requirements of the selection formula and therefore can be indisputably recommended as the most viable selection method.

VERIFICATION

This is the second method of selection; it is a faster, less involved selection process where an initial viewpoint is referred to the facts (of form) for verification. Consequently it is not a truly objective method of selection because:

(a) Each runner is not equally thoroughly scrutinized;

(b) The viewpoint is a bias implanted in the process of selection;

(c) A bias limits or negates the free use of the critical faculty essential in an impartial examination of facts.

The verification process of selection in its practical application is:

(a) An assessment of the selection probable(s) made after only a superficial investigation of a race.

(b) This assessment of the selection probable(s) is then subjected to examination by the facts (of form) for confirmation or denial.

The verification approach to be consistently successful requires the selector:

(a) To make a sound initial judgement in the assessment of the selection probable(s);

(b) To make objectively a thorough and factual examination of the selection probable(s);

(c) To revoke or support the selection probable(s) only in response to the factual evidence.

Verification as a method of selection demands the use of the finest skills of judgement and can therefore only be considered as a viable and appropriate selection method for only the most able and experienced selector.

Verification is not a strictly factual process of selection. It is a method or selection which purports to provide a factual background that will endorse or deny the validity of a superficial assessment decision. Verification originates from a viewpoint (hence its lack of complete objectivity) and therefore has to be practised extremely judiciously before it may be regarded as an able abbrieviated substitute for the more involved elimination process. However, the observance of factual consideration does not prevent the interpretation of these facts from being tempered to confirm a viewpoint and thereby to undermine the power of objective reasoning. This is the inherent weakness constantly to be found in the verification approach and which is exemplified in the selection articles of most racing journalists.

The pressures of meeting copy deadlines every day precludes the possibility of there being an in-depth analysis made of each selection, resulting in selection decisions originating from memory of form, visual impressions of races and snippets of racecourse information, with the Form Book used only finally to provide the source of factual confirmation. In these circumstances the tendency will be to ratify rather than attempt to verify an initial decision. This tendency can be seen to prevail regularly in the selection articles of many racing journalists who propose a distorted interpretation of facts to support preconceived selection judgements. Verification practised in this pernicious manner produces only an inconsistent and poor record in selection results and is highly discredited. Unfortunately, however, by assuming these practices as typical, a doubting shadow is cast publicly over other more reputable selection processes that are correctly practised as reasoned factual methods.

The verification method badly practised can be seen as confusion masquerading as logic whereby a selection having evolved from an attitude based on presumed facts is then verified by a further biased interpretation of fact. Verification will only serve as a reliable method of selection if consistently practised in a manner which is judicious and scrupulously honest.

PRE-DETERMINED SELECTION

This is the third approach to selection. It cannot be presented as a method of selection with a definable process because it exists only as a preconcluded opinion which has been accepted as the selection decision. A predetermined selection is fixed, it does not desire or need any further factual qualification and is therefore *not an objective method of selection*.

A predetermined selection approach is based on the principle that the qualities of the horse selected so exceed its rivals that further considerations are unnecessary. The success of a predetermined selection is entirely dependent on the acuteness in perception of its original judgement which is subject to no further examination.

Predetermined selection may be concluded as a disregard for the opposition in a race. It is a viewpoint transcended into a selection opinion and normally emanates from someone who has had some connection with a horse's performance(s) (i.e. race-watcher, trainer, jockey, etc.) and is influenced to attribute to a horse qualities which make it worthy of automatic selection in its next race. This approach represents either a subtle awareness in observation or an irrational bias – the difference only to be ascertained after the result of the race is known.

The three approaches to selection have been described in order of merit and degree of objectivity.

Predetermined selection is an unobjective method of selection that is also likely to have no factual basis. It is a popular approach to selection because it is instantaneous, and has the alluring attraction of removing the element of self-responsibility involved in making protracted factual decisions. An unrestrained opinion can manifest itself as a selection decision. The success of predetermined selection is entirely dependent upon the quality of perception from which a formed opinion originated and over which there may be no control. Therefore, a predetermined selection can never be unequivocably accepted as a reliable approach to selection – as a decision must be subject to the scrutiny of detached objective questioning. Practical examples of predetermined selection are: *subjective opinion, tips, systems.*

Subjective opinions

These can emanate from reasons that are bizarre or rational and range from a selection made because of liking a horse's name to choosing a horse because of the way it performed in its last race (i.e. it ran well, it was unlucky in running, etc.)

Tips

These can be those obtained from daily newspapers or racing publications, by subscription to a racing tipping service or from private inspired racing sources.

Systems

These are similar to subjective opinion and may be rationally or irrationally based. They can be loosely or rigidly defined, and include following jockeys in form, trainers in form, certain jockeys, a list of horses, beaten favourites, horses for courses, etc.

Predetermined selection, although not to be considered as a recommended approach to selection, is still favoured by some selectors as their only method of making a selection. It is therefore essential for the selector who insists on practising such a method of selection to be aware of and understand the motives which produce predetermined selection (i.e. the reasoning behind a tip, a subjective opinion or the employment of a definable system). Unless an understanding is obtained of the reason for a selection the selector will always be at the mercy of uncontrolled, incomprehensible forces.

This method of selection is a presupposition of a situation and not an examination of a situation in its immediacy. Therefore, it can have no role to play in the immediate objective assessment of information demanded in the proper use of the selection formula.

SUMMARY OF SELECTION

1. The aim of selection is consistently to produce successful results.
2. This aim will be achieved by promoting the functioning of a clear, detached and reasoning mind.
3. Elimination is the practical method of selection which most efficiently promotes this function.

A correctly practised elimination method requires that the selection process be approached and conducted in an impassive manner. Each decision that is taken should be a reasoned undistorted interpretation of fact, with improbabilities systematically eliminated until the remaining option(s) constitutes the selection decision. A selection concluded by this method relies entirely on the clarity of reasoned thought, thereby removing the emotional attachment associated with a selection which has been formulated through choice and opinion.

The practical steps necessary in the approach to making a selection are as follows:

1. The method to be used.
2. The manner in which the method is practised.
3. The confidence gained in practising the method.
4. The conclusion drawn during the process of selection.

1. *The method* to be used must be positively decided and persevered with – elimination is the *best method* and the one most applicable to the selection formula. (Accrding to skill and experience a selector may more easily relate with one of the other methods.)
2. *The manner* in which a selection is made should always be in an atmosphere of unhurried calm, every consideration being given to the relevant factors without the pressures of a time deadline being allowed to influence and to intrude into the process. This will mean that sufficient time must be carefully allowed to complete the selection process.
3. *Confidence* must be gained from and in practising the chosen selection method. The final selection decision should always be made confidently (the result of judgements supported by factual evidence). A tentative selection decision has the implication of being supported only by hope and irrationality.
4. *The conclusion* to the process of making a selection is that a confident reasoned selection has emerged or that no confident and reasoned selection decision can be made. If the latter conclusion is drawn the selection process must immediately stop without further effort to resolve the puzzle of selection while the former conclusion brings the selection process to a more satisfactory resolution.

This last concluding decision is the most important and often the most finely balanced judgement to be made throughout the selection process, providing a thorough test of the selector's power of will and reasoning. It is the vital decision constantly taunted and tempted by the consuming force which constantly may seek to encroach into the selection process – **betting**.

7 BETTING

The purpose of betting is to win money!

Betting is defined: 'To risk money on the result of an event – to back an opinion with money.'

Betting can be described as the practical act which is confirmation of a commitment to a selection decision/opinion.

Betting seeks to exploit for profit a selection decision/opinion. Successful betting is therefore subject to correct selections (i.e. selecting winners); it is dependent upon, complementary to and secondary to selection.

Horserace selection is subject only to its own process and can exist without betting. Betting cannot exist without a race selection opinion.

Race selection (the means) must remain separate from and dictate to, betting to win money (the purpose). A confusion or an intrusion of betting in the selection process undermines and perverts the selection decision and thereby defeats the purpose.

Betting will only be financially viable if practised as a calculated reasoned act.

TO WIN AT BETTING

The obvious and fundamental necessity is betting on winners. If selections recorded are 100 per cent correct there are no modifying factors that can prevent winning at betting. This is an ideal to be aimed for with selections but is an unlikely practical reality.

THE MODIFYING FACTORS

These factors which prevent winning at betting, are as follows:

1. The percentage of winners to selections (ratio winners : losers);

2. The *odds* of winners betted;
3. The staking method or system used or not used.

These modifying factors clearly divide the total betting operation into two distinctly separate parts; *selection* and *betting technique selection* which are the basis of betting. It must always be a confident and reasoned decision. If this criteria is not entirely fulfilled a *selection must not be made.* Time and effort may be required in the making of a selection decision but this can never be used as a justification for selection.

BETTING TECHNIQUE – '*If*' and '*How*' to bet

Betting technique is basically simple, it revolves around one question that must always be asked: 'To bet or not to bet.' Even with the conclusion of a confident reasoned selection decision this question is evoked, because the factor still to be considered that will limit successful betting is 'The odds'.

In the assessment of odds the following should be considered:

- The purpose of betting is to win and the odds place a limit on what can be won.
- The backer has no control in the formation of odds – odds are controlled by the layers (layers of odds bookmakers) who manipulate the odds for the distinct purpose of restricting winnings and limiting their own financial liabilities.
- The backer has one and only one action to combat this power of the odds held by the bookmaker – he has the power of veto.

THE 'IF'

'To bet or not to bet' till the odds be considered fair, reasonable and/or completely in the favour of the backer. It is an advantage which must never be surrendered by the backer. The bookmaker has to lay odds all the time for each and every race – the layer has no choice – but the backer can choose if and when to bet.

In assessing the odds the backer, supported by a confident reasoned selection, needs to pose the monetary questions: 'What can I win?' Specifically, 'How will the money returned be comparable to the money risked?' Money used for betting is the highest risked capital and it is suggested that the minimum acceptable return be at least equal to outlay – 'even money'. *The backer must consider odds of less than evens unacceptable in all circumstances.*

STAKING SYSTEM (part of the 'how' to bet)

The obvious and most simple to operate 'level stakes' is the best method. In level stakes every bet is of the same value, every bet is of equal importance and no particular relevance is attached to any single bet. Therefore, no single selection decision is less or more important than the previous, and one loser places no financial loss out of proportion to other losers.

Successful betting is dependent upon the following:

1. *Selecting winners.* It is deemed that selections formulated without prejudice or enticement to bet, based upon proven factors of reasoned probability, are selections that hold the most likelihood of winning.
2. *Betting at fair and reasonable odds.* Only betting at odds where gain is appropriate or favourable to the amount of money risked.
3. *Staking system.* One which places no undue emphasis on one particular bet to the instant detriment or enhancement of the previous betting record.

A successful outcome to betting required that betting be conducted as a calm reasoned act, paying due regard to these modifying factors. This will mean applying discipline to refrain from betting in unfavourable circumstances and practising only good betting habits.

Selection, odds and staking are theoretically the only commanding factors in the betting process, but in practice there is another all-pervading aspect which can conspire to play a dominant role. This is the *financial consideration.* Although the purpose of betting is to win money, betting entails the risk of losing money. Lucid betting requires the removal of that fear of losing, whether money be in the form of hard cash, markers, credit or encapsulated ego and pride. The financial involvement, therefore, must be considered, realized and placed in its true perspective.

Money used for betting is high-risk money
It is therefore essential that a bank or pool of money be set aside to be used solely for the purposes of betting. The size of the bank may be large or small, but with the prerequisite that losing the whole or part of the bank places no financial burden on the backer.
- It must be money that the backer can afford to lose.
- It must be money that the backer is not attached to.
- It must be money the backer considers already lost.
A weakening from this rigid viewpoint will serve only to promote the unwelcome influence of the financial consideration. This influence unchecked will grow to affect the selection process adversely and thereby undermine the basis upon which successful betting is founded.

THE 'HOW' TO BET

The way

Betting is the simple act of supporting an opinion/selection with money. Placing a bet is an uncomplicated operation – writing instructions on a slip/voucher or verbally giving instructions by telephone. There are three ways to bet on a single selection: (1) to win; (2) place (only); (3) each way (win and place combine). Single selections may be joined together to form doubles, trebles and accumulators in myriad combinations.

Besides single selection bets there are forecast bets:

- Straight forecast – predicting the first two finishers in correct order.
- Dual forecast – predicting the first two finishers in either order.
- Forecasts can be similarly joined together to form doubles, trebles, etc.
- Tricasts – selecting first three finishers in correct order in handicap races of 12 or more runners.

SINGLE SELECTION BET

To win   is the simplest and most economic bet. It demands decisive selection.

Place only   is an uneconomic bet; SP and Tote place bets of selections with positive chances of being placed are normally odds-on. It encourages timid and indecisive selection.

Each way   the place part of the bet is uneconomic at one-fifth of the odds. If the selection wins, half the stake has been wasted in an endeavour to protect whole or part of the stake.

Tote odds are not guaranteed for any type of bet.

The single win bet is the best possible way to bet. It is uncomplicated, economically sound and no part of the stake is wasted if the selection is successful. Selection is focused on predicting decisive positive results; its aim is unmistakably understood from the outset.

There are other methods besides single selection bets which include the following. Combined selection bets (doubles, trebles, etc.) designed to give a large return on a small outlay by multiplying the odds together. The increase of odds signifies a decrease in the chances of winning and should be considered an over-ambitious, uneconomic way of betting. Forecasts similarly have the attraction of multiple odds and large possible gain for small outlay, but the inherent weakness of numerous combinations of possible results. Forecasts can only be economically viable when the possibilities of the result are numerically small and the multiplication of odds large (i.e. in small fields of five or less – a combination forecast made of the highest priced runners. This is a proposition based on mathematical speculation and without any regard necessarily to selection based on reasoned probability.)

Single selection bets contain enough unpredictable factors without the further additions introduced when combining selections. It is said that doubles were invented for anyone not satisfied with one loser but preferring two.

ODDS (PRICES)

Odds are the means by which the layers of odds make a profit whatever the result. Bookmakers make a book of prices/odds on an event, giving each competitor or runner price or odds against its chances of winning. These prices are carefully mathematically balanced against the money betted, so after settling payment of all winning bets the bookmaker takes a percentage profit on the overall money that has been taken.

The odds are formulated and controlled by the major bookmakers at a race meeting. After an initial write-up or opening 'show' of prices, market forces operate, with prices adjusted to accommodate varying amounts of money wagered. This betting market continues until the start of the race. The starting price odds are the mean average price for each horse calculated by independent assessors, from the lists of the leading bookmakers at the end of trading. They are a fair representation of the amount of money wagered on each horse. In the market exchanges before the start of the race, prices continually fluctuate according to supply and demand and a bet struck during these exchanges will be at a 'board price' which may be more or less than the final or starting price.

THE THREE TYPES OF ODDS

Starting price (SP) odds

The official, independently calculated average odds, that were offered at the close of trading at the start of the race.

Board price odds

The odds laid and taken in the market exchanges before a race. These odds are fixed, guaranteed and not subject to any later market fluctuations.

Tote odds

The odds calculated after the division of the pool of money wagered on a race with the Totalisator Board. These odds are not fixed or guaranteed. They are variable and unpredictable, depending on the size of the pool and how this relates to the number of winning ticket holders (i.e. a large pool with few winning ticket holders pays high odds, a small pool with many winning ticket holders pays low odds).

BOOKMAKER'S PERCENTAGE

Bookmakers win in the long run and most backers lose in the long run because the odds available are balanced in favour of the book-maker. Take the most simple case of all, the two-horse race where both animals are believed to have equal chances of winning. The situation is exactly the same as spinning a coin, heads and tails are both even-money chances. That gives the bookmaker no profit margin, so in a two-horse race if one horse, A, is evens the other, B, will be odds-on say 4–5, to give the bookies their percentage. If the odds-makers have got things exactly right their book on the race may look like this:

£55.55 to win on B at 4–5 – liability £99.99
£50 to win on A at Evens – liability £100.00
Total £105.55

Whichever horse wins, the bookie wins £5.55.

The more runners there are in the race the bigger the bookmaker's percentage can be without it appearing bad value to the backer. On average the bookmakers will have around 30 per cent built into the odds in their favour, but in a two-horse race that would mean odds of approximately 8–15 on both horses which would be completely unacceptable. So they are prepared to accept around 5 per cent on two-horse races but ask for, and get, more than 50 per cent in big fields.

The discerning backer must be able to calculate when the book-makers' margins are unacceptable and be able to work out the odds. To do this requires a little skill in arithmetic, but it is well worth while practising on a few races.

The odds of each horse must first be worked out in terms of a per-centage that it represents towards the bookies' profit. To do this write down the odds of a horse as a fraction, putting the left-hand part of the odds on the bottom and the right-hand part on top. Then add the top part of the fraction into the bottom part, divide it out and show the answer as a percentage. A few examples are shown below:

$$2-1 \text{ is } \tfrac{1}{2} \text{ becomes} _1 \div _2 = \tfrac{1}{3} = 33.3\%$$
$$3-1 \text{ is } \tfrac{1}{3} \text{ becomes} _1 \div _3 = \tfrac{1}{4} = 25.0\%$$
$$4-6 \text{ is } \tfrac{6}{4} \text{ becomes} _4 \div _6 = \tfrac{6}{10} = 60.0\%$$
$$13-8 \text{ is } \tfrac{8}{13} \text{ becomes} _8 \div _{13} = \tfrac{8}{21} = 38.1\%$$

To calculate the theoretical percentage profit for the bookies in a given race, calculate the percentages for every runner and add them up. The resulting figure is the so-called *overround* figure or the percentage in favour of the bookies. An example taken from the 1981 St. Leger is given in Table 7.1.

TABLE 7.1   Bookmaker's percentages

Horse	Starting price			Percentage towards profit
Shergar	4 – 9	9/13	=	69.2
Glint of Gold	4 – 1	1/5	=	20.0
Bustomi	13 – 2	2/15	=	13.3
Cut Above	28 – 1	1/29	=	3.4
Riberetto	66 – 1	1/67	=	1.5
Magikin	250 – 1	1/251	=	0.4
Brigadier Hawk	250 – 1	1/251	=	0.4
Total				108.2
Percentage in bookmaker's favour			=	8.2

In broad terms the bookmakers are prepared to work on smaller margins in small fields, at big meetings and on the first race at a meeting. They work on big margins in large fields, on bank holidays and in sellers.

It is also important to note that the bookmakers make least out of bets on favourites and short-odds horses and most on long-odds chances. An analysis of the prices of all the horses that ran on the Flat in 1981 is given in Table 7.2.

TABLE 7.2

Prices	Winners	Runners	Profit or loss	Loss percentage
Odds on	223	375	−11	−3
Evens – 2–1	533	1404	−43	−3
9–4 – 5–1	962	4768	−389	−8
11–2 – 9–1	569	5454	−1725	−32
10–1 or more	552	20557	−10951	−53

Odds are the factor which decides how little or how much is returned on the money staked. To win money successfully demands betting only at the right odds.

THE RIGHT ODDS

This can be termed as getting 'value for money', when it is clearly understood to mean obtaining fair and reasonable odds on a well-formulated selection which has a positive reasoned chance of winning. However, value for money often tends to be a term totally misunderstood to mean obtaining fair and reasonable odds on a well-formulated selection which has a positive reasoned chance of winning. This is a misunderstanding nurtured when a selection decision has not been fully realized and/or concluded and when betting and the selection process are allowed to become entwined.

It is impossible to state categorically what are the right odds without examining the factors particular to any given situation. It can only be left to the personal judgement of the backer to decide what odds in the circumstances are appropriate, always placing supreme importance on two questions: What can I win? and What do I stand to lose? (And how these two factors relate to the practical chances of the selection winning, i.e. form/fitness, strength of opposition, etc.)

Before suggesting what may be considered the right odds it can be emphatically stated what can be considered 'bad odds'. 'Odds-on' are bad odds as they are unfair and unreasonable.

They can never favour the backer who stands to lose more than can be gained.

They always favour the bookmaker whose risk is less than possible gain.

At odds-on the onus is firmly placed on the backer being correct in selection, at 'evens' less than a 50 per cent winning ratio produces financial loss. In such circumstances the only viable response to bad, unfair, restrictive odds is not to bet.

A guide to the 'right odds'

Getting the 'right odds' can be termed as the fine balance of the odds that can be fairly and reasonably demanded by the circumstances and the odds realistically likely to be offered by the bookmakers.

The circumstances reveal and are the subject of the following factors

1. The proven quality of the form of the selection.
2. The number of runners, particularly the number with probable chances of winning (i.e. the more competitive the race, the more open should be the betting odds).

3. The type of race (e.g. mdn races basically have a reliable predictability value. All types of handicaps are by their nature unpredictable. Chases are similarly laced with drama and surprises that
   can thwart even the most reasoned of selections.)

These prominent factors have to be carefully considered when making
a calculated assessment of true, fair, appropriate odds which may not
bear close relationship to the odds offered and calculated solely to
favour the layers.

The realistic view of the odds actually offered by the bookmakers
is subject to the following:

1. The popular predictability of the selectors (i.e. how strongly have
   the racing press tipped or ignored the selections).
2. Information/rumour private to bookmakers, of a horse's chances
   which causes them cautiously to shorten or speculatively lengthen
   prices.
3. Weight of money wagered before the opening show of prices
   which restricts the possibility of a fair price being offered.

After giving due regard to the odds which may be realistically
offered; a guide can be suggested upon which to base the 'fair' right
odds. This should be constructed on the understanding that 'evens'
are the lowest acceptable odds, and that upward price adjustments be
made to accommodate competition and conditions.

A 'fair price' for a horse in a race in which there is no foreseeable
competition is evens. When betting tax and unforeseen circumstances
are taken into consideration there will still remain a good profit for
the backer in this situation. Odds-on is not acceptable because the
profit for the backer is reduced to unacceptable or non-existent levels.

If there is a serious danger to a selection the backer must look for
longer odds to compensate for the additional risk; 2–1 is the least
acceptable odds.

Two serious rivals, the backer must look for 3–1 or more; three
serious rivals warrants 4–1 or more and so on.

N.B. It is considered that a race comprising of three or more serious
     rivals to a selection is too competitive to contemplate a selec-
     tion, and any selection still formulated in these circumstances
     is likely to be most injudicious.

While favourable conditions such as weight, distance and/or going
require the reduction of odds by a fraction of a point, similarly, if
these and/or other elements are to the disadvantage of a selection, then
fractions of a point should be added.

By this method the backer can calculate odds that are fair and equivalent to the practical elements influencing the winning chances of a
selection. The backer with this formed and detached assessment of the

odds can readily make a reasoned comparison with the actual odds offered by the bookmaker, and not be unknowingly beguiled to accepting less than a fair value. The value offered to backers does vary considerably from course to course according to the strength of the market.

BETTING VALUE HINTS

Every backer knows how difficult it is to beat the bookie because the satchel man fixes the odds. Ask a bookmaker if you can have a bet on the toss of a coin and he will offer you 4–5 for each of the two so he can make his profit.

What few backers realize is that the bookie's profit margin varies from race to race and that the off-course bookmaker and backer is in the hands of the on-course bookmaker who fixes the prices.

The backer can obtain a vital edge by knowing when the odds are in his favour and avoiding betting on races when the bookies' take is high.

A survey was made of flat races run in 1981 and, using a computer to make the many thousands of calculations involved, it produced the following results. The average mark-up was just over 20 per cent which gives the odds fixers a reasonable profit. However, in some races the mark-up went to over 60 per cent and in many it was less than 10 per cent.

By and large, the more runners there are in a race the bigger the bookies' margin becomes. In our coin-tossing example, the layers would have to go to 4–6 heads and tails to get their average 20 per cent margin and who would bet at those odds? It can be seen from Table 7.3 that betting in fields of 5 runners or less is a much better proposition than betting in fields of 16 or more runners.

The other major factor is the strength and make-up of the on-course market. In this survey, Salisbury gave the backers the worst value and

TABLE 7.3

Size of field	% Mark-up
5 and under	9.4
6–15	21.0
16 and over	43.0
All races	20.1

Lingfield the best. But when we take into account the number of runners in the races concerned, the position changes and we get the *Backers value table*:

Very Good	Ascot, Brighton, Catterick, Kempton, Leicester, York
Good	Epsom, Lingfield, Newbury, Ripon, Sandown, Warwick
Average	Beverley, Chester, Folkestone, Goodwood, Nottingham, Pontefract, Thirsk, Wolverhampton
Poor	Bath, Doncaster, Haydock, Newcastle, Newmarket, Redcar, Yarmouth
Very poor	Ayr, Carlisle, Chepstow, Edinburgh, Hamilton, Salisbury, Windsor

The Tote is changing its methods of collecting dividends so often we do not know where we stand. But it should be worth while betting on the Tote at the poor value meetings and on the book at five-star meetings.

TOTE ODDS

These are not guaranteed and can always be subject to very unpredictable elements; they are not usually considered a professional or reliable way to bet. Tote punters tend to be small stakes, fun punters who dislike the atmosphere of the bookmakers' betting ring and prefer the more respectable demure approach of the Tote officials. Few serious backers will ever bet on the Tote because the risks are unknown. Tote dividends are calculated on the basis of the number of winning tickets on the successful animal and the backer cannot know in advance what the pay-out will be. The backer, therefore, gambles twice – once on the outcome of the race and then again on the dividend.

Because the Tote take-out is constant there are occasions when on average it will pay to bet on the Tote rather than with bookmakers. This is when the bookmaker's percentage is known to be high in big fields, outsiders, bank holidays, sellers, etc.

Never back on the Tote in small fields, on favourites or on fashionable jockeys. The dividends in these circumstances are invariably disappointing. Tote backers by and large bet names, numbers, fashionable jockeys, trainers, and famous horses, and herein lies the essence of which is a guide to predicting Tote odds.

Fashionable jockeys, trainers (or ones with good records at a course particularly the provincial ones)	Pay bad odds (i.e. odds that are invariably worse than SP)
Well-tipped horses	
Untipped horses, from unfashionable stables with little-known jockeys (i.e. unfashionable ones, new apprentices or inexperienced amateurs)	Pay good odds (i.e. odds invariably considerably better than SP)

STAKING

Stakes

The amount of money bet is of equal importance and fully complementary to odds in betting technique. Winning money is the outcome of developing a successful betting technique, and this will only be established by forming and maintaining a disciplined staking method. Although many staking plans abound, the best, most efficient, obvious and simplest to practice is *level stakes betting*. Level stakes ensures every bet be treated with equal importance. No particular significance or stress is placed upon winning or losing a single betting battle in a campaign that is only a part in the continuous betting war.

The size of the stake

This essentially must be left to the personal consideration of each backer. For practical guidance it is recommended that a bank of money (solely set aside for betting purposes) be divided into 20 equal parts to represent 20 bets at level stakes. Such an approach enables the betting operation to commence without any financial pressure of looming insolvency.

Level stakes may appear a cautiously mundane method of betting – but results testify to its effectiveness and sound economic basis. There are occasions, however, when favourable circumstances demand a deviation from its rigorous enforcement, these modifying factors being: *favourable odds* – introduction of an accumulative (roll-up) level stakes method.

FAVOURABLE ODDS

When odds are offered that are well above their real value (i.e. 5–1 is offered for a selection whose reasonable fair odds should be 2–1) such favourable odds demand an increase of the stake. The amount of increase in the stake can only be left to the personal judgement of the backer to assess; the guiding factors being: 'the greater the value the greater the increase in the stake'.

The occasions when bookmakers generously error in the odds offered is extremely rare – they do exist – but only enforce the wisdom of maintaining level stakes at most times. Real over the odds value from bookmakers is comparable to 'solid gold' watches being sold cheaply – it is a situation to be viewed with great scepticism.

In the fluctuations of the betting market, drifting odds can become favourable odds if they reach well above a prescribed level thought to represent fair value. This situation justifies considering making another bet, if one had already been struck at lower odds or increasing the stake if a bet has yet to be made.

In the charged atmosphere of the betting ring, where rumours are rife, and sinister implications can be drawn without justifiable cause if prices drift, it is essential to understand that the drifting or lengthening of odds are simply the bookmakers' only method to attract money to balance their 'book'. The drifting of the odds of any carefully formulated selection should not persuade the backer to lose nerve but rather to be spurred to take full advantage of the opportunity to obtain extra value by increasing the stake.

Shortening odds are unfavourable odds

If odds shorten no attempt must be made to increase stake to compensate for loss of the price value. If a bet was not made at the fair 'right odds' a bet must not be made later at shorter odds (especially when there is a temptation to increase stakes).

An increase of stakes to offset shortening of odds is at best an extreme method of buying money, which if habitually practised will quickly lead to betting bankruptcy.

ACCUMULATIVE STAKING (BASED ON THE LEVEL STAKES PRINCIPLE)

This accumulative level stakes plan is a method of raising while at the same time always maintaining a consistent equal level of stakes, not subject to fluctuations of success. Winnings are added to the betting (bank/pool) for immediate reinvestment in a systematic increase of stakes.

The bank – divided into 20 equal units representing 20 equal bets – allows for 20 consecutive losers before the bank is lost completely. The profit from winnings is added to the bank, which is divided to immediately raise the level of stakes of the remaining bets, i.e.:

If the first bet is a winner, e.g. 2 pts profit:
    2 pts + bank 20 pts = 22 pts
    22 pts ÷ 20 (bets) = 1.1 pts (20 remaining bets)
If the first bet was a loser and the second bet a winner, e.g. 2 pts profit:
    2 pts + (remaining bank) 19 pts = 21 pts
    21 pts ÷ 19 (remaining bets) = 1.105 pts (19 remaining bets)
If it were desired to keep the bank intact in the second instance, then:
    21 pts ÷ 20 (original no. of bets) = 1.05 pts (20 bets)
N.B. The rate of increase in stakes is subject to the odds and consistency of winning selections.

Accumulative staking seeks to make full use of winnings by immediate reinvestment to produce further profit. It requires strict and constant attention to be paid to the accounting side of betting.

Level staking makes no immediate use of winnings. It requires little attention to be paid to the accounting side of betting.

SUMMARY OF BETTING

A guide to successful betting may be summarized in the following formula:

S	O	S
Selection	Odds	Stakes

These alone are the three factors which govern betting.

Selection

This is the first and fundamental element. Selection is the *means* – without winning selections there is no possibility of achieving successful betting results.

Odds

These are a modifying element, secondary to selection. Odds are the modality which impose a limit on how much can be won. Objectively they must evoke the question: 'Is the reward worth the risk?'

Stakes

These are the other modifying element – complementary to both odds and selection. Stakes are the method which serves to apply the means. Stakes raise the question: 'How much should be risked?' Stakes are the vital monetary aspect whose inconsistent or ordered application will frustrate or promote the successful outcome of betting.

The outcome of successful betting is to win money. This objective can only be consistently achieved by supporting successful selections at the 'right odds' with a rational system of stakes.

BETTING AND BOOKMAKERS

BOOKMAKING

This is the making of a book (set) of odds on the outcome of an event. The odds are mathematically calculated to provide the maker of the book with a percentage profit on turnover irrespective of the outcome of the event.

BOOKMAKERS

These are the layers of odds – they form the betting market which they endeavour to control and manipulate to maintain an advantage over the betting public. The layer of odds seeks to obtain the minimum of liability (pay out) coupled with the maximum of income from betting stakes. This therefore makes odds-on the most attractive and favourable bet to the bookmaker and the most unfavourable bet to anyone taking those odds.

Bookmakers operate through the British Isles 'on' and 'off' the course, some are strictly on-course or off-course bookmakers, while others combine and are both kinds. The betting market, however, is formed and controlled solely at the racecourse (except for ante-post betting) by the on-course bookmakers.

Types of on-course bookmakers

There are three separate groups of on-course bookmakers who can be immediately recognized from the position where they trade on the racecourse: (i) the 'rails' bookmakers; (ii) The 'Tatts' bookmakers; (iii) the Silver Ring (or public enclosure) bookmakers.

The 'rails' bookmakers

These are the foremost and, at most race meetings, the group of bookmakers which hold a commanding influence in the betting market. They take their position on the racecourse lining the railings which divide the members' enclosure from the Tattersalls enclosure. They are the hierarchy among bookmakers, the senior, often longest established and largest firms of bookmakers, wielding considerable power in the trading activities of the betting market. Betting transactions are made verbally with them and recorded on large boarded sheets of paper which give them an immediate visual indication of their commitments.

Business is conducted almost entirely in credit, and therefore only with clients that have been vetted and are of a reliable standing; these include other bookmakers, professional racing people who often bet in larger sums than the average 'Tatts' bookmaker can or wishes to lay, and racing stables who, when they place their commissions on course, prefer the credit facilities offered by the 'rails' bookmakers.

The 'rails' bookmakers do not visually display the odds they have on offer and it is necessary to ask or listen to their exalted barker-like calls to discover what odds they are prepared to lay. These odds will be subject to market fluctuations and therefore change in response to the on-course betting activities conveyed to the 'rails' bookmakers by strategically placed and frantically signalling 'tic-tac' men. Off-course betting developments are conveyed to the 'rails' bookmakers with equal swiftness and efficiency via the 'blower' (the racecourse–off-course direct telephone link) and will produce an appropriate response in odds.

The 'rails' bookmakers with their off-course betting links and their facility to lay the larger on-course bets command the most powerful and dominating influence in the betting market. Significant market acitivity which permeates through to affect prices in the other betting rings is sure to have emanated from trading moves of the 'rails' bookmakers (i.e. 'laying off' money – the bookmaker's method of limiting liability by placing whole or part of an accepted commission with other bookmakers). Such moves which bring a volume of money suddenly into trading activities causes an immediate depression of prices as money chases odds and the market forces of supply and demand are intensified.

As the betting market closes at the 'off', it is from the 'mean' or average prices laid by the 'rails' and leading 'Tatts' bookmakers that independent assessors who have observed and recorded the foregoing market trading compile the SP odds.

The 'Tatts' bookmakers

The 'Tatts' bookmakers usually form the majority of bookmakers to be found on the racecourse; they are located in the Tattersalls Ring which is the focal point of betting at a racecourse. The Tattersalls area represents the medium-priced entrance fee for racecourse enclosures, attracting the racing enthusiast who is non-professional and whose principal interest is likely to be a moderate flutter (i.e. betting in sums from £1 to £2 up to perhaps a maximum of £100). The Tattersalls bookmakers exist principally to accommodate these punters, offering 'cash only' betting and visually displaying the prices they have on offer on boards.

'Tatts' bookmakers form the cornerstone of bookmakers in the betting market, they offer odds which are competitive among themselves and often with those on offer by the 'rails' bookmakers. It is necessary for them to be (as their well-earned reputation confirm), sharp in their dealings and forever vigilant of the constant change of currents in market trends which unheeded would quickly swamp them. 'Tatts' bookmakers have for long provided colour to the racecourse betting scene epitomized in the caricature of 'Honest Joe' standing beside a board of prices, with a satchel heavily laden with the money of losing punters.

The Silver Ring bookmakers

The Silver Ring bookmakers are the least influential of bookmakers found at a racecourse, they are located and operate in the Silver Ring or public enclosures (the cheapest entry admissions on a racecourse). They provide a betting service for the amateur racegoer more likely interested in a day's outing in the open air than any hearty ventures into betting. Silver Ring bookmakers like their 'Tatts' counterparts insist on cash-only bets, and being at the lower end of the market take only the smaller bets. They compensate for this lower turnover by usually offering undervalue odds (prices that are lower than what is on offer in the other betting ring).

Silver Ring bookmakers play no influential role in the betting market, and will be given a wide berth by the more experienced racegoers and backers. Their role is to serve the needs of the amateur, inexperienced and indiscriminate backers, the prices offered by the Silver Ring bookmakers have no influence on the eventual SP odds.

The on-course betting market

The on-course betting market except for the larger prestigious races and meetings (Flat and National Hunt) tends to be extremely sensitive and quite unable to withstand any sizeable bets without a violent depression of odds. This is because without strong market activity (a considerable flow of money), the aim of bookmaking (making a rounded book of prices, with money proportionally evenly spread to show a percentage profit whatever the result) is challenged and threatened. In such circumstances any large influx of money in an inactive market will be met with the counterbalancing response of an immediate reduction in the odds. If the influx of money is too great for even this guarded response, the bookmakers will enforce their strongest weapon: 'We maintain the right to refuse a part or whole of any commission.' In other words they will choose what bets, and what size of bets they are prepared to lay – usually refusing whole or part of sizeable bets at odds which are attractive to the backer. This attitude is the source of all the friction between backers and bookmakers because it originates from and reveals the bookmaker's fundamental and undisguised posture towards betting: 'We'll take any sort of bet except a winning one' (especially a sizeable winning bet) – the bookmaker demonstrating what a big brave fellow he is when the backer who has both hands tied behind him and then makes a promise not to hit the bookmaker. It can be stated that the bookmaking fraternity are extremely sensitive and nervous people when faced with the possibility of accepting – or even worse if having already accepted – sizeable bets at long odds on a horse with a real winning chance. Such fears by bookmakers have forced any determined backers who want sizeable bets at less than derisory odds to find undetectable methods of 'getting on'.

On-course or off-course, large single bets at long odds will just not be taken by bookmakers except in the most competitive of races and where there is an extremely large and strong market (i.e. Derby, Grand National, or popular handicaps where there is ante-post betting). Large bets for other races at best will usually only be accepted in part and then only at reduced odds; occasionally bookmakers will accept them whole or in part at SP (if they have sufficient time to 'lay off' the bet). This will result in a sweeping depression of the SP as the bookmaker quickly lays off the bet and in the process gains free trading points profit. (By retaining a bet in such instances because of the impossibility of making a round 'book' in an uneven market the bookmaker stands to gain only if the bet is a loser.) However, by laying off the bet the bookmaker will seek to profit from the horse winning and yet stand in no liability. Laying the bet off will immediately reduce the SP to lowly odds as money floods in one direction in a weak market. The SP returning perhaps at evens when as the money was laid off (spread with a number of other bookmakers) the odds may have varied in this process from 5–1 to 2–1 giving the original bookmaker who laid the bet off 2, 3 or 4 points profit on a winning bet.

The only hope any intrepid backer has to defeat such ploys, is to get the bet laid without the bookmakers being aware of its real size. It will mean 'spreading the money'. This can be achieved on-course or off-course, but will require careful planning and skilful execution. On-course it will require a team of people simultaneously to place small bets (in total equivalent to the large bet) and having them accepted at prices before the significance of such prices on the market is realized. Off-course money may spread over a wide area in small amounts and with the hope of a reasonable SP as the market activity on-course will be uneventful.

The off-course bookmakers

There are two types of off-course bookmakers representing cash or credit business, although some do combine both.

Cash bookmaking

This is the more dominant feature of off-course bookmaking and is represented by betting shops/offices which adequately cater for the needs of the majority of the betting population. Business which is strictly 'cash only' is conducted in a casino-like atmosphere where some events for betting (i.e. horse-racing or greyhound racing) are occurring normally every 10 to 15 minutes throughout the late morning and afternoon. Commentaries of races may be interspersed with, and are supplemented by, betting shows conspiring to engulf the betting-shop customer in an intrigue of constant action and excitement. Bets of almost any size from a nominal minimum to a fairly high maximum will be accepted in betting offices, and there is no discrimination between the large or the small backer. The smaller backers are in fact encouraged to bet small stakes in myriad combinations which if successful at good/long odds would produce a considerable return on a small investment (a possibility which to the dismay of the punter and the expectation of the bookmaker seldom happens). The cash bookmakers involved with betting offices play no significant role in the on-course betting market, although themselves always subject to the results of its trading in the SP. Occasional large bets taken in the offices may be phoned through to be 'laid off' on-course to depress the SP; or similarly threatening commitments from the final leg of a successful but incomplete accumulative bet may warrant the same response and have an influence in the on-course market. Normally, betting offices passively lay the Board prices shown which represent the 'on-course' market trading and rely completely on the SP to settle all other bets. Off-course bookmakers are therefore very vulnerable to any coup in on-course trading which could inflate starting prices and have to remain extremely alert in preventing such situations from arising.

Betting offices, the only legal places for off-course cash betting, have become social institutions providing warmth and a meeting-place for those of like mind and disposition among the betting classes.

Credit bookmaking

Although smaller in volume this is normally of greater significance than off-course cash betting and bookmaking. Credit bookmaking is usually conducted by telephone, with backers conveying their instructions verbally and betting in larger amounts than the normal cash customer. The larger credit bookmaker is likely to have or represent professional racing interests (i.e. trainer, owner, etc.) whose betting habits are likely to be a specific indication of a horse's real chances of winning. The value of such information to a bookmaker amply compensates the retaining of these possibly regular winning accounts which would otherwise not be tolerated because of their unsound economic basis. Precise reliable information from these sources will prompt bookmakers to anticipate market trends and act accordingly, being ready to hold or lay off bets as the situation demands. All the larger credit bookmakers have or have access to course representatives with whom they will be in constant contact, entrusting them to initiate or regulate market activity with the aim always of limiting the bookmaker's liability.

Credit clients are only accepted by bookmakers from reliable personal references or after scrutiny of financial references (i.e. bank), to their credit-worthiness. Transactions of often such a delicate financial nature require goodwill and trust by both parties, of which bookmakers with their years of experience have designed safeguard systems which seldom give rise to any disputes over bets. Credit accounts work well and provide excellent service to the backer; accounts are rendered for settlement weekly or fortnightly and they can be recommended as the easy comfortable way of betting for all except the impulsive, and uncontrollable gambler.

Ante-post betting

Ante-post betting is the betting that takes place on an event some time before it actually occurs – any time from 24 hours to up to a year or more before the event. All the large races (i.e. Derby, Guineas, Classics, Grand National, etc.) have an ante-post betting market and they are constantly engendered by bookmakers to create betting activity at all times. The rule of ante-post betting is that all bets stand whether a horse runs (competes) in the event or not (i.e. horses entered a long time in advance for a race may become injured, ill or sometimes prove inadequate and are then withdrawn from the race). All the bets on these horses are lost, and herein lies the weakness and uncertainty of ante-post betting. The only attraction to ante-post betting is the chance of obtaining good odds and the possibility of holding a winning voucher on 20–1 chance whose starting price is returned at possibly 4–1 or 5–1. Ante-post betting to be successful usually requires professional racing knowledge as to a horse's aims and more than a fair share of luck – it cannot be recommended to the fun-loving amateur punter who will lose out more often than not with the horse failing to run.

Ante-post betting, where all are in, run or not (there are some concessionary ante-post bets on the morning of the race which offer the backer possible longer than SP odds without risk of losing the stake if the horse be withdrawn) cannot normally be recommended as a good betting medium. Ante-post betting can fairly be said to be

designed by bookmakers solely for their self-development and publicity. Cash ante-post bets where bookmakers have the backer's
money a considerable time before settling day must appear an
extremely attractive proposition to bookmakers and be a conclusive
argument against this form of betting.

Bookmakers are kept to the standard of living they have for long
grown accustomed and now expect, by a large army of backers whose
principal interests are to be involved in the act of betting irrespective
of the consequences and without regard to their supposed aim of
actually winning money.

8 THE SELECTION FORMULA ANALYSED

FORM

Form is the first and foremost constituent in the selection formula.

Form is the record of a horse's race performances and the factual evidence of racing ability.

Form is therefore the primary consideration in race analysis and the fundamental element upon which to base selection.

In the evaluation of form it is necessary to ask: 'What horses has the horse beaten?' or, 'What horses have finished behind it?' The only satisfactory answer is previous and/or subsequent winners. Such confirmation establishes the form as of value, it means a horse has finished in front of horses which have previously or subsequently beaten many other horses. It is the best and most reliable criterion of form, the soundest foundation upon which to base selection and applicable to races of all types and class.

FORM ANALYSIS

The unbiased assessment of only proven factors is the guiding principle of objective *Form analysis*.

The selector is seeking to identify the following:

1. The abilities of a horse.
2. The modifying factors responsible for the probable reproducing of these abilities (i.e. similar distance, going, weight, class, course, jockeys, handicap).
3. After the assessment of this information, the concluding assembly of a form probable or probables.

It is revealed in the process of analysing form that a horse's ability can be identified as corresponding to one of three distinct categories: **proven positive ability; unproven ability; proven non–ability.**

Proven positive ability

This is solely the positive aspects of ability proven by race performances. It is where a horse produces a race performance of definable
positive value (i.e. winning or being placed, etc.) displaying proven
ability.

The more race experience a horse has, the more information there
is upon which to judge ability; patterns in performance become established from which a horse will make only discernible and probable
deviations (i.e. its racing style will be predetermined).

Proven positive ability is only what a horse has achieved in race
performance, it is exposed ability, and it can be identified in horses
of all types, ages and class.

Unproven ability

This is ability that is unexposed and can be said to exist where the
evidence from race performance is insufficient to confirm a horse has
either proven positive ability or proven non-ability. It applies to
inexperienced horses, some of which display potential ability, and to
horses that have not previously raced. The less experienced a horse,
the less opportunity it has had, and the less information there is upon
which to assess ability. In these circumstances it is judicial to consider
such a horse's ability as unproven.

Potential ability and supposed abilities emanating from off-course
reputation all remain unproven until confirmed in race performance;
this applies to horses of all types, ages and class.

Proven non-ability

This is where a horse of experience has shown no ability in its race
performances, or at best moderate ability which shows no sign of
improvement. In such instances the horse can be considered to have
proven non-ability, this also applies to horses of all types, ages and
class.

It is revealed in the defining of the three categories of ability that
the key to a reasoned interpretation of form is the careful use and
understanding of words. These are the symbols used to describe,
record and communicate perceptions, they form the basis of the
thought and reasoning process. In form analysis words represent race
performances; it is therefore essential they be used precisely and their
meaning accurately understood. It becomes apparent that the inac-
curate use of words in the process of analysing form leads to an
erroneous interpretation of form (i.e. potential, unproven ability and

reputation can become insidiously regarded as proven ability). In such cases speculative opinion assumes the role of proven fact.

It is essential that the selector carefully examines the use and meaning of words and never accepts assumption as proven fact. The confusion of fact with fiction (unsupported fact), proof with speculation is the main cause for misinterpretation and miscomprehension of form.

Assessment relying on factors of proven ability is the most reasoned approach to form analysis and the surest foundation upon which to base selection. Proven ability can only be assessed from past performances. Form is a record of past performances, and by its very nature it is always past form. This can be considered and graded as: (i) recent/current form; (ii) less recent form; (iii) distant past form.

Recent current form

This is the highest grade; it is the most reliable indication of whether or not a horse is likely to reproduce its known proven abilities. Recent form undeniably reflects a horse's current form, fitness and general well-being (especially within the previous 7 days) and thereby indicates whether or not a horse is likely to reproduce its abilities.

The time-scale for considering form as current is (as recent as possible) preferably within the past 7 days but allowing up to 16 days approximately.

Less recent form

This is of middle grade in value; the less recent form is, the less reliable it is as an indication of a horse's current ability. This applies particularly when assessing the form of inexperienced horses (i.e. 2–3 y.o. mdns, novice hurdlers, novice chasers) who often make rapid and varying degrees of improvement which demands the reappraisal of less recent form. In these instances current/recent form continually supersedes less recent form. Less recent form can only be relied upon when 'top class' (i.e. Classics, Group Races or their National Hunt equivalent). Any time from 20 to 28 days+ can be considered less recent form.

Distant past form

This is the lowest grade in value; it can be termed 'old form'. The older form becomes, the less relevant it is likely to be to the present. Distant past form is a record of what a horse is capable of, while current form reflects its present abilities. A comparison of the two will indicate whether a horse has maintained its form, improved or deteriorated. If distant past form is top class it can never be completely disregarded as a horse with proven ability may always reproduce it. However, a horse which has lost its form is unlikely to suddenly return to form without prior indication, which will be evident from its most recent performance (current form).

Distant past form can be considered as 42 days+ for 2-year-olds, 42–56 days+ for 3-year-olds, 3 months+ for older horses (especially National Hunt).

FORM INTERPRETATION

The interpretation of form, is the selector's personal assessment of a horse's ability and form as revealed during form analysis. It is the moment which first commits the selector to decisions that will command a dominating influence in the final selection judgement. Form interpretation is the comprehending, balancing and resolving of factors which often contain elements that are contradictory and inconsistent. It is an uncompromising test of a selector's experience and skill that will be fully exposed by selection results.

The presence of the speculative aspect inherent in all areas of prediction exists in the interpretation of form. It is necessary for the selector to keep this firmly within the bounds of reasoned probability by applying a disciplined logic and basing judgements upon proven facts.

Form interpretation for the purposes of the selection formula requires a defined quality evaluation of proven ability. This has required the establishing of three degrees of merit: (1) **proven;** (2) **promising;** (3) **improving.**

Proven

This is form verified by analysis to be clearly superior. It means a horse has already beaten – or appears through the comparison of form to having the beating of – its rivals.

It has the proven form – this is form of the highest merit – and requires a horse to have to deteriorate, or not improve, while its rivals have to improve, for the form to be reversed. This is the best and most desired form evaluation.

Promising

This is the description given to form that after careful analysis, while acknowledged to be of value, cannot indisputably be proved to be the best. It is form that is second degree in value and which is often the most common evaluation of the form of horses of proven ability. It is form that in many instances 'promises' to be considered the best but cannot be confirmed as such because there is no direct, immediate or reliable comparison with the form of the other probable(s). Form considered 'promising' will apply to performances almost verifiable as 'proven' (the best form) and range to lesser definement where differences in proven ability may be so marginal that they be considered the same. A horse's form described as 'promising' will need to improve to beat 'proven' form.

Improving

This is form that is of third degree in value. Its merit is its clear evidence of a horse having improved on its previous form and being in the process or having the possibility for further improvement. Objectively, it is form that appears of lower quality than 'promising' form, but may have a greater potentiality for further improvement.

'Improving' is the unpredictable category of merit which can bring surprising reverses to superior form. It contains the speculative element – improvement.

Also involved in the assessment of merit are previously unmentioned elements of form: **CONSISTENCY; INCONSISTENCY; DETERIORATION; IMPROVEMENT**. These have to be carefully considered when interpreting form. Their existence can be established by examination and comparison of current with past form.

Consistency is shown by form which contains performances of constant equal merit.

Inconsistency is displayed in form where performances are unpredictable and of varying merit.

Horses of top-class proven ability are usually consistent in performance. Horses of moderate ability tend to be unreliable and inconsistent in performance.

Deterioration is form that is worsening and displays present performances which are inferior to past performances. It can be apparent in horses of all types, ages and class (but it is especially found in National Hunt horses who fail to recapture their previous form after injury, in younger horses (Flat and National Hunt) who suffered from physical ailments, and in horses whose enthusiasm for racing has been soured).

Improvement is form which shows that a horse's performances has become better. It applies to horses of all types and class, and is a particular prominent feature in the assessment and interpretation of the form of younger inexperienced horses. Improvement can be positively established and calculated in respect of past performances, but its existence in the present and/or (the race to be competed) future is purely speculation.

It is the unprovable conjecture which provides form interpretation with the greatest imponderable.

The defining of the categories of merit value in form interpretation reveal the difficulties of creating and precisely maintaining these distinct divisions.

Proven form is the only category clearly discernible and of consistent reliable value. It is the verified evidence of superior ability. The two other categories, 'promising' and 'improving', are less clearly discernible or reliable as they contain intangible elements which demand yet defy a precise objective merit value. **A positive value cannot be attributed to form without verified evidence**.

In the process of form interpretation, practicalities require that some assessments be made that cannot be based on positive proven evidence. When this is the situation, it is essential that these judgements remain within the realms of reasoned probability and there is a balanced viewpoint established which encompasses an understanding of the *intangible elements* of form. These are aspects of form which cannot be adequately measured or proven, and yet by this expression demand close consideration. Intangible elements are encased within the merit descriptions of form, 'promising' and 'improving' evoking as a major factor the proposition of improvement – to become better.

Improvement

This is the manifestation of positive change, and which from its confirmation incites the possibility of still further development in the future. It is this assessment of its future development which pose the imponderable issues. The issues to be considered are as follows:

1. Is further improvement necessary?
2. Is further improvement likely to continue or can it be considered that a peak has been reached?
3. If further improvement is likely/possible by what degree?

1. Is further improvement necessary? Improvement is essential for horses that carry a weight penalty, and for horses raised in class. In both instances they must better their previous performance to have a winning chance.

Constant improvement is an essential need for all inexperienced horses if they are to maintain their ability status with their peers. This applies to 2-year-olds – many show early season form of promise whether by a victory or in defeat, but as the season progresses they fail to maintain this superior position either through insufficient improvement or complete lack of improvement while their rivals

FORM

Form is the undisputed record of a horse's race performance. The smaller the margin of victory or defeat the more possible a reversal of form. The greater the margin of victory or defeat the less likely a reversal of form.

An example of a close margin finish.

An example of a wide margin finish.

Close-up showing the proximity of horses – typical of a close margin finish.

Close-up showing distance between horses – typical of a wide margin finish.

Horses can gain a vital advantage by jumping fences and hurdles accurately and quickly.

While horses may brush through hurdles and only lose impetus . . .

horses that hit the much sturdier fences in chases are likely to pay the higher price of falling.

make considerable development. Consistency alone in these events is likely to be inadequate (e.g. the form figures read 33232 which unless they belie a raising in class reveal admirable consistency by insufficient improvement to win without a lowering in class).

The criterion for improvement being a necessity, applies to all horses (3–4 y.o. mdns, novice hurdlers novice chassers – and even handicappers) if they are to maintain their status. It is, however, more particularly apparent when applied to 2-year-olds where rapid growth and improvement exist as very dynamic factors. The only time improvement is not a required necessity is when it is applied to a current proven champion (i.e. Classic champions, sprinters, milers, middle distance horses, stayers and their National Hunt equivalents) where if challenged at equal conditions (weight – distance – going) it is the challenger who must improve – and the consistent reproducing of proven ability will be enough for the champion to win.

2. Is further improvement likely? The likelihood of improvement will be indicated in the previous performance and will be dependent on three factors:

(a) The manner of its performance (i.e. whether it won easily, all out, ridden out, stayed on, run on).

(b) Its physical fitness at the time (i.e. was it at peak fitness, and is there scope for physical development?).

(c) The methods and ability of the trainer to improve a horse progressively.

(a) *Manner of performance.* A horse that has not won may be judged as having to improve to win. A horse that has won displays proven ability which can be assessed for further development.

Every horse can have a style of racing peculiar to itself (i.e. a horse which can win only if held up and then wins only by the narrowest of margins; a horse which will do no more than it has to to win, every race it wins is hard fought; or a horse that can only win if not seriously challenged by opponents), but the guiding principle in a horse improving upon its performance is the ease with which it wins. A horse that wins 'easily', 'unchallenged', can do no more – if an inexperienced horse (e.g. 2 y.o.) running for the first time this is a highly commendable performance which suggests in all probability it will improve. Although particular to 2-year-olds first time out, any horse winning easily suggests further improvement. The more hard fought the victory, the less obvious scope in ability a horse has for improvement.

(b) *Physical fitness* at the time of performance.

A horse that wins unfit (not at peak race fitness) easily can be almost guaranteed to improve.

A horse that wins in a hard-fought race (unfit) is very likely to improve as it obtains peak fitness.

A horse that wins easily (when fit) can still improve, especially if inexperienced.

A horse that wins in a hard-fought race (when at peak fitness) is less likely to improve. The modifying factor here will be the scope for further physical development in the horse. This is not a factor that can be satisfactorily abstracted or adjudged from form; it can only be assessed by seeing the horse and observing its physical conformation. It is a speculative personal judgement.

(c) *The methods and ability of the trainer*. Improvement is always subject to training methods. It is noticeable that some trainers in their racing preparation of inexperienced and experienced horses allow themselves an area in which to improve a horse i.e. racing it initially short of peak race fitness, allowing weaker horses (2-year-olds that are growing) time to recover from races and gain strength, and generally allowing a horse to fulfill its physical potentiality.

Other trainers similarly run their horse 'fully wound-up' (peak race fit) and have less scope to improve them, in fact will in some instances 'burn out' a horse (especially 2-year-olds).

Improvement is dependent upon the skill, method and in some instances patience of the trainer.

3. Degree or rate of improvement   If a horse is likely to improve, what degree of improvement could be expected? This is an almost unanswerable question and there can be no proven answer, only speculation. The likelihood of the rate and/or degree of improvement will be strongly influence by the following:

(a) The horse's physical scope (allowing for the possibility of any rapid or slow development).

(b) The trainer's method, which may be to allow the horse to mature slowly and not be rushed (i.e. in the case of 2 y.o. who is bred to stay as a 3 y.o., or a backward National Hunt horse which is considered primarily as a staying chaser and is allowed as much as two seasons to develop).

Improvement can be compared to growth and/or learning; it is a gradual process that occurs in stages. There will be instances of progress and of consolidation, and for a short time the rate of improvement is likely to be equivalent to the degree of improvement (i.e. a horse makes seemingly considerable improvement quickly).

The degree, or the progress of improvement, is not one of improbable and incomprehensible leaps.

● The improvement to winning form is normally from progressively better performances (this is not always apparent from mere abbreviated form figures – closer analysis may be required to establish this fact).

93

- The improvement on winning form, often originates from the impetus of winning. (The experience of winning to an inexperienced horse gives it an added confidence in its ability to initiate further success.)

An understanding of the degree on this basis places it within the discernible reaches of probability.

The rate, the quickness or slowness of improvement. It will be closely linked with the type of horse (i.e. Flat or National Hunt, sprinter, stayer, 2m hurdler, 3m chaser) and whether the horse is precocious or slow maturing. As a rule, the shorter the distance the faster maturing the horse is likely to be, and the longer the distance the slower maturing the horse will be. Sprinters 'come to hand' quicker than potential stayers, and are likely to be trained with a short-term viewpoint. Stayers (especially National Hunt 3m chasers) are trained with a long-term viewpoint. Between the extremes there are numerous rates of progress.

Once a horse (of whatever type) begins improving, its rate and range should not be underestimated. For example, early season 2-year-olds 'sharp types', often run up a sequence of wins over the minimum 5f distance (in the first months of the Flat season). Similarly, 2-year-olds without previous experience, or with moderate form over shorter distances suddenly improve extensively and rapidly when running over a distance 7f–1m (late season). Three-year-old mdns can, during their second season, improve quickly and considerably when racing at longer distances, although sometimes not developing until late in their 3 y.o. season. Novice hurdlers usually learn quickly (immediately) after a few races, but some may take a whole season.

Whatever type—once a horse shows improvement, its rate of improvement will be closely attached to its degree of improvement and its abilities must then be considered carefully.

The misuse and misunderstanding of the term 'improvement'. Improvement as a proposition is always an entirely speculative judgement, and only exists as a proven fact when it is a comparison judgement of past and current form. The misuse and misunderstanding of the term 'improvement' as associated with horse-racing often emanates from journalistic copy which has presented opinion as fact.

'Has improved' is a statement of fact that can be disputed or verified by examination of form. Correctly understood, this statement provides concisely defined information upon which to make a judgement. 'Has improved', however, can have the unfortunate connotation of implying more than it can represent, arousing speculation and exceeding the limit of its accurate definition. 'Will improve' – 'sure to improve' – 'can only improve' have become commonly used and accepted terms in horse-race parlance, but from the objective view-point are meaningless. They insinuate proven fact, but are and can only ever be subjective opinion.

'Is improving' literally is another misleading term from any objective viewpoint of form. It has been confused with and often mistakenly used instead of the term 'has improved' which is an observed comparison of past and present form. 'Is improving' correctly used means 'getting better now' – at this time a fact that cannot be verified from form which concludes assessment at the horse's last race performance. 'Is improving' is an unproven assertion of no value to objective form selection, and can only be assumed as a meaningful term for consideration when it can be an attributed view of a trainer who has witnessed improvement in its ability since the horse last raced. This information, however, is not discernible from/or required by purely impartial objective form analysis; and its explanation and inclusion is only for the purpose of providing a further understanding of 'improvement'.

FORM EVALUATION

Form is evaluated during analysis and interpretation by comparison with other form. Accurate evaluation depends upon a constant acquaintance with up-to-date form, a realization of what constitutes better-quality form and a flexibility to adjust views to accommodate changes in the value of form (i.e. as the value of new form supersedes that of previously valued form).

The comparison of form can immediately reveal a great or slight difference of ability or require a closer examination to make a judicial evaluation.

1. Great and/or obvious differences are revealed by a disparity in class.
2. Slight differences are usually found when there is no disparity in class.

Form evaluation is easy when there are obviously great differences in comparable abilities, but difficult and sometimes almost impossible when the differences are slight. If there is no immediately obvious comparison of form (i.e. horses have either not run against each other and there is no disparity in class), form evaluation may be made by comparison through *collateral form*.

Collateral form

This is form of two horses (A and B) which have not competed against each other, but have commonly raced against a third horse (C). It is by comparison of their separate performances with the third horse (C) that the abilities of *A and B* can be assessed.

95

Collateral form to be a reliable indication requires that:

1. The third horse is a proven consistent performer;
2. The conditions of the two races should be similar (i.e. distance, going, jockey, course);
3. The conditions of weight can be clearly calculated.

Collateral form is most reliable when applied to top-class horses and cannot be confidently accepted when applied to moderate horses. If after the examination of collateral form the differences between horses appear indefinably balanced it is suggested (except in the case of the very top-class horses*) that no evaluation be undertaken and the Selector refrains from Selection.

It is essential the evaluation of form be based strictly on proven fact, and the interpretation should not be stretched to consider what might have occurred (i.e. excuses for poor performances).

Form evaluation which accepts the conjectures of excuses retreats from a stronghold of reasoned objectivity to the meandering of speculation and will be rewarded with a perversion of judgement.

In the maintenance of a reasoned balanced and consistency an excuse(s) for one horse would demand the consideration of excuses for each of the other horses and this renders any attempt at such an exercise as impractical. The accurate evaluation of form is the bulwark of selection and to be successfully obtained requires an objectivity and flexibility of a reasoning mind.

Assessment of recent, up-to-date form

The value of form, although essentially and eventually adjudged by events has in practice often to be assessed more immediately without the benefit of such hindsight. It is therefore necessary to adopt a reliable method of assessing and evaluating recent up-to-date form. The previously unconsidered aspect of *time* (assessment of form by the time factor) will act as an informative aid in this role.

Time. This means race-time and is the time taken to run a race. As a general rule, the faster the time of a race, the better the value of form. It can be expected that race times will be faster on firmer going and slower on softer going – this consideration, and weather conditions, must always be fully taken into account.

A fast time invariably represents form of value – a race in such a

---

* Top-class horses usually produce extremely consistent performances and it may therefore be possible to conclude an evaluation from a careful balancing of the pertaining modifying factors (fitness and conditions).

time will have been a true and searching test; the winner will have had to provide a noteworthy performance, as would other horses who finished within close proximity.

A slow time usually represents form of little or no value – it does not require a noteworthy performance to win and may suggest the race was falsely run and not a true test over the distance, and therefore any margins between horses are likely to be misleading.

The actual time of the race (NB. Only the times of flat races are official times.) In reading of form, the actual time of the race is recorded, next to which will be its comparison to the average or standard time for the race:

(b0.0) represents below average time in seconds and tenths of a second
(a0.0) represents above average time in seconds and tenths of a second
(eq) indicates equally average time.

Below average time is always a fast time – and of the highest value in assessing time.

Equal average time is a good time, but its exact value can only be ascertained by comparison with other times on the day and consideration of the going (i.e. it is not of much value when the going is firm/hard and the times of other races at the meeting are below average).

Above average time is of least value; however, the degree of such time must be considered, as well as comparison with other race times on the day and the state of the going.

Race time applies both to Flat and National Hunt racing – good form in both codes is usually in faster comparable times. Time has been thought to be more applicable to Flat racing where the emphasis is purely on speed, there are no obstacles to contend with and ground conditions tend to be more consistent during the summer. A fast time, however, is a fast time, and cannot be disputed as to the merits of a fast-run race under either code of racing.

Race time is a most reliable guide to assessing the value of recent unproven form. This applies especially to 2 y.o. races of whatever class and value, for unless they are run in 'good' (fast) time the value of form is likely to be suspect. GOOD 2 y.o. form demands fast, truely run races placing emphasis on race fitness and a horse being in a forward physical condition to compete throughout the race. On the Flat where times are most important the last furlong of true run races is completed in around 12 seconds, thus in 1 second a horse travels approximately 18 yd or 6 lengths. Time can therefore be translated into weight using the following scales:

5–6f	1 sec =	18 lb =	6 lengths
7–8f	1 sec =	15 lb =	6 lengths
9–11f	1 sec =	12 lb =	6 lengths
12–14f	1 sec =	9 lb =	6 lengths
15f+	1 sec =	6 lb =	6 lengths

A comparison of race times for horses of different ages over the same distance on the same day (similarly handicaps with non-handicaps, etc.) give a reliable indication in the assessment of form.

Horses racing on the same race programme but in different races can be compared from their finishing positions in the race and the corresponding race time. In novice hurdles, which usually open and end the programme at a race meeting, in heavy/soft going the earlier divisions are likely to be faster than the later divisions as the course becomes more ploughed-up with horses racing on it. This consideration is of paramount importance in the comparison of time. Therefore a major factor affecting time is the going. A selling plater can run a faster time on firm ground than a top-class horse can return when the going is heavy. Before the value of a time can be assessed the nature of the going must be known and the time adjusted accordingly. As a rough guide the following can be used:

Firm   Add 0.2 secs per furlong to recorded time
Good   Subtract 0.2 secs per furlong from recorded time
Soft   Subtract 0.8 secs per furlong from recorded time
Heavy Subtract 1.2 secs per furlong from recorded time

For example, a horse that runs 6f in 70 seconds on firm ground may take 76 seconds on soft ground and 72.4 seconds on good ground. Really firm ground does not make for faster times because few horses stride out freely when the ground becomes hard.

Other points to consider in respect of time. Shorter races, i.e sprints 5–6f and races up to 1 m (Flat) and 2m hurdles (National Hunt), are invariably run in faster comparable times (i.e. to standard) than longer races. Shorter races are less contests of race tactics (i.e. making sure a horse gets the trip) and more tests of pure speed. Longer races are often subject to smaller fields, muddle pace, 'cat and mouse' tactics and the resulting slower times.

The more fiercely contested races (conditions and 'going' allowing) produce fast times. This can be observed by examination of the times of top-class races (i.e. the classics, group races), races at Ascot and other top meetings, the Cheltenham Festival (usually soft ground) and the Aintree Festival (going usually good) which produce races of below average times.

SUMMARY OF FORM

1. Form is the record of past performance; it is the most reliable indication of ability.
2. Recent form is the most positive guide to assessing current ability.
3. Good top-class form is extremely reliable.
   Form of lower class is generally unreliable.

4. The Accurate interpretation of form is dependent upon translation being made only of objectively assessed proven facts.
5. The evaluation of form will be most throughly served by the persistent inquisition:
   What? When? Where? How?
   What has the horse done?
   When, where, how – did the horse do it?

FITNESS

Fitness is the second constituent in the selection formula and the major modifying factor to form. Unless a horse is fully race fit it is unlikely to produce its true or best race form.

Fitness can never be absolutely assured – a degree of fitness has to be left to trust (i.e. to the good judgement of the trainer) yet it must not be assumed just because a horse is declared to race that it is fully fit to reproduce its best form. The fact that a horse is competing in a race is not alone proof of its race fitness, and must not ever be arbitrarily accepted as such.

A horse competing in a race should have no physical ailments, be sound of eye, wind, heart and limb, but if it has not raced for a time its race fitness is not assured and cannot be assumed. This applies particularly to inexperienced horses (2 y.o., 3 y.o., mdns. novice hurdlers, novice chasers), for until they have proved themselves on the racecourse, the trainer has little information upon which to assess what constitutes fitness in an individual horse, and off-course preparation is problematic.

Physical and race fitness, although closely related and dependent upon one another must not be regarded as the same. A horse's fitness on the day of the race will be dependent upon its natural health (wellbeing) and the training preparation it has received prior to the race. Race fitness may be defined as peak physical fitness which gives a horse (if good enough) a positive chance of winning, as opposed to fitness which enables a horse merely to complete the race without physical injury.

The general term 'race fitness' from the selector's viewpoint should be understood as *peak race fitness*.

Although there can be many imponderables surrounding the race fitness of a horse, surprisingly, much unquestioning trust is placed on a horse being in peak physical condition when there is no evidence to support this assumption (i.e. horse making its racecourse début, or reappearance after a lengthy absence, are in fact indications to the contrary).

FITNESS

A horse will usually have to be at peak race fitness if it is to have a real chance of winning a race. The most reliable indication of a horse's fitness is a recent race performance.

This horse, photographed in the paddock prior to winning a race is instantly recognisable as being fit by the well defined and developed lines of muscle running down its hindquarters and the lack of fatness around its girth and ribs. The skin is clear and healthy and this is borne out by the diamond pattern that is glowing across the top of its hindquarters, evidence that the horse has been well-groomed as part of its pre-race preparation.

This horse, photographed prior to finishing well beaten in its race can be instantly recognised as still having to reach peak race fitness. Whilst appearing as a strong robust horse, there is a lack of well defined and developed muscle on its hindquarters and an excess condition around its girth and ribs. The markings on the coat however, are where the horse has been trace clipped, a common feature on many National Hunt horses once they have grown their winter coats.

The most reliable evidence of a horse being 'racefit' is proof from a recent race performance. 'Recent' is the operative word – within the previous 7 days is the most favourable time span.

In this recent race performance: (i) a horse of proven ability must display a semblance of that ability; (ii) a less experienced horse (of promising or improving ability) must have shown form of discernible merit, having figured prominently at some stage during the race. (This will indicate that peak fitness has, or is about to be, reached.) Applying the above stipulations it can be almost 100 per cent guaranteed that a horse is at or will have gained peak race fitness from competing in a race. This is not private or inspired information but public to anyone prepared to examine recent form.

SEVEN-DAY RACE FITNESS

This is the most reliable confirmation of peak race fitness, and without this confirmation there always exists elements of doubt as to a horse's race fitness. It is necessary there to allay the fear that a horse may be racing just to gain peak fitness for a future engagement by becoming acquainted with the methods of various stables and their motives for racing and preparing their horses.

Many of the leading stables with good success records seldom race their horses twice within a 7-day period yet still ensure that their horses are generally well prepared and in good race condition when they run, but even these are often defeated by the peak race fitness of other horses which had raced more recently (i.e. within the last 7 days). Seven-day race fitness has a particularly dominating influence upon: (i) all inexperienced horses; (ii) horses of moderate ability (selling class); (iii) during the times in the season (Flat and National Hunt) when unfavourable weather conditions disrupt normal race fixtures and/or training schedules (i.e. snow and rain in winter, hard 'baked' going in summer).

Seven days may appear as an arbitrary time span that has been applied to race fitness; it is, however, a well-tried and tested response formulated to combat the otherwise ambiguous assessments of race fitness.

The essential quality of race fitness is that it is the peak of physical condition and therefore it allows the fullest expression of racing ability. It is, however, a transitory state which can only be maintained for a short time – 7 days is that approximate time. In practice, this means a horse will remain (without further training preparation) in physical peak condition for about a week. A horse, having displayed peak race fitness in its last race, will have still retained it if raced again within 7 days, while a horse brought to peak race fitness from its last race will also have maintained that condition if raced again within 7 days.

The previously unstated but obvious qualifying factor with regard to a horse racing again within 7 days is that the horse must have suffered no injury during its previous race. This factor can only be left to trust on the reasonable assumption that a trainer would not race a horse again so quickly if it had suffered any injury. Similarly, races in quick succession may not be suitable for (i) horses of a weak constitution or wayward temperament who require a longer interval between races, (ii) those who have suffered from the effects of long-distance travel (travelling can blunt a horse's vitality as much as hard races). In all of these instances, after paying due regard to the facts available, the selector must trust that the trainer's judgement to race the horse is the correct decision.

The general guiding rule to race fitness is the more recently a horse has run, the more likely it is to be race fit. The longer the time since a horse last raced, the less likely it is to be in peak condition.

On a time-scale:

1–7 days – is the most assured confirmation of fitness;

8–14 days – is a reasonable length of time, particularly appropriate to National Hunt horses;

15–28 days – is an immoderate length of time that sheds doubts on a horse's fitness;

29+ days – cannot be accepted, without knowledge of the trainer's methods.

This is further reinforced by the statistics given for both the Flat and National Hunt in Table 8.1.

The statistics of Flat race winners in 1981 suggest that the shorter the time span in which a winner races again, the greater its winning chances. A closer examination of the record of previous winners racing again reveals that when the time span is concentrated in 1–6 days or 7–14 days the results shown in Table 8.2 are obtained. This table clearly indicates the advantage of horses racing again within a short period and confirms their form and fitness.

The exceptions to this rule are the particular methods employed by certain trainers (the leading ones especially) who have the staff, the skill and facilities to prepare horses off-course, on home gallops. It applies particularly in the cases of top-class horses of experience (Flat and National Hunt) which may have an advance programme of races marked out for them at the beginning of a season, and time and effort will not be spared in these preparations.

In cases of inexperienced horses and of trainers without the staff, facilities or abilities, recent race fitness is the determining factor in the consideration of a horse's fitness and must never be lightly overlooked.

103

TABLE 8.1   Winners (horses with proven fitness) racing again

Days	Two-year-olds Winners – runners	Three-year-olds+ Winners – runners	Total Winners – runners
1–7	14 – 81 = 17%	82 – 318 = 26%	96 – 399 = 24%
8 – 14	50 – 201 = 25%	94 – 577 = 16%	144 – 788 = 18%
15–28	76 – 298 = 25.5%	135 – 660 = 20%	211 – 958 = 22%

N.B. Two-year-olds need an extra few days to recover from a race compared with older horses.

National Hunt 1980–1 (2m handicap hurdle – the most competitive race, requiring peak fitness to win) – the record of previous winners racing again

Days	Winners – runners
1–7	13 – 31 = 41.9%
8–14	9 – 64 = 14.0%
15–28	8 – 60 = 13.3%
29+	4 – 24 = 16.6%

TABLE 8.2

Days	Two-year-olds Winners – runners	Three-year-olds+ Winners – runners
1–6	10 – 45 = 22%	59 – 196 = 30%
7–14	54 – 237 = 23%	117 – 699 = 17%

Proven fitness is the most dominating factor when considering a horse's chances of winning – and in this sphere there can be no substitute for 7-day race fitness which may finely tune a horse's performance to give it a winning edge.

CLASS

Class is the third constituent in the selection formula and an important modifying factor.

Class in the racing sense means the quality of opposition a horse has competed against. In respect of quality this can range from the very best – 'top class', Classics, group racing (Flat) and the National

Hunt equivalent – Champion Hurdle, Gold Cup – down to selling races which have been designed for the worst horses.

A 'class' horse, or 'class' in the colloquial sense accurately used means the very best horses (type and age applying).

A horse can be raised or lowered in class or compete in the same (similar) class.

A horse raised in class must improve to have a winning chance.

A horse lowered in class has only to reproduce its known form to win.

A horse in the same class, may have either to improve upon or simply reproduce its best run form, depending on the evaluation of that form. The most favourable situation, for consideration in Selection is when a horse with consistent proven ability is lowered (dropped) in class. A horse must never be considered to have a winning chance just because it has been dropped in class. It must have discernible positive ability in the higher class to be considered a leading form probably when dropped in class.

The more extreme example is when a horse has been raised initially well above its class (e.g. a mdn 3 y.o. competes in the Derby to fulfil wishes of an ever-optimistic owner and finishes tailed off 2f behind the rest of the field) fails or struggles when dropped in class to win a modest mdn race later in the season. It is therefore necessary to examine carefully all the facts of form before making any judgements which may be presumptive.

The evaluation of class plays a dominating role in the evaluation of form, and while differences are easily definable at the extreme ends, differences are less distinguishable in the middle range of class. Prize-money and the grade of course (Group I, II, III or IV according to Jockey Club ruling) provide the obvious indications of class.

One of the easiest and perhaps obvious methods of defining the class of races, horses and their form is by identification and comparison of racecourses. A graded list of racecourses is given in Table 8.3. It has been compiled in respect of the quality value of the form of most of the races contested in accord with the level of allocated prize-money (i.e. the greater the level of prize-money, the more competitive are the races, the better are the horses and therefore the higher the value of form). This list is closely based on the Jockey Club's own grading of racecourses in regard to the amount of prize-money and subsidies allotted to each course, but also with special consideration placed on experience of form selection.

The Flat racecourses have been divided into five grades and the National Hunt courses into four grades. It may be seen that while there is a clear-cut distinction between the top and bottom grades of courses, this distinction can become much less clear in assessing the value of form as between two of the lower grades of courses. It will, however, serve as a basic and most reliable guide.

CLASS

Class is the quality or type of race contested by a horse. Top class horses usually have the conformation and looks to match their ability whilst slower, moderate horses are correspondingly lacking in these features.

Champion Sprinter Lochnager who can be clearly seen as a strong imposing horse with a muscular athletic appearance – he is well proportioned and of good conformation.

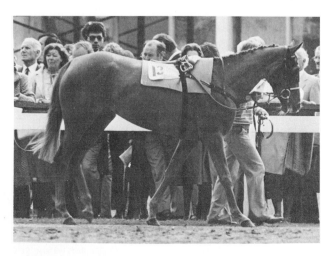

In contrast to the previous photograph, this horse is of moderate selling plate class ability and can be clearly seen to lack physical quality.

TABLE 8.3 Grading of racecourses

Flat

Grade I	Ascot, Goodwood, Newbury, Newmarket, Sandown, York
Grade II	Ayr, Chester, Doncaster, Epsom, Haydock, Kempton, Newcastle
Grade III	Bath, Brighton, Leicester, Lingfield, Nottingham, Redcar, Ripon, Salisbury, Yarmouth
Grade IV	Beverley, Chepstow, Pontefract, Thirsk, Windsor, Wolverhampton
Grade V	Carlisle, Catterick, Edinburgh, Folkestone, Hamilton, Warwick

National Hunt

Grade I	Ascot, Cheltenham, Doncaster, Haydock, Kempton, Liverpool, Newbury, Sandown
Grade II	Ayr, Chepstow, Lingfield, Newcastle, Nottingham, Wetherby, Wincanton
Grade III	Carlisle, Catterick, Folkestone, Huntingdon, Leicester, Market Rasen, Newton Abbot, Stratford, Towcester, Warwick, Windsor, Wolverhampton, Worcester
Grade IV	Bangor, Cartmel, Devon and Exeter, Fakenham, Fontwell, Hereford, Hexham, Kelso, Ludlow, Perth, Plumpton, Sedgefield, Southwell, Uttoxeter, Taunton

The most valuable races, fiercely competitive on the most testing courses, can be considered top class. The lowest prized races on the smaller, easier racecourses which attract the same regular group of contestants can be considered the lowest class. Class plays an important role in the selection formula as it is the factor which requires improvement as a necessity or requires no more than a reproducing of known ability.

The old adage suggested to racehorse owners: 'Run your horse in the worst company and keep yourself in the best company', applies with equal wisdom for those seeking selections from horses lowered in class.

CONDITIONS

Conditions are the fourth constituent in the selection formula, they are modifying factors which may act as the vital balancing role in forming the selection decision.

If these modifying factors are of proven positive value, they can only act as an endorsement to a decision. If they contain the negative aspect, they may serve as the eliminating element in the balance of decision-making. Occasionally these modifying elements may assume the role of the salient factor in the forming of a selection decision.

The conditions affecting the reproducing of form are as follows:
1. Distance (the distance of a race).
2. Going (the ground conditions on which the horse must race).
3. Weight (the weight carried, and whether it involves penalties or allowances).
4. Courses/draw (the variation of courses, and the fixed starting positions in Flat racing).
5. Jockeyship (the quality).
6. Sundry factors (i.e. blinkers).

DISTANCE

A horse can only be considered *proven* over the distance by winning at that distance, or showing form of proven value at the distance. A change of a 'horse's' distance from its proven distance(s) places it in the area of the unknown – and means the horse is unproven at that distance.

Most horses specialize and perform best at only one distance (i.e. sprinters may be only 5f horses or be equally proficient at 5f and 6f). Milers may only act best at 1m or may act equally well between 7f

CONDITIONS

DISTANCE

Most horses, whether Flat or National Hunt produce their best form over one particular distance. A change in distance often produces a change in form.

These two photographs, looking up the July Course at Newmarket clearly show the difference in distance between one and two furlongs. In the top picture the disc on the rails to the right is the two furlong marker from the winning post while in the bottom picture the disc to the right is the one furlong marker from the winning post.

TABLE 8.4 Leading sires of Flat horses
† Young sires details not available   * Stands abroad

Year of birth	Sire	Sire's sire	Av. no of 2 y.o. wins	Best dist. for 3 y.o.+	Sires winning distances minimum – maximum
70	African Sky	by Sing Sing	7	5f	7f–8f
72	Auction Ring	by Bold Bidder	13	7–8f	5f–6f
71	Averof	by Sing Sing	7	5–8f	5f–10f
71	Bay Express	by Polyfoto	9	5f	5f–6f
74	Be my Guest	by Northern Dancer	11	10–11f	6f–8f
66	Blakeney	by Hethersett	5	10f+	7f–13f
70	Blue Cashmere	by Kashmir II	8	6–8f	6f–7f
64	Bold Lad (Ire.)	by Bold Bidder	7	5–8f	5f–7f
68	Brigadier Gerard	by Queen's Hussar	4	8–12f	5f–12f
63	Busted	by Crepello	3	10f+	10f–12f
76	Bustino	by Busted	6	10f+	10f–14½f
68	Comedy Star	by Tom Fool	6	5–6f	6f–8f
65	Connaught	by St Paddy	4	8–12f	10f–12f
71	Dragonara Palace	by Young Emperor	10	7–8f	5f–8f
72	Gay Fandango	by Forli	6	7–10f	7f–8f
74	Godswalk	by Dancer's Image	13	6–8f	5f–6f
63	Great Nephew	by Honeyway	7	Various	6f–10f
72	Grundy	by Great Nephew	3	10–12f	6f–12f
66	Habitat	by Sir Gaylord	11	7–8f	8f
66	High Line	by High Hat	1	10f+	7f–16f
69	High Top	by Derring Do	5	8–12f	5f–8f
69	Home Guard	by Forli	8	7–10f	5f–7f
66	Hotfoot	by Firestreak	7	6–12f	6f–10f
72	Lochnager	by Dumbarnie	8	6–7f	5f–6f
65	Lord Gayle	by Sir Gaylord	7	8–12f	7f–10f
69	Mansingh	by Jaipur	9	5–6f	5f
69	Martinmas	by Silly Season	7	8–10f	6f–8f
68	Mill Reef	by Never Bend	7	8f+	5f–12f
68	Mummy's Pet	by Sing Sing	19	5–6f	5f–6½f
73	Music Boy	by Jukebox	11	5–6f	5f–6f
67	Nijinsky	by Northern Dancer	*	10f+	6f–14½f
71	Nonoalco	by Nearctic	5	8–10f	6f–8f

Year of birth	Sire	Sire's sire	Av. no of 2 y.o. wins	Best dist. for 3 y.o. +	Sires winning distances minimum–maximum
68	Northfields	by Northern Dancer	6	7–10f	5½f–9f
64	On Your Mark	by Restless Wind	9	6–10f	5f–8½f
75	Persian Bold	by Bold Lad	15	†	6f–7f
70	Pitskelly	by Petingo	10	Various	7f
67	Prince Tenderfoot	by Blue Prince II	10	7–10f	5f–6f
72	Raga Navarro	by Reform	12	†	5f–8f
67	Realm	by Princely Gift	10	5–8f	6f
71	Red Alert	by Red God	12	7–10f	5f–7f
69	Rheingold	by Faberge	4	10f+	6f–12½f
69	Roberto	by Hail to Reason	★	8–12f	6f–12f
68	Run The Gauntlet	by Tom Rolfe	3	12f+	6f–12f
69	Sallust	by Pall Mall	15	6–8f	5f–8½f
70	Sandford Lad	by St Alphage	9	6–8f	5f
69	Sharpen Up	by Atan	17	7–8f	5f–6f
65	So Blessed	by Princely Gift	12	8–10f	5f–6f
66	Song	by Sing Sing	11	5–6f	5f–6f
70	Star Appeal	by Appiani II	?	10–12f	6f–12f
68	Swing Easy	by Delta Judge	8	5–7f	5f–6f
70	Thatch	by Forli	7	6–10f	6f–8f
67	The Brianstan	by King's Leap	5	5–7f	5f–6f
74	The Minstrel	by Northern Dancer	★	†	6f–12f
66	Tower Walk	by High Treason	6	6–8f	5f–7f
64	Tumble Wind	by Restless Wind	11	6–8f	5f–10f
69	Warpath	by Sovereign Path	3	12f+	9f–11f
66	Welsh Pageant	by Tudor Melody	3	8–12f	6f–8½f
66	Welsh Saint	by St Paddy	8	Various	6f–6½f
69	Windjammer	by Restless Wind	7	8f	4½f–8f
73	Wollow	by Wolver Hollow	4	7–9f	6f–10½f
64	Wolver Hollow	by Sovereign Path	6	7–12f	8f–10f

and 1m 1f. Middle-distance horses, similarly, may only race well at 1¼m or be versatile between 1m 1f and 1m 4f. Stayers also may need 1½m, 1¾m, 2m or 2m+ or may act over a range of extreme distances. National Hunt horses have equal speed and stamina restrictions, ranging from 2m hurdlers to 3½m+ chasers.

Distance can and does alter performances. This may apply particularly to mdn horses (Flat and National Hunt) which may suddenly improve when they find their best distance. Breeding is likely to be the strongest indication of a horse's most suitable distance, but is only an assumption that cannot be accepted as face – proven fact can only be accepted from the test on the race course.

Breeding is not an exact science, but by examining the records of leading sires given in Table 8.4 it is possible to identify the characteristics and influences inherited by a sire's racing stock. Change of distance is one of the fundamental reasons for reversals in form, and improvement of form when the correct one is found.

N.B. All mdn. 2-year-olds and 3-year-olds – novice hurdlers and chasers who show considerable improvement when raced over a different distance (normally a longer one).

Experienced racehorses are often given a 'pipe-opener' over a shorter distance than they need to bring them to peak race fitness with a race to obscure the value of their form. The oldest and easiest ploy to disguise a horse's true form and ability is to race it over its wrong distance. In the case of many mdns, however, often to the frustration of a trainer, and to confound all laws of breeding, a horse's best distance is only discovered by trial and error from racing it over various distances.

Distance can be a salient factor in the consideration of form.

GOING

Going, on a level par with distance, is often the culprit responsible for reversals in form. A horse can only be considered to act on going if proven from the racecourse test – similar going or slight variations are unlikely to affect a horse, but extreme changes which have not been previously encountered can have devastating effects (i.e. changes from good to heavy or good to hard).

It has been said that a 'good horse' will act on any going, and while there is a certain truth in this remark, it must strongly be stated that most horses have strong preferences and act best on particular ground. A horse's action and physique will allow it to perform better and with greater ease on certain going, and this allows some horses to display specialist capabilities in/on extremes of going (i.e. the soft ground specialist who revels in the mud in heavy ground and cannot act and may even get jarred up on other going; then there is the other type

GOING

Variations in going can have a vital influence on form

Typical going that is encountered during the summer months – officially described as firm.

Going officially described as soft with clods of turf being visibly kicked up.

of specialist who only acts on ground when hoofs can be heard to rattle). Breeding often produces characteristics such as these passed down from one generation to the next (e.g. some sires, themselves soft ground specialists produce stock of similar tendency, other sires who preferred good or firm ground pass on this characteristic and have offspring only able to act on this type of surface). Although breeding will give strong indications of a horse's likely preferences, each horse is an individual, whose requirements can only be confirmed by the test on the racecourse which may confound presumptions of breeding.

A horse's ability to act in particular ground conditions cannot or should not be assumed positive/or negative until proven by the racecourse test.

In extremes of going – going can be the salient factor to affect form.

WEIGHT

Weight as a factor is the great leveller of ability. It applies to all types of horse and in all classes of races. Enough weight given to even the very best horses will stop them from winning. At level weights a race is a contest only of comparative ability and fitness, but as differences occur (weight penalties or concessions) a more involved consideration begins to dominate the assessment process.

The changes in conditions of the weight carried brings about changes in form, as revealed by handicaps and the myriad of solutions to the questions posed by the unequal distribution of weight. The consideration of weight always creates certain imponderables and it is necessary as part of the selection analysis to be acquainted with the conditions of weight and their influence in the outcome of a race.

Races where horses carry level weight (within certain prescribed limits) are the most readily discernible for analysis and assessment. The weight variations within this basic criterion are as follows:

1. Sex allowances (Flat racing). Colts giving a weight concession of 3 lb to fillies and geldings. Sex allowances have been extended to National Hunt racing from 1983–4. Colts, horses and geldings giving a weight concession of 5 lb to fillies and mares in all chases, hurdles and National Hunt Flat races.
2. Weight-for-age (Flat and National Hunt). Horses of different ages giving or receiving weight according to an official scale.
3. Weight penalties (incurred for winning and/or differing according to the value of the race won).
4. Weight allowances (Flat and National Hunt for mdns at starting). A special allowance (Flat only) for horses which have previously not run.

WEIGHT

Weight is a major factor which can produce a reversal of form and can defeat even the best horse. Burdened with enough weight even a fast horse can be beaten by a normally slower rival who is carrying less weight.

A comparison between a 1 lb saddle (left) and a 5 lb saddle (right) to illustrate part of the dead weight which a horse has to carry.

Weight variations (and the effects)

A weight allowance of 3 lb is given by colts to fillies (and often to geldings); this was introduced to counterbalance the basic differences of physical strength and development between the sexes. Colts are normally more robust and faster maturing than fillies or geldings, and would without this compulsory weight concession hold initially an unfair advantage in races.

Sex allowance. The effect of the sex allowance in practice is therefore to resolve the physical imbalance and give equal opportunity to colts, fillies and geldings racing against each other.

N.B. The sex weight allowance at certain times may, however, not represent the true differences between colts and fillies and therefore be to the positive advantage of one or the other:
    1. Early in the season 2 y.o. colts with racing experience have

115

a distinct physical advantage over fillies likely to be more than 3 lb sex allowance.
2. In the summer of their 3 y.o. careers (late July and throughout August and September) fillies tend to develop considerably physically, to the extent that suddenly they reach a par with colts. The 3 lb weight concession then is to their advantage and it is noticeable at these times how the rapidly improving fillies defeat colts in mdn races.

Weight for age (Flat and National Hunt). Weight for age is an official scale of weights formulated by the Jockey Club to give horses of different ages racing against each other equal opportunity, by apportioning them varying weights. On the Flat it applies to 2–4-year-olds (older horses considered equal), and in National Hunt to 4–6-year-olds (older horses considered equal) and pays due regard to the varying distances (5f–2½m Flat, 2m–3m National Hunt). The scale changes throughout the season to accommodate the normal rate of maturity of younger horses (i.e. in March/April Flat racing a 4 y.o. would be expected over 5f to give a 3 y.o. 12–13 lb and a 3. y.o. to give a 2 y.o. 31–32 lb, but by October the scale would have fallen – the 4 y.o. gives a 3 y.p. 0–1 lb and the 3 y.o. gives a 2 y.o. 16–17 lb – similarly weight changes apply to National Hunt racing). Tables 8.5 and 8.6 give the scale of weight for age for Flat and National Hunt respectively.

Although the Jockey Club have an official weight-for-age (WFA) Scale this serves only as a guide to the clerks of courses who can frame the conditions of their races differently. It is therefore advisable to examine the conditions of WFA races and note whether conditions would seem to favour one age rather than another or if the race conforms strictly to the Jockey Club Scale.

N.B. The conditions of all races where WFA applies particularly consider *novice* hurdlers. where especially in heavy going a weight concession can be a decisive factor.

Weight penalties (Flat and National Hunt). Weight penalties are incurred by all horses that win except if the conditions of the race preclude them, i.e. Classic races, most group races, handicaps where the horse has been rehandicapped after winning, some specially conditioned races where prize-money value determines penalty, etc. and the National Hunt equivalent.

Weight penalties apply particularly to mdns at closing Flat, all novice hurdlers and nov. chasers, National Hunt. A horse with a penalty must be considered handicapped by this extra burden of weight – it will mean that whatever performance has been achieved, the horse is likely to have to improve further to overcome this new handicap of weight.

TABLE 8.5 Scale of weight-for-age for Flat races

	Age (yrs)	Mar & Apr 1–15	Apr 16–30	May 1–15	May 16–31	June 1–15	June 16–30	July 1–15	July 16–31	Aug 1–15	Aug 16–31	Sep 1–15	Sep 16–30	Oct 1–15	Oct 16–31	Nov
5f	2	32	31	29	27	26	25	25	23	21	20	19	18	17	16	15
	3	13	12	11	10	9	8	7	6	5	4	3	2	1	—	—
6f	2	—	—	30	29	29	28	27	26	26	24	22	21	21	20	18
	3	15	14	13	12	11	10	9	8	7	6	5	4	3	2	1
7f	2	—	—	—	—	—	—	—	—	—	—	24	23	23	22	21
	3	16	15	14	13	12	11	10	9	8	7	6	5	4	3	2
1m	2	—	—	—	—	—	—	—	—	—	—	27	27	26	25	24
	3	18	17	16	15	14	13	12	11	10	9	8	7	6	5	4
9f	3	18	17	16	15	14	13	12	11	10	9	8	7	6	5	4
1¼m	3	19	18	17	16	15	14	13	12	11	10	9	8	7	6	5
11f	3	20	19	18	17	16	15	14	13	12	11	10	9	8	7	6
1½m	3	20	19	18	17	16	15	14	13	12	11	10	9	8	7	6
13f	3	21	20	19	18	17	16	15	14	13	12	11	10	9	8	7
1¾m	3	21	20	19	18	17	16	15	14	13	12	11	10	9	8	7
15f	3	22	21	20	19	18	17	16	15	14	13	12	11	10	9	8
2m	3	22	21	20	19	18	17	16	15	14	13	12	11	10	9	8
2¼m	3	23	22	21	20	19	18	17	16	15	14	13	12	11	10	9
2½m	3	25	24	23	22	21	20	19	18	17	16	15	14	13	12	11

Note: Allowance assessed in lb which: 3 y.o. will receive from 4 y.o. 2 y.o. will receive from 3 y.o.

TABLE 8.6 Scale of weight-for-age for National Hunt races

Distances (miles)	Age (yrs)	Jan (st lb)	Feb (st lb)	Mar (st lb)	Apr (st lb)	May (st lb)	June (st lb)	July (st lb)	Aug (st lb)	Sep (st lb)	Oct (st lb)	Nov (st lb)	Dec (st lb)
2	4	—	—	—	—	—	—	11 0	11 1	11 2	11 3	11 5	11 6
	5	11 7	11 8	11 9	11 10	11 11	11 11	11 12	11 12	11 12	11 12	11 12	11 12
	6	12 3	12 3	12 3	12 3	12 3	12 3	12 3	12 3	12 3	12 3	12 3	12 3
2½	4	—	—	—	—	—	—	10 11	10 11	11 0	11 1	11 2	11 3
	5	11 6	11 7	11 8	11 9	11 10	11 11	11 11	11 11	11 12	11 12	11 12	11 12
	6	12 3	12 3	12 3	12 3	12 3	12 3	12 3	12 3	12 3	12 3	12 3	12 3
3	4	—	—	—	—	—	—	10 7	10 7	10 11	11 1	11 2	11 3
	5	11 5	11 6	11 7	11 8	11 9	11 9	11 11	11 11	11 11	11 11	11 12	11 12
	6	12 3	12 3	12 3	12 3	12 3	12 3	12 3	12 3	12 3	12 3	12 3	12 3
2	3	—	—	—	—	—	—	10 7	10 7	10 11	11 0	11 1	11 3
	4	11 0	11 2	11 3	11 5	11 6	11 6	11 7	11 7	11 10	11 11	11 12	11 12
	5	12 1	12 2	12 2	12 3	12 3	12 3	12 3	12 3	12 3	12 3	12 3	12 3
	6	12 3	12 3	12 3	12 3	12 3	12 3	12 3	12 3	12 3	12 3	12 3	12 3
2½	3	—	—	—	—	—	—	10 6	10 9	10 11	11 0	11 1	11 3
	4	10 13	11 1	11 2	11 4	11 5	11 6	11 9	11 11	11 11	11 12	11 12	11 13
	5	12 0	12 1	12 2	12 2	12 3	12 3	12 3	12 3	12 3	12 3	12 3	12 3
	6	12 3	12 3	12 3	12 3	12 3	12 3	12 3	12 3	12 3	12 3	12 3	12 3
3	3	—	—	—	—	—	—	10 5	10 8	10 9	10 11	11 0	11 2
	4	10 12	11 0	11 2	11 4	11 5	11 5	11 8	11 8	11 10	11 11	11 11	11 12
	5	11 13	12 0	12 1	12 2	12 2	12 3	12 3	12 3	12 3	12 3	12 3	12 3
	6	12 3	12 3	12 3	12 3	12 3	12 3	12 3	12 3	12 3	12 3	12 3	12 3

Individual penalties range from 3 lb to 10 lb (Flat) and 5 lb–10 lb (National Hunt). These are often cumulative in novice hurdlers and chasers or may be 7 lb for one race and 10 lb for two races won; similarly, the conditions of some races (both National Hunt and Flat) require varying weight penalties according to the value of the races won.

TABLE 8.7   Winners defying weight penalties during the 1981 Flat season

Penalty	5f handicaps (all ages) Winners – runners	2m handicaps Winners – runners
Up to 5 lb	1 – 3 = 33.3%	4 – 27 = 14.8%
6 lb or more	16 – 90 = 17.8%	1 – 17 = 5.9%
Total	17 – 93 = 18.3%	5 – 44 = 11.4%

TABLE 8.8   Weight penalty scale

Flat		National Hunt	
5–6f	3 lb per length	2m	2 lb per length
7–8f	2½ lb per length	2½m	1½ lb per length
9–11f	2 lb per length	3m	1 lb per length
12–14f	1½ lb per length	3m+	½ lb per length
15f+	1 lb per length		

The effect of the weight penalty. Weight has a greater effect the longer the race. The larger the penalty the less likely it is a horse will be able to defy that penalty. This is the guiding principle to the effect of weight as can be seen from Table 8.7. The penalty scales given in Table 8.8 are those most widely applied.

On fast ground the allowances need to be increased and on soft ground decreased. For example, some judges believe that 4 lb represents a length over 5f on firm ground, and ½ lb a length may be the best yardstick over 2m on soft going. The selector should use his own judgement within the broad guidelines.

Many situations demand the practical consideration of penalties and the likelihood of a horse defying a penalty can be said to depend on:
1. The size of penalty;
2. The scope it has to make the necessary improvement.
   The size of the penalty.
Penalties are allotted in the following categories:
3 lb–5 lb The lowest and easiest penalties for a horse to overcome
   – many horses can improve the necessary amount to over-

119

come these low penalties, for example simply by winning a race. Early season 2-year-olds would normally develop this amount from a winning experience.

7 lb This requires greater improvement and defeats most horses unless slightly lowered in class.

10 lb and 10 lb+ This requires considerable improvement and will defeat all but the very best horses.

Scope for improvement is essentially connected and bound to the horse's physical constitution and scope for development; this information can hardly be gleaned from examination of form but requires experienced observation of the horse.

Scope for improvement will also be indicated from the manner of the horse's winning performance (i.e. the ease or difficulty of winning). A horse that wins easily can hardly do more and is likely to improve upon that performance, while a horse that wins 'all out' suggests that it is unlikely to improve.

Weight allowances can be described as the weight concession for unproven ability, as a penalty in weight is the handicap for proven ability. Weight allowances are normally framed in the conditions of races as a concession to lack of achievement (due to ability or experience), i.e. mdn allowance for horses that have not won a race; a weight allowance for horses which had not run previously; a weight allowance for horses that have not won a race since a certain date or a race of a prescribed value.

COURSES

There are over 50 racecourses spread throughout Britain, some specializing in Flat or National Hunt racing while others can accommodate both types. These courses can vary as much in size, shape and gradients of their surfaces as they do in location.

Courses range in extremes from a sharp flat track at Chester which is approximately 1m in circumference to the wide-open galloping expanses at Newmarket where there is a course a straight mile long. This variation of courses can and does strongly influence a racehorse's performance, ensuring that some horses become course specialists. These horses only seem able to produce their best form under the conditions prevailing on a certain course, and at other tracks produce below-par performances.

The variation of courses is as wide for National Hunt racing as for Flat racing. Extremes personified at one end of the spectrum by figure-of-eight-shaped circuits at Fontwell and Windsor and the other by wide galloping tracks at Aintree and Haydock. The former two tracks have easy fences while the latter have large awesome fences which, having a drop on the landing side of the fences, are negotiated only by the safest of jumpers.

COURSES

The different characteristics of race tracks can have an effect on a horse's performance. British racecourses vary as much in their shape, size and undulation as they do in location.

These photographs illustrate the two extremes. The top one is looking down the July Course at Newmarket – a wide, straight galloping track, while the bottom one shows Chester which is a tight round track of approximately 1 mile circumference.

121

TYPES OF FENCES

In National Hunt racing there are two types of obstacles – fences in steeplechase races (chases) and hurdles in hurdle races. In chases there are three different types of fence – plain fence, open ditch and water jump. On National Hunt steeplechase courses there is only one water jump, one or two open ditches, the remaining fences being plain fences. A water jump has a fence not more than 3 feet in height pre-ceeding it and an expanse of water not less than 12 feet in width. An open ditch consists of a fence not less than 4 feet 6 inches in height with a ditch not less than 6 feet in width on the take-off side of the fence. All plain fences are sturdily built non-moveable structures made of firmly-packed birch and trimmed gorse and are not less than 4 feet 6 inches in height. Hurdles are portable structures consisting of two bar wooden frames covered with gorse and are staked to the ground. They are not less than 3 feet 6 inches in height from the bottom to the top bar. The stiffness and type of fences can vary from course to course.

These differences combine to endorse the maxim 'horses for courses' especially where the course is of extreme character. *Flat*: Chester – small circuit with tight bends; Epsom, Brighton – rolling gradients; Newmarket – straightness and openness; Windsor – figure-of-eight shape. *National Hunt*: Fontwell, Windsor – figure of eights; Newton Abbot – tight flat track 1m circumference; Haydock, Aintree – big fences, galloping courses; Cheltenham – tough fences, large circuit, stamina-sapping gradients.

Some courses are right-handed, others left-handed, some suit front runners others benefit long-striding horses who need a galloping course to be seen to best advantage. The variety of racecourses in Britain is one of the intriguing and attractive features of British racing, allowing a horse to keep its own characteristic individuality and not necessarily have to conform to the stereotype conditions of racing that exist elsewhere. Therefore, it is always necessary when assessing a horse's chances to pay attention to the special features and require-ments of the course. The characteristics of both Flat and National Hunt racecourses in the UK are given below.

Flat racing

ASCOT (RH)	Round course 1m 6f with a run-in 2½f. It is a galloping-type course. Straight course 1m is undulating with a stiff 3f, uphill finish.
AYR (LH)	Round course 1m 4f with a run-in 4f. Straight course 6f.

TYPES OF FENCES

The mammoth fences at Aintree.

An open ditch at Sandown Park.

The usual type of plain fence encountered on a park course.

The type of hurdle encountered on National Hunt courses.

BATH (LH)	Round course 1m 4f with a run-in 4f. It is a galloping-type course. Straight course 5f 167yd and uphill.
BEVERLEY (RH)	Round course 1m 4f with a run-in 3½f and stiff uphill finish. Straight course 5f.
BRIGHTON (LH)	U-shaped course 1m 4f with a run-in 3½f. It is an undulating course.
CARLISLE (RH)	Pear-shaped course 1m 5f that is undulating with a run-in 3½f uphill. Straight course 6f.
CATTERICK (LH)	Oval course 1m 2f with a run-in 3f. It is a sharp course. Straight course 5f that is downhill most of the way.
CHEPSTOW (LH)	Oval course 2m with a run-in 5f. It is an undulating course. Straight course 1m.
CHESTER (LH)	Tight, round-shaped course of 1m with a run-in 2f. Sprint races are run on the round course.
DONCASTER (LH)	Round course almost 2m with a run-in 4½f. It is a galloping course. Straight course 1m.
EDINBURGH (RH)	Oval course 1m 2f with a run-in 4f. It is a flat, sharp course. Straight course 5f.
EPSOM (LH)	U-shaped course 1m 4f with a run-in 4f. It is an undulating course. Straight course 5f downhill and very fast.
FOLKESTONE (RH)	Pear-shaped course 1m 3f with a run-in 3f. It is a sharp course. Straight course 6f.
GOODWOOD (RH)	Is a loop-shaped course that allows races up to 2m 5f to be run, run-in 4f. Straight course 6f. It is a sharp, fast course.
HAMILTON (RH)	Loop-shaped course allowing for races up to 1m 5f, run-in approximately 5f. Straight course 6f. It is an undulating course.
HAYDOCK (LH)	Round course 1m 5f with a run-in 4f. It is a galloping course. Straight course 5f.
KEMPTON (RH)	Triangular-shaped course 1m 5f with a run-in 3½f, plus a dog-leg-shaped course 10f (Jubilee Course). Separate straight 6f across in the centre of the course. It is a flat course.
LEICESTER (RH)	Oval course 2m with a run-in 5f. It is a galloping course. Straight mile which is downhill at first.
LINGFIELD (LH)	Round course 1m 4f with a run-in 3f. It is an undulating course. Straight course 7f 140 yd.
NEWBURY (LH)	Oval course 1m 7f with a run-in 5f. It is a galloping course. Straight course 1m.

NEWCASTLE (LH)	Oval course 1m 6f with a run-in 4f. It is a galloping, testing course. Straight course 7f.
NEWMARKET (RH)	*Rowley Course.* Long course of 2m 2f with a gentle bend into the straight 1m 2f from finish. It is a wide, galloping course.
(RH)	*July Course* – is of similar shape with a gentle bend into its straight 1m from the finish. It is slightly more undulating.
NOTTINGHAM (LH)	Round course 1m 4f with a run-in 4f. It is a flat course. Straight course 7f.
PONTEFRACT (LH)	Pear-shaped course 1m 4f with a run-in 2f. It is a sharp, undulating course. There is no separate straight course.
REDCAR (LH)	Round course 1m 6f with a run-in 5f. It is galloping course. Straight course is 1m.
RIPON (RH)	Round course 1m 5f with a run-in 5f. It is a sharp course. Straight course 6f.
SALISBURY (RH)	Loop-shaped course with races up to 1m 6f with a run-in 7f. Straight course approximately 1m. Last 4f are uphill and provide a stiff test. It is a galloping course.
SANDOWN (RH)	Round course 1m 5f with a run-in 4f. Stiff galloping course. Separate straight course 5f in the centre of the course and steadily rising throughout.
THIRSK (LH)	Round course 1m 2f with a run-in 4f. It is sharpish course. Straight course 6f.
WARWICK (LH)	Circular course 1m 6f with a run-in 3f. It is a sharp course. The 5f course bends left with the junction of the round course.
WINDSOR (RH)	Shaped as a figure of eight. Flat races bend right-handed. Has almost straight 5–6f courses.
WOLVERHAMPTON (LH)	Triangular course 1m 4f with a run-in 4½f. Straight course 5f.
YARMOUTH (LH)	Oval course 13f with a run-in 5f. It is a flat course. Straight course 1m.
YORK (LH)	U-shaped course 2m with a run-in 5f. It is a galloping course. Straight course 6f.

COURSES

National hunt

	Circumference	Run-in (from final fence) (yd)	Type of course		Fences
ASCOT (RH)	1m 6f	160 (Uphill)		Testing	Stiff
AYR (LH)	1m 4f	210	Flat	Average	
BANGOR (LH)	1m 2f	325	Flat	Sharp	
CARLISLE (RH)	1m 5f	250	Undulating	Stiff	
CARTMEL (LH)	1m	800	Undulating	Easy	
CATTERICK (LH)	1m 2f	240	Undulating	Sharp	
CHELTENHAM (LH)	1m 4f	350 (Uphill)		Testing	Stiff
CHEPSTOW (LH)	2m	240	Undulating		
DEVON & EXETER (RH)	2m	250	Hilly	Sharp	
DONCASTER (LH)	2m	250	Flat	Galloping	
FAKENHAM (LH)	1m	220	Undulating	Sharp	
FOLKESTONE (RH)	1m 3f	220	Undulating	Easy	
FONTWELL					
(Chases – figure of eight)	1m	220	Flat	Tricky	
(HURDLES) (LH)	1m	220	Flat	Easy	
HAYDOCK (LH)	1m 5f	440	Flat	Testing	Stiff
HEREFORD (RH)	1m 4f	300	Flat	Easy	
HEXHAM (LH)	1m 4f	250 (Uphill)	Undulating	Stiff finish	
HUNTINGDON (RH)	1m 4f	200	Flat	Galloping	
KELSO (LH)	1m 3f	490	Flat	Average	
KEMPTON (RH)	1m 5f	200	Flat	Easy	Stiff
LEICESTER (RH)	1m 6f	250	Undulating	Stiff	
LINGFIELD (LH)	1m 2f	200	Undulating	Sharp	
LIVERPOOL (LH)					
Grand National Course	2m 2f	494	Flat	Galloping	Stiff
Mildmay Course	1m 2f	260	Flat	Sharp	
LUDLOW (RH)	1m 4f	450	Flat	Stiff	
MARKET RASEN (RH)	1m 2f	220	Flat	Sharp	
NEWCASTLE (LH)	1m 6f	220	Undulating	Stiff	
NEWBURY (LH)	2m (approx)	255	Flat	Galloping	Stiff
NEWTON ABBOT (LH)	1m	300	Flat	Sharp	
NOTTINGHAM (LH)	1m 4f	240	Flat	Galloping	
PERTH (RH)	1m 2f	450	Flat	Average	
PLUMPTON (RH)	1m 1f	200	Undulating	Sharp	
SANDOWN (RH)	1m 5f	300 (Uphill)		Stiff	Stiff
SEDGEFIELD (LH)	1m 2f	525	Undulating	Sharp	
SOUTHWELL (LH)	1m 2f	250	Flat	Sharp	
STRATFORD (LH)	1m 3f	200	Flat	Sharp	
TAUNTON (RH)	1m 2f	150	Flat	Average	
TOWCESTER (RH)	1m 6f	300	Undulating	Stiff	
UTTOXETER (LH)	1m 2f	300	Flat	Galloping	
WARWICK (LH)	1m 6f	240	Flat	Sharp	
WETHERBY (LH)	1m 4f	190	Flat	Galloping	
WINCANTON (RH)	1m 3f	200	Flat	Galloping	
WINDSOR (figure of 8)	1m 4f	200	Flat	Average	
WOLVERHAMPTON (LH)	1m 4f	220	Flat	Average	
WORCESTER (LH)	1m 5f	220	Flat	Average	

THE DRAW (APPLIES ONLY TO FLAT RACING)

It is the position across the course from where a horse must start, whether placed in a starting stall or lining up behind a barrier (tape) or by flag.

THE DRAW

The draw only applies to Flat racing and the position of the draw can have a significant influence in sprint races where an advantage at the start may never be overcome at a later stage of the race.

Horses are usually started from stalls in Flat racing.

The tape barrier start used in National Hunt racing allows a jockey to pick his starting position. The horses are started as far as possible in a straight line and at a reasonable distance from the tape.

It is really only a significant factor in most races up to 1m with perhaps the Derby, Cambridgeshire Handicap (where there are large fields) and some longer races at Chester the exception. The draw is of particular importance in the shorter distance races of up to 1m where ground advantage lost at the start cannot be regained. The draw plays a more important role on some courses more than others, and in certain prevailing ground conditions more than others.

In considering the draw a number of factors must be taken into account:

1. The use or non-use of starting stalls. Stalls are used on most occasions (when stalls are not used, especially in races for 2-year-olds it is essential that a jockey be experienced and competent).
2. The positioning of starting stalls. The position of the starting stalls may be moved from their normal position close to the rails, to a position either to the far side or middle of the course and thus the advantage of the draw can be radically affected. (The movement of stalls occurs usually only in emergency situations, but the effect can be dramatic.)
3. Change of going. While under normal going conditions certain numbers (high, low, middle) will be favoured by the draw, a change of going could nullify and/or reverse this advantage. For example, at Windsor the high numbers, on the stand side, are normally favoured in 5–6f races, but on very soft or heavy going the advantage reverses to the low or middle numbers on the opposite side.
4. The size of the field. In a small field of 5 or 6 runners the runners will not be spread across the course so their is little advantage from the draw but in fields of 16 or more runners with horses spread across the course, favourably drawn horses have a distinct advantage.

Form books, guides and newspapers regularly carry the information regarding the considered favoured draw positions on each course and this needs careful consideration when assessing the chances of a horse.

Course	Draw	Distance	Affect of going
ASCOT	No Advantage	(round course)	
	Low numbers	5f–1m straight course	
AYR	High numbers	5f, 6f	
	Low numbers	7f upwards	
BATH	Low numbers	Up to 1m	
BEVERLEY	High numbers	5f and 1m	
BRIGHTON	Low numbers	5f, 6f	
CARLISLE	High numbers	Up to 1m	

Course	Draw	Distance	Affect of going
CATTERICK	Low numbers	5f, 6f, 7f	
CHEPSTOW	High numbers (straight course)	5f–1m	
CHESTER	Low numbers	All distances	
DONCASTER	High numbers (straight course)	5f–1m	
	Low numbers (round course)	1m	
EDINBURGH	High numbers	5f	
EPSOM	Low numbers	5–8f	
	Middle numbers	10–12f	
FOLKESTONE	Low numbers	5f, 6f	
GOODWOOD	High numbers	5f, 6f	
HAMILTON	High numbers	5f, 6f	
HAYDOCK	No advantage	5f	
	Low numbers	6–8f	
KEMPTON	No advantage	5f, 6f	
LEICESTER	Low numbers	5f, 6f	
LINGFIELD	High numbers	5f–7f 40 yd	
	Low numbers	5f–7f 40 yd	Heavy
NEWBURY	High numbers	5f–1m	(Particularly heavy)
NEWCASTLE	No advantage		
	Low numbers	5f–7f	Heavy
NEWMARKET	Variable	5f–1m	
(Rowley, July courses)			
NOTTINGHAM	High numbers	5f, 6f	
	(but variable as stall positions alter)		
PONTEFRACT	Low numbers	5f, 6f	
REDCAR	High numbers	5–8f	
RIPON	Low numbers	5f, 6f	
	High numbers	8f	
SALISBURY	High numbers	5–8f	
SANDOWN	Low numbers	5f	
	High numbers 7f,	7f, 8f	
THIRSK	High numbers	5f, 6f	
	Low numbers	7f, 8f	
WARWICK	Low numbers	5–8f	
WINDSOR	High numbers	5f, 6f	
	Low numbers	5f, 6f	Heavy
WOLVERHAMPTON	High numbers	5f	
YARMOUTH	No advantage	—	
YORK	No advantage	—	

The draw affects only the distances stated and can be assumed to be of no advantage at other distances.

JOCKEYSHIP

'Fear runs down the reins' – this statement proclaims the importance of good jockeyship. Jockeyship can be the marginal difference between winning and losing in evenly balanced contests, and only when a horse is vastly superior will it overcome the disadvantage of poor handling. Good jockeys cannot win without a good horse underneath them, but bad jockeyship will certainly ruin a horse's chances of winning.

A jockey needs certain qualities:

1. To be competent and reliable in ability and judgement;
2. Honest in application;
3. Have tactical ability (independently to devise a strategy for a race, or to carry out proficiently the instructions given by the trainer, and yet be adept to improvise should the situation demand);
4. To control and impose authority on a horse while encouraging it to give of its best.

The first two qualities mentioned can be said to be the basic requirements common to all the leading riders. It is in the varying degrees of development of the other desired qualities plus character and ambitious purpose which determines the great from the merely good riders.

1. Competence of ability and a reliability of judgement

These are the fundamental and least-considered aspects of jockeyship, requiring no further elaboration because they are qualities constantly observable in the actions of the leading riders.

2. Honesty in application

This is the aspect of a jockey's integrity and requires close examination. It is usual to hear disgruntled punters loudly claim that a jockey's dishonesty was responsible for a horse's defeat when seldom is there anything further from the truth. A jockey, it must be understood, has his first allegiance to whoever engages him to ride (i.e. the trainer/owner) and it will be expected that the race instructions he is given be followed whether or not they comply strictly to the rules of racing. While making this declaration, it must be stated unequivocally that the advantages for winning far outweigh the considerations for deliberately losing a race. A jockey may not try to win a race for the following reasons:

(a) Because he has been instructed to do so by the horse's connections/trainer. The reasons may be numerous – ranging from preparing a horse for a future betting coup to giving an introductory educational race to an inexperienced horse.

(b) Because he has received inducement (financial or otherwise) from a third party (not connected with the horse) who seeks to benefit from a horse not winning. (The implication is that benefit will most likely have a connection with betting.)

In the first instance, a horse that a trainer may condone not winning the race, will usually not have on the day more than an extremely tenuous chance of winning. For example, in the case of a proposed future betting coup the horse is unlikely to be fully fit, and the conditions of the race – going, distance, weight – are likely to be equally unfavourable, and an inexperienced horse is likely to lack the physical maturity or racing 'know-how' at this stage in its career. Instances of trainers stopping a horse with a real winning chance from trying to win is most unusual, for most have learned from experience that a certain winner today (at any odds) is better than risking waiting for the uncertainty in the future.

On the second count the favourable financial advantage or other powerful inducement will have to be considerable to counterbalance the discredit to career and reputation should the act of dishonesty be detected. For a jockey the financial rewards in the long term and sometimes in the short term by successful honest endeavour so outweigh the benefits of malpractice that such acts appear as a most unattractive proposition. The close-knit racing community demands a code of loyalty and integrity which once broken immediately deems a jockey unemployable.

The basic prescribed qualities of jockeyship applies to both Flat and National Hunt riders with, however, defined and distinct physical characteristics which reflect the particular demands in each code of racing.

Flat racing is a manifestation of speed, the maximum racing distance is 2m 6f and the maximum weight carried by a horse is normally 10 st. National Hunt racing is a combination of speed, strength and endurance, the minimum distance is 2m with eight flights of hurdles to jump and the minimum allotted weight is 10 st. Flat race jockeys are therefore small, of light weight (approx. 8 st) and rely on speed of thought and reflex to practise their skill. *National Hunt* jockeys are of normal average height, with a riding weight of 10 st (approx.). Strength, courage, durability and clear understanding are essential elements in their make-up.

The riding lifetime of National Hunt jockeys is a short one; while not gaining the full physical strength to fulfil their full potential until their mid-twenties, within a decade the effects of falls and the rigours of race riding will signal their retirement. Meanwhile Flat race jockeys not subject to the continuous effects from the hazards of injury improve with age and experience, often reaching a plateau of maturity in their thirties which they are able to exploit with notable effect.

Good National Hunt jockeys need the full complement of skills in horsemanship and race riding possessed by their Flat race counterparts with some additional ones as well:

1. The jockey's skill of bringing a horse with a well-timed challenge at the end of the race, and keeping in a position during a race.
2. The horseman's skill of placing a horse well at its fences so that it may jump them in the easiest and most efficient way.
3. The physical courage to keep a horse racing even after it may have made bad errors in jumping – this confidence by example being transferred to the horse.
4. A strong physical constitution, to withstand the rigours of riding long distances, and crushing falls, with a resilience to make fast and complete recovery from injury and to be healthy to resist normal winter ailments, such as colds and flu.

A National Hunt jockey should epitomize the balance between horseman and jockey with a particular emphasis on courage, strength and endurance with a fortitude and optimism to overcome setbacks that may always be only the next jump away.

Jockeys (Flat racing)

In the cause of brevity it is quite impractical here to analyse every good jockey riding in the British Isles. A concise list of jockeys has been compiled composed of those riders which have ridden an English or Irish Classic winner or a race of equivalent stature. An omission of any jockey from this list is not an intended slur on his ability, but a present lack to meet the qualifying requirement.

The list begins with the four great jockeys: **W. Carson, S. Cauthen, P. Eddery** and **L. Piggott**. It is completed by G. Baxter, P. Cook, E. Hide, E. Johnson, J. Mercer, A. Murray, J. Reid, B. Rouse, G. Starkey, W. R. Swinburn, and B. Taylor. 'Good horses make good jockeys' is a statement given full testimony by the exploits of the preceding list of jockeys, each of whom have made marked improvement by their association with very good and/or great horses.

All good jockeys are a combination of horseman and race rider:

Race riding requires the skill of judging pace, tactical awareness and ability to anticipate situations, plus the drive and power to ride a horse in a finish.

Horsemanship is command, control and empathy with a horse. Balancing a horse, enabling it to maintain its stride pattern, settling and imparting confidence in a nervous and/or free-running horse, galvanizing and/or inspiring a faint-hearted or ungenerous one.

The many skills a Flat race jockey needs to develop means that many jockeys only reach the height of their powers with maturity. A fact personified by the more senior jockeys: L. Piggott, J. Mercer, G. Starkey, E. Hide and B. Taylor; and their predecessors in the upper echelons: A. Breasley, R. Hutchinson, F. Durr, G. Lewis and W. Williamson.

'Great riders are born not made' is a statement inspired by observing the empathy great jockeys have with a horse, a oneness in action and of purpose. Great jockeys, although not immune from making errors of judgement, make far fewer and less vital ones than the average rider. It is also an ability to extricate themselves from difficult or potentially difficult situations that separates the great jockeys from the others. The startling difference that divides great jockeys from the others is captured in the statement: 'Great jockeys win races they had no right to win, while other jockeys lose races they had no right to lose.'

Lester Piggott (*riding weight 8 st 5 lb*). 'The best jockey riding' is the simple but true accolade that must be paid to Lester Piggott. A star apprentice from his early teens, Lester Piggott was only 12 years of age when he rode his first winner and became champion apprentice in the 1950 Flat race season before reaching his fifteenth birthday. He was only 18 when he rode his first Derby winner on NEVER SAY DIE in 1954, having 2 years previously finished second. Lester Piggott has ridden more English Classic winners than any other jockey in this century, and has been champion jockey on 11 occasions (including the 1982 championship), gaining his first title in 1960. The established top international jockey throughout the 1960s and 1970s, Lester's formidable record and reputation is all the more noteworthy when it is considered he has confounded a personal weight problem which would overcome the resolve of any lesser man.

Although Lester Piggott has a riding style which in some purist's eyes does not conform to beauty, no one can doubt its effectiveness. A characteristic sight during a race is to see him perched high over a horse's withers with his rear cocked in the air, indicating the ease with which his horse is travelling. He has ridden many winners in this manner, looming alongside opponents under pressure whose jockeys, dismayed by the ease with which Lester's horse appears to be racing, are beguiled into accepting defeat without a prolonged struggle. Similarly, on other occasions, horses which appeared to be going so easily on the 'bridle' suddenly have no more to give when their challenge meets a heartened response, and it would appear it has only been the Piggott 'magic' which has nursed them into such a prominent challenging position.

Technically in race riding there are no departments in which Lester Piggott can be found truly wanting; for while capable of the most tender handling, he has renown for his most persuasive all-power finishes. He is an excellent judge of pace and a master of riding a waiting race, whether coming from behind or skilfully imposing his challenge from the front. As a race rider he has the priceless ability of all the great jockeys to be able to dominate a race, seizing the initiative from rivals, being placed throughout a race in a position of his own choosing and being able quickly to anticipate and extricate himself if situations during a race conspire against him. Such qualities demand a coolness of purpose exemplified by Lester Piggott on the big occasion when he seems always inspired to great performances. While his power finishes are legend, it must be said he rarely gives a horse a hard race if he cannot win, and win or lose horses are seldom soured by his riding. This is the sign of a great horseman as well as jockey to have the innate understanding with and of a horse to be able to get the horse to give of its best in performance. Whether it be on a nervous filly who needs coaxing or a robust colt who requires strong handling, Lester has an immediate authoritative and calming effect on a horse.

Lester Piggott has perfected his own riding style, but it is one which it would be unwise for any aspiring young jockey to emulate, for he rides incredibly short but somehow maintains from this position a sense of balance which never ceases to amaze. His strength and skill can be seen to maximum effect on an inexperienced and/or tiring horse which he always seems to be able to keep so immaculately balanced. His skills are supplemented by an audaciousness and ability to improvise that none of his rivals can or dare to match. The big occasions hold no fear but rather inspire him to excellence, for there is no jockey who can ride the Epsom Derby course better or the stamina-testing Ascot racecourse with its short straight. He similarly excels on his favourite racetrack at York and the wide flat courses at Newmarket.

Lester Piggott, while never having sought public acclaim is simply by the magnitude of his exploits unable to avoid it. He is a professional who thoroughly knows his business, seldom voicing an opinion in racing which is not uncannily accurate and therefore always to be respected. He has an acute perception of what is going on around him in a race, thus enabling him, when as a free-lance jockey, to have the choice of many horses with a real winning chance for his next riding engagement.

The final compliment to pay to Lester Piggott is to say that it is a pleasure and a privilege to witness him riding at his peak.

Willie Carson (*riding weight 7 st 9 lb*).   The ebullient Willie Carson is a rare jockey, who in spite of being at the top of a highly competitive profession exudes a joyfulness in his work.

Willie Carson, the first Scottish-born champion jockey, comes from a non-racing background and his rise to the top of his profession was hardly a meteoric one. He was not champion apprentice and did

THE SELECTION FORMULA ANALYSED

not ride his first winner until late into his apprenticeship. The tenacity and will to succeed which marks his riding style eventually gained him the opportunities his natural abilities could fulfil. A determination to win is what Willie seems to be able to implant in the horses he rides, from his crouched position on a horse he seemingly is able to get right inside and behind a horse to urge it along. This style characterized by his 'push-push' action has tended to allow his other skills to be dismissed or overlooked.

Willie Carson is a good judge of pace, he is able to control and place his authority on a race, riding a waiting race from in front or coming from behind with a late rousing challenge. Tactically adept, he gives little ground away, having his horses in positions where they are given every chance if good enough to win. He excels in tight finishes, driving his horse without over-use of the whip but by the rhythmic propulsive action of his whole body.

Horsemanship is a quality not normally associated with a small Flat race jockey, but Willie Carson has this quality in abundance. He keeps horses well balanced, gripping his legs around them and using his whole strength to balance hanging or inexperienced horses.

The racing public really warms to a trier, and no one epitomizes this more than Willie Carson; he can be justly described as the saviour of lost causes. So often he has been seen to inspire a horse, getting tired and apparently beaten horses to respond to his urging and grasp victory from the gaping jaws of defeat. Willie Carson is a true professional who goes about his business with an engaging pleasure that is transmitted to horse and human like. His association with great horses (especially TROY) and the quality horses of W. Hern's stable has elevated him from being merely a very good jockey to a great one.

Steve Cauthen (*riding weight 8 st 2 lb*). In the spring of 1979, Steve Cauthen 'the Six Million Dollar Kid' first came to England. A mighty reputation preceded him and his arrival was not greeted in some quarters with immediate approval. However, by his return to America in the autumn, he had won over any initially hostile critics with the cool assurance of his riding and the maturity with which he conducted himself, whether in victory or defeat.

The acknowledgement of him as a top international rider is full vindication of his decision to widen his experience as a jockey in England and Europe. He adapted quickly and successfully to the varying conditions of racing, and before his return to America had ridden a worldwide total of 1,000 winners in a short yet phenomenally successful career.

As a rider, Steve Cauthen is well developed in the skills of jockeyship. In particular he is a superb judge of pace, a skill refined by the demands of American racing, where races are shorter and horses have always to be prominently placed to have a chance of winning.

JOCKEYS

Action photographs of 4 of the leading Flat race jockeys

Lester Piggott

Willie Carson

Steve Cauthen

Pat Eddery

He is therefore master in the art of riding a waiting race from the front. This requires an acute judgement of time, allowing a horse to dominate the pace of a race without over-exerting itself. Steve Cauthen is equally capable of riding a waiting race from behind, as he displayed when bringing TAP ON WOOD with a final-furlong flourish to win the 2,000 Guineas. As a jockey Steve Cauthen has a proficient command of tactics, he ensures that his horses are prominently placed giving them every winning opportunity if they are good enough. Like all the great jockeys, he is a great horseman, has a natural empathy with a horse and the priceless attribute to get them to run generously for him. He has the ability to balance a horse in a manner that is second to none. A unique feature of his riding is the stillness with which he sits on a horse yet obtains maximum effort, counteracting the more strenuous efforts of whip-waving rivals.

Racing is a powerful test of character and Steve Cauthen has shown the dignity and resolution to pass that test. Although promoted to super-star status by the media, he has never acted less than modestly in public. He has been unassuming in victory and has responded to sequences of losers with a grace and fortitude that can be held as an example to other more temperamental media stars.

Steve Cauthen is a great young jockey whose ambitions and abilities will take him to further heights.

Pat Eddery (*riding weight 8 st 4 lb*). Pat Eddery, the classic size and build for a Flat race jockey, has the full complement of skills to match these physical attributes. Irish born, Pat comes from a family with a racing tradition, yet this hardly explains his remarkable rise from champion apprentice in 1971 to the first of four consecutive champion jockey titles in 1974. He is now an established top international rider serving as a fine ambassador to the quality of British jockeyship.

Pat Eddery's style combines a cool, neat, commanding action with an efficient, dashing purposefulness. During a race he portrays a dominating air, able to stamp his authority on how a race is run and taking the initiative from less decisive rivals. He positions his horses prominently and is noted for giving little ground away, preferring the shortest route home. He excels in a final dashing challenge which few other jockeys can match in persuasiveness and seldom fail to be overwhelmed by. He is a good judge of pace, tactically resourceful, adept at laying off the pace if it be too fast or quickening if it be too slow.

Pat Eddery, like all the great jockeys, is a good horseman possessing a fine ability quickly to balance a horse perfectly, keeping it well balanced throughout a race and particularly in the highly pressurized closing stages. He is a thorough professional whose services are constantly sought, a particularly good jockey to engage for opinion of a horse, or give an inexperienced one an encouraging introduction.

Pat Eddery's association with GRUNDY and that horse's King George

139

VI Stakes and Derby triumphs brought him to be justly regarded as a great jockey, a view his performances since have only served to endorse. His grip on the jockeys' championship has loosened over the past few seasons, firstly due to the demise of P. Walwyn's all-conquering stable where he was the retained jockey, and more recently his appointment to Robert Sangster and Vincent O'Brien's Irish-based international stable. This latter development which has resulted in his riding engagements being divided between England and Ireland have limited his chances of maintaining the constant challenge necessary to retain the champion jockey's crown. However, this has meant that whenever circumstances allow his services are in constant demand by all the leading trainers. These opportunities he has fully exploited, highlighted recently by the 1981 Benson Gold Cup success on BELDALE FLUTTER and previously the 1979 Oaks success on SCINTILLATE. Despite this less than full commitment to English racing, Pat Eddery has continued consistently to ride over 100 winners per season, and should he decide to concentrate his activities solely in England he will again be most vigorously challenging for the jockey's title, an honour he has worn so majestically.

E. Hide (*riding weight 8 st 3 lb*).   One of the senior jockeys riding, champion apprentice in 1954–56 although never graduating to champion jockey, Edward Hide has consistently been among the top 10 riders during the 1960s and 1970s. Although based in the north of England and considered COCK O' THE NORTH, Edward Hide has ridden successfully in the South as a retained jockey for Sir G. Richards, P. Nelson and C. Brittain. In the space of 20 years he has ridden 5 Classic winners. Edward Hide has a compact style of riding, he is a good tactician, judge of pace and can ride a waiting race from in front or behind. A reliable jockey, Edward Hide is a very good horseman and particularly suited to introducing a 2 y.o. or an inexperienced horse to racing.

He is a good professional jockey, an expert rider on all the northern courses, and thorough in application. A jockey who will walk a course and carefully choose the best ground for the prevailing ground conditions, his opinion of a horse should always be carefully considered when given.

E. Johnson (*riding weight 7 st 9 lb*).   Overshadowed by the arrival of S. Cauthen as first jockey to B. Hills in 1979, Ernie Johnson whose light weight may limit his opportunities in the very top-class races, is pound for pound as good as almost any jockey riding. Champion apprentice in 1967, Ernie Johnson has ridden two Clasic winners, but most of his best rides are restricted to handicaps where his services are always in demand. A serious riding accident in 1977 nearly curtailed his race-riding career, but he has since made a spirited come-back, having his best total of winners in 1978. Ernie Johnson is a forceful rider, sound in judgement and tactics who is well up to the task if he has a horse to match.

J. Mercer (*riding weight 8 st 4 lb*). A very popular and senior jockey, Joe Mercer was champion apprentice in 1952 and 1953, but had to wait until 1979 to accede to the full champion jockey title. Joe Mercer and his then retained stable of H. Cecil had their best-ever season, and Joe's experience was seen to full advantage partnering most of Henry Cecil's record-breaking total for training winners, including a Classic success on ONE IN A MILLION. Joe Mercer had previously ridden five Classic winners, and throughout the past decade has always promi-nently figured among the leading riders.

His neat riding style has been described as classic, and one on which all aspiring jockeys would do well to model themselves. His rhythmic urgings where he is seen using his hands, arms and legs in harmony with his horse's action is very effective and keeps a horse well balanced. Joe Mercer is a good tactician who always ensures his horses are per-fectly positioned in a race and he is an excellent schoolmaster for a young, inexperienced horse. Joe has proved that age is no barrier to class and ability, producing riding performances of a rare vintage in the 1979 season that marked his third decade in racing and first crown-ing as champion jockey.

G. Starkey (*riding weight 8 st 5 lb*).   Greville Starkey is a stylish rider whose riding abilities received long-overdue public acclaim after his exploits on SHIRLEY HEIGHTS in the 1978 English/Irish Derbys and an English Oaks win on FAIR SALINA. Greville Starkey rode his first win-ner in 1956, was champion apprentice in 1957, consistently among the top leading riders during the 1970s, yet it was not until his 1975 Arc de Triomphe success on STAR APPEAL that he gained international repute.

Greville Starkey had a tremendous riding season in 1978, having purple patches of riding important race winners and ended the season with, for the first time, over 100 winners. He is a strong, forceful jockey who is particularly powerful in a finish and renowned for late pounding challenges that can be devastating. However, he is equally adept at 'making all' if required, and a feature of his riding is to see that his horses, always prominently placed, are given every chance. Greville Starkey is a good horseman, well suited to riding 2-year-olds and a professional whose racing opinions are always of account.

Recent associations with so many good horses have allowed Greville Starkey's latent abilities to be fully realized, and his cool mature riding will bring future success.

B. Taylor (*riding weight 8 st 4 lb*).   Brian Taylor is a senior and popular jockey who after riding his first winner in 1956 took a number of years to become established as one of the leading riders. Always a good reliable jockey, Brian Taylor's transformation was marked by his appointment as retained jockey to H.R. Price's stable. This provided opportunities consistently to ride good-class horses, heralding an immediate rise in his total of winners, and in 1976 for the first time he rode over 100 winners in a season. Brian Taylor has always shown he is equal to the task, given a horse of ability, a point clearly demonstrated by his masterly and adventurous riding on SNOW KNIGHT to win the 1975 Derby.

Brian 'Ernie' Taylor is large in size for a Flat race jockey, but rather than be hampered by this circumstance uses his extra weight and strength to positive advantage. He excels in a power finish and is an excellent judge at making a well-timed challenge, yet can equally effectively ride a race from the front.

Brian Taylor is a thoroughly reliable professional rider who has learned his trade with years of experience, and once given the horse is most capable to the task at hand.

J. Reid (*riding weight 8 st 2 lb*).   John Reid is a younger jockey than most of the leading riders and still very much an unrecognized and underrated rider by the public at large. Irish-born John Reid, apprenticed to C. Bewicke, rode his first winner in 1973 and has made a steady rather than spectacular rise to prominence as a jockey. His retainer by the R. Johnson–Houghton stable in 1978 met with some surprise, and initially he had the indignity of being replaced by more fashionable jockeys on the more prestigious rides. His appointment was fully vindicated, however, by a successful partnership with ILE DE BOURBON, emphasized by the cool emphatic victory in Ascot's King George V Stakes.

John Reid has a riding style characterized by his assured yet unassuming manner, belying a fine judgement which allows him to almost ghost into a challenging position. He rides with a longer length of leather than some riders, loses nothing in effectiveness in a finish but rather gains extra grip to keep a horse well balanced. He is a good horseman whose calm approach makes him a very suitable jockey for 2-year-olds.

John Reid has seized with aplomb the opportunities that have befallen him, displaying all the qualities necessary for a great jockey in the making.

G. Baxter (*riding weight 7 st 13 lb*).   Geoff Baxter is a good professional jockey, who was apprenticed to A. Budgett and rode his first winner in 1963. During the 1970s he has consistently had good totals of winners each season, achieving successes in many top handicap races.

He is a strong, stylish rider who can be accurately described as a thoroughly reliable professional who can be engaged with confidence. He is determined in a finish, a good judge of pace given to making few errors of judgement. Geoff Baxter cannot be considered a fashionable jockey and has been limited in opportunities outside his retained stable. He needs the association with top-class horses to allow his undoubted abilities to develop fully.

B. Rouse (*riding weight 7 st 13 lb*).   Brian Rouse is one of the senior jockeys whose rise to public prominence has taken a number of years, but was finally heralded with a confident, finely judged riding performance that captured the 1980 English 1,000 Guineas. After a less than distinguished early career and a period away from racing, Brian re-embarked on a jockey's career in the early 1970s gaining his first winner in 1972. Since then he has made consistent and continuous progress, steadily increasing his total of winners each season. Southern based and initially associated only with the Epsom-based stables, his reputation has spread until now his services are widely in demand among all the informed racing fraternity.

Brian is a cool determined jockey with an undemonstrative manner and style which should not serve to understate his ability, for he is a good judge of pace, strong and resolute in a finish with the calm commanding quality of an accomplished horseman. He is a jockey who can and will ride to instructions, can be trusted to forward a clear constructive opinion after a race and therefore an excellent rider to engage on young or inexperienced horses. Brian Rouse has established himself as a thoroughly professional jockey who once given the right opportunity is equal and able to meet the challenge against the very best opposition.

W. Swinburn (*riding weight 8 st 3 lb*).   It is seldom that a young jockey within 3 years of riding his first winner in public and still before his twentieth birthday should ride the winner of the premier English Classic race. This, however, is the achievement of Walter Swinburn, scarcely out of his apprenticeship and only in the first season of becoming stable jockey to M. Stoute's powerful establishment in riding the 1981 Derby winner SHERGAR. Normally one would not promote such an inexperienced jockey to join the ranks of the leading riders, but having gained the rare qualification of riding the winner of the most important Classic, coupled with the maturity of his performance in a meteoric rise to prominence, Walter Swinburn may be placed in this esteemed league.

A son of famous Irish-based jockey Wally Swinburn, young Walter has displayed from the earliest days of his apprenticeship a rare brand of professionalism comparable only in another generation to a young Lester Piggott. Walter Swinburn's outstanding quality as a jockey is an uncanny ability to do the right things at the right time. His personal manner and performance epitomizes this quality of quiet confidence to master each new experience and situation. As a rider he is commanding in action, exhibiting in races a calm poise not subject to intimidation and therewith raising himself high above his contemporaries on the road to developing into a truly great jockey.

A. Murray (*riding weight 8 st 1 lb*). Tony Murray returned to the English Flat racing scene in 1982 after an absence of 6 years, in which time he was based firstly in France and more recently in Ireland. These experiences have widened his reputation and elevated him to the status of a jockey of international repute whose services are eagerly sought after. This development follows an early career which saw him as a star apprentice, before establishing himself as senior jockey in the middle and early 1970s with H. R. Price's powerful stable. This partnership was highlighted by two Classic successes, GINEVRA in the 1972 Oaks and BRUNI's facile win in the 1975 St Leger.

A. Murray is a strong resourceful rider equal to almost anyone in a finish and who combines the finest attributes of horseman and jockey. He is tactically astute, with a calm persuasive style that is aptly suited to the big occasion and likely to be rewarded with many future successes.

P. Cook (*riding weight 8 st*). Paul Cook, after a swift rise to prominence as champion apprentice in the mid-1960s when he gained his first Classic success in the 1966 1,000 Guineas on GLAD RAGS has taken until the 1980s to be fully accepted as one of the leading jockeys. This acceptance marked by his enterprising riding to win the 1982 English and Irish St. Leger's on TOUCHING WOOD. After initial success his career, like other riders before him, experienced a time in the doldrums as he struggled in a transition period to become established at senior status. Mildly mannered Paul, however, is nothing if not determined and by the latter part of the 1970s his season's total of winners improved until he equalled his best-ever total in 1980.

P. Cook is a cool, confident rider with a neat, quiet style that may disguise its persuasive effectiveness. He is a most experienced and reliable jockey, able in the most competitive company, with an approach that can quickly adapt to circumstances. He is a jockey who at last has come of age and who should now enjoy much future success.

National Hunt jockeys

A list of top National Hunt jockeys has been compiled covering the leading riders of the 1982–3 season. Comments have been made as to their particular abilities, noting which jockeys have been champions yet refraining from categorizing them into degrees of excellence, but allowing their past record and current form to be sufficient testimony.

National Hunt racing is nothing if not a test of fate, and the jockey who is a hero and victor one day in one race can just as swiftly be cast in the role of an accident victim the following day or the next race. Fitness and durability are therefore two essential qualities needed by any National Hunt jockeys who hardly expect to sustain their riding career for as long as their Flat counterparts. In these circumstances it is hardly surprising that opportunities constantly present themselves to aspiring riders, and no jockey can rule absolutely supreme.

There were four jockeys riding in the 1982–83 season who had held the champion National Hunt jockey title:

J. J. O'Neill (*riding weight 10 st*). The 149 winners in the 1977/78 season is a record number of winners in a season for a National Hunt jockey and pays full testimony to the brilliance and consistency of Irish-born Jonjo O'Neill. He has a dashing fearless style which can get the last ounce of effort from a horse and this has made him a firm favourite with the racing public. His boldness and drive on a horse should not belie his tactical skill epitomized by his many late rousing challenges which always makes him a formidable opponent until the finishing post has been reached.

R. Barry (*riding weight 10 st 6 lb*). 'Big Ron' Barry, champion jockey on two occasions in the 1970s, was the rider who had previously ridden most winners in a season – 125 winners in 1971/72. Ron Barry is a strong determined rider, known as the 'iron man' for his durability after many hideous falls and injuries. His services are constantly in demand both in the North and in the South, and his calm style is seen to excel, especially when riding chasers. Ron Barry's experience and coolness make him an excellent tutor for young inexperienced horses which are educated to reach their full potential.

J. Francome (*riding weight 10 st 7 lb*). Champion jockey on four previous occasions and joint reigning champion during 1982/83. John Francome is the stable jockey to the powerful F. Winter establishment with which he has been associated througout his racing career, and has ridden a Gold Cup and many big race winners. He has an assured undemonstrative style that marks him as a superb horseman, noted for his ability to get horses to jump quickly and accurately and presenting them correctly at a fence. His horsemanship should not, however, undermine his abilities as a jockey, who is tactically astute and seldom beaten through errors of judgement. John Francome's cool, balanced style is supplemented by a powerful determination to win and places him among the leading post-war National Hunt jockeys.

P. Scudamore (*riding weight 10 st 2 lb*). Peter Scudamore, son of famous National Hunt jockey Michael Scudamore, is one of the new generation of jockeys to emerge in the 1980s. He has in a remarkably short time established himself as one of the top National Hunt riders, sharing the championship in 1982, whose services are now eagerly sought after by many leading trainers. Peter is a determined vigorous young rider whose straightforward style and manner seems to epitomize modern National Hunt racing. While forceful in application, Peter's approach contains a cool, calculation aspect that makes his appraisal of horses and races uncomplicated and accurate. There seems no doubt that providing he can avoid encountering the constant adversary of all National Hunt jockeys, serious injury, Peter Scudamore will for many years remain one of the leading riders.

Two other leading riders who have yet to reach the status of champion, but are good riders are as follows: R. Lamb, S. Smith-Eccles.

R. Lamb (*riding weight 10 st 2 lb*).   Northern-based Ridley Lamb has risen to prominence from the amateur ranks, and has visibly grown in stature as a rider from his association as retained jockey to W. A. Stephenson's large stable. Although he has been adequately supplied with mounts from this stable, he has made the most of opportunities of riding for outside stables. Ridley Lamb is tactically an astute rider, who has the ability to get horses to jump well for him and run kindly. He is a tall upright but stylish rider, a good horseman and a jockey with a strong finish who should only continue to flourish as a leading rider.

S. Smith-Eccles (*riding weight 10 st*).   Steve Smith-Eccles is one of the new generation of emerging mature jockeys set to replace the retired and fading senior riders. He is a forceful jockey, noted for his brave determined riding, likely to inspire a faint-hearted horse and provide very competitive opposition to any rival. Steve Smith-Eccles has grasped most efficiently the opportunities that became available to him, and providing he can withstand the punishing injuries he has been prone to receive, will remain established as one of the very leading jockeys.

Other younger jockeys who have emerged during recent seasons and have become established among the leading riders are R. Rowe, H. Davies and R. Earnshaw.

Besides the above-mentioned jockeys there are a number of other competent professionals seeking to establish themselves amongst the ranks of leading riders needing possibly only consistent opportunities to fulfil their ambitions. These include R. Linley, P. Leach, D. Goulding, P. Barton, A. Webber and S. C. Knight.

Action photographs of 4 of the leading National Hunt jockeys

Jonjo O'Neill

John Francome

Steve Smith–Eccles

Peter Scudamore (left)

OTHER POINTS TO NOTE REGARDING CONDITIONS

Blinkers

The overnight declaration of blinkers is compulsory for Flat racing and National Hunt racing.
Blinkers are fitted to a horse for the purpose of inducing it to run faster. It is therefore of particular significance to establish when a horse wears blinkers for the first time, as it is on this occasion that they are likely to have their most dynamic effect. When blinkers are fitted to a horse its field of vision is reduced, thereby forcing it to direct its attention forward and hopefully concentrate its efforts into running faster.
In practice the fitting of blinkers to a horse for the first time can have three effects:

1. They encourage a horse to concentrate its energies and run faster.
2. They discourage a horse so much that it does not want to race at all and therefore goes slower.
3. They over-excite a horse to run too quickly in the early part of a race and so it exhausts itself before the finish.

The effect of blinkers fitted for the first time in a race is always problematic and the outcome can never be guaranteed. An indication of the outcome may be drawn from observing a horse's behaviour after blinkers have been fitted and the manner in which it cantered to the start. The questions to consider are as follows:

1. Did the fitting of blinkers appear to markedly affect the horse's attitude and behaviour?
2. Did they appear to over-excite the horse, causing it to break out in sweat and become disturbed?
3. Did the horse canter to the post in an uncontrolled manner, was it pulling too hard or was it reluctant to canter at all?

Those are negative aspects which tend to indicate the bad effect blinkers have and will continue to have. However, if the horse appears galvanized by their application (i.e. gently on its 'toes', excited without undue nervousness) and canters to the start, keenly taking a firm hold of its bit, these are the indications it is responding favourably and blinkers are likely to have the desired effect and improve its performance.
Of nearly 32,000 runners on the Flat in 1981, 3,306 wore blinkers. Of these only 6 per cent won their respective races compared with over 10 per cent for horses without blinkers. *Winning favourite* statistics of horses that wore blinkers is dismally only 22 per cent – a survey of horses winning who wore blinkers for the first time produced stat-

BLINKERS

Blinkers restrict a horse's area of vision. They are fitted with the desire to concentrate a horse's attention forward and thereby induce it to run faster.

A horse's head fitted with blinkers – the horse can only see forward and cannot be distracted from the rear.

istics that were even worse. The conclusion from this survey is to beware of all horses wearing blinkers unless they have previously won when so equipped and wear them on a regular basis. Horses wearing blinkers for the first time should be similarly viewed with caution as an extra element has been introduced which cannot be calculated in advance.

THE TRAINER'S METHODS AND RECORD

For a racehorse trainer producing winners can be described as a two-fold process. Firstly consisting of the art of training a horse to attain physical and peak race fitness, and secondly involving the often underestimated skill of successfully 'placing' a horse (deciding the when and where to run it) so that it may have more than a hopeful chance of winning.

TRAINERS' METHODS

Training methods vary from trainer to trainer and are likely to be a reflection of the varying practices encountered by a trainer during an apprenticeship of gaining training experience.

The older trainers can be expected to be found practising the well-tried and tested methods of preparing racehorses (i.e. using only established food products and feeding habit patterns, having a pre-scribed amount of work and method of exercising horses in prep-aration and using only conventional methods of treating injuries). Newer and/or younger trainers may be more inclined to innovation and prepared to experiment in their training methods (i.e. new or different foodstuff, varying exercise in training with perhaps bouts of swimming for horses, seeking and being aware of other treatments to cure illnesses and heal injuries).

With so many possible ways of training a horse it is hardly sur-prising that there can be no restrictive uniformity of training methods. Individual methods can only be judged by the results they produce which will be subject to certain factors – but especially to the character and ability of the trainer himself who will be limited by the facilities and staff at his disposal and restricted by the type, quality and physical constitution of the horse in his care. These considerations will be fun-damental in establishing whether a horse will receive a careful, thorough off-course preparation to be brought to peak race fitness or whether it will only achieve its peak fitness by running in races. Some trainers are noted for having their horses always extremely well prepared before they are raced, ensuring that their horses are fully race fit for their seasonal racecourse reappearance or on their racing debut.

Leading trainers (Flat)

Henry Cecil *Newmarket.* Born 11 January 1943, first licence 1969. An outstanding trainer to follow, as Cecil's ratio of winners to runners is regularly better than one in three. He has turned out more than 100 winners in a season on several occasions. The Warren Place trainer has a tremendous record with his runners first time out and is the only man worth supporting at Newmarket, his home track. As many as half of Cecil's runners at the minor northern courses win their races. Stayers are a speciality, with LE MOSS and ARDROSS springing most readily to mind. Whoever is riding this stable's runners must never be ignored.

Dick Hern *West Ilsley, Berks.* Born 20 January 1921, first licence 1957 No British-based trainer can match Dick Hern's record in the Classics as all five have gone West Ilsley's way at one time or another. His Epsom double in 1980 with HENBIT and BIREME was especially memorable. An expert at preparing his horses at home, Hern captured the 2,000 Guineas with BRIGADIER GERARD in 1971 without giving the colt a preliminary outing. A level stake profit can be made from following Dick Hern's horses in most seasons, as his is clearly not a gambling stable.

Michael Stoute *Newmarket.* Born 22 October 1945, first licence 1972 An ever improving young trainer, Michael Stoute became widely known to the general public following SHERGAR's brilliant efforts in 1981. Two-year-olds are a speciality and only Henry Cecil has a better record with youngsters, although few are seen out before the end of May and they hit peak form in July and August. A meticulous planner, Stoute leaves little to chance. Take particular note of any of his runners at Brighton.

Barry Hills *Lambourn.* Born April 2nd 1937, first licence 1969 Many top-class horses have been handled by Barry Hills since his early training successes with HICKLETON, bought out of a seller back in 1968. The most famous was RHEINGOLD, the Prix de l'Arc de Triomphe winner in 1973. Despite that victory, Hills is most highly regarded for his training of fillies. The trainer's overall strike rate averages 16 per cent, but reaches double that level at the minor northern courses.

Guy Harwood *Pulborough, Sussex.* Born 10 June 1939, first licence 1966 After spending his early days as a trainer handling a mixture of jumpers and handicappers on the Flat, Guy Harwood burst into the big time with some shrewd purchases made jointly with James Delahooke, including ELA-MANA-MOU and TO-AGORI-MOU. His strike rate is generally around 20 per cent and together with some long-odds winners this has produced some handsome returns. The Pulborough 2-year-olds are generally useful and any Harwood runners at Folkestone can usually outclass the opposition.

John Dunlop *Arundel, Sussex.* Born 10 July 1939, first licence 1966
Patience is the key to John Dunlop as he rarely rushes his horses in the early stages of their careers. This approach has paid dividends with Classic winners such as SHIRLEY HEIGHTS and QUICK AS LIGHTNING, but the Arundel trainer does especially well with handicappers. Dunlop's strike rate averaged only 17 per cent, several points behind the top three and a substantial degree of selectivity is needed when following the yard.

Leading National Hunt trainers

Michael Dickinson *Harewood, Yorks.* Born 3 February 1950, first licence 1980
The dedication shown by Michael Dickinson first as a jockey and then as assistant trainer to his father Tony, paid handsome dividends when SILVER BUCK won the 1982 Cheltenham Gold Cup. Chasers are the primary objective of the stable and are much more worthy of betting attention than the Dickinson hurdlers which are trained with their long-term careers in mind. Around a half of all the trainer's runners over the bigger obstacles win their races and a level stake profit from this sector is a regular occurrence. Any Dickinson horses sent to southern tracks are worth extra consideration.
M. H. (Peter) Easterby *Great Habton, Malton, Yorks.* Born 3 August 1929, first licence 1950
The Gold Cup/Champion Hurdle double achieved by Peter Easterby in 1981 with SEA PIGEON and LITTLE OWL was a fitting tribute to an outstanding trainer who carried all before him in the late 1970s and early 1980s. An outstanding strike rate in excess of 25 per cent coupled with some generous starting prices has resulted in regular level stake profits for followers of the stable. Peter Easterby's record of success with his seasonal débutants is especially noteworthy and horses sent south strike fear into the hearts of southern-based trainers.
Fred Winter *Lambourn.* Born 20 September 1926, first licence 1963
Following a long career as a jump jockey including a hat-trick of champion jockey titles in the mid-1950s, Fred Winter has enjoyed equal sucess in the training sphere. A stream of top-class animals have been through his hands including the Champion Hurdle winners BULA and LANZAROTE and the 1978 Gold Cup victor MIDNIGHT COURT. Winter's runners are dangerous in any company and his overall strike rate is consistently above 20 per cent. First-timers are generally fit to do themselves justice while stable runners at Chepstow and Lingfield are well worth support.

TRAINERS

Leading Flat race trainers of the 1980s

Henry Cecil

Barry Hills

Dick Hern

J. Dunlop

Guy Harwood

Michael Stoute

Josh Gifford *Findon, Sussex.* Born 3 August 1941, first licence 1970 Another champion jump jockey to make a success of training, Josh Gifford hit the national headlines with the fairytale victory of ALDANITI in the 1981 Grand National. The Findon horses are generally a little below the top class, but do well around the minor tracks, especially Huntingdon and Towcester. The trainer's strike rate is generally around 17 per cent which makes level stake betting unprofitable. Stable runners are usually at their best in the first half of the season, notably November.

The trainers portrayed above are a selection of those who besides producing a large number of winners each season have had and usually have many of the best horses that compete in the most prestigious races. The selector will gain a fully comprehensive understanding of the many trainers in British horse-racing by referring to the publication *Trainers Record* from which two annuals are produced – *Flat Race Edition* and *National Hunt Edition.*

TRAINER'S RECORDS

A trainer's record is a testimony of the methods he employs and provides a further factor for consideration in the selection process. A trainer's record portrays how he races his horses, and it is useful to be acquainted with the training records of the leading trainers (Flat and National Hunt), establishing the following:

1. *The racecourses where they are most successful* (i.e. where they are the leading trainers or figure prominently as one of the leading trainers.)
(a) Courses where a trainer has a high percentage of winners to runners, i.e. this may be where southern/Newmarket horses (Flat) are sent by their stables for rare but successful visits to minor courses – North, South, East or West or vice versa – northern stables visiting southern courses.
   N.B. (This may apply particularly in National Hunt racing where the standard of racing throughout the country is more evenly balanced and some northern stables have a particularly high ratio of winners to runners at courses such as Ascot, Newbury, Kempton and Sandown).
(b) *Adversely* There are courses where trainers have a very high ratio of runners to winners – and no particular importance can be placed on their horses running there. For example, Newmarket-based horses racing at Newmarket; Lambourn based horses racing at Newbury; Northern (Malton)-based horses racing at York/Doncaster (invariably 2-year-olds, inexperienced 3-year-olds, novice hurdlers, etc. are given introductory races at these meetings close to their base).

Leading National Hunt trainers of the 1980s

Michael Dickinson

Fred Winter

M. H. (Peter) Easterby

Josh Gifford

2. *The times of the season a trainer has most winners* and *the meetings at which a trainer is consistently successful.* Trainers often have the major proportion of their winners at a certain time in the season – early, mid-season or late.

A disposition for a trainer to produce winners at certain times in the season may be by circumstance or design or by a combination of the two. For example, southern trainers based at Epsom and on the South Coast have a reputation of producing winners in the early part of the Flat season, being favoured by the supposed more clement winter weather conditions. Yet certain northern trainers not blessed with the supposed milder weather conditions of their southern counterparts, have a reputation for similarly producing early season winners. Design then appears to have an equal role with circumstance, a fact which is borne out by the number of trainers who are mid-season specialists focusing their training schedule to have their horses in top condition in mid-season (Flat – July and August; National Hunt – January, February and March) when the racing fixtures are heaviest and prizes on average more valuable. Similarly, some trainers avoid the strong competition of mid-season and concentrate early or late in the campaign. For example National Hunt trainers with the more moderate horses are seen regularly to contest prizes at the lower grade courses at the seasons opening in August, September, October or at its close in April and May.

The leading trainers, however, usually manage to have winners constantly throughout the season, yet with particular months when their crop of winners reaches a height. Circumstance and design merged when stables stricken by the virus (which has blighted a number of Flat race stables) were forced to readjust their training programmes and make the most of their opportunities whenever possible.

Meetings. Certain meetings hold a particular significance for some trainers. The most important of these are (Flat) Newmarket, Newbury meetings, Epsom's Derby and spring and bank holiday meetings Royal Ascot, the Goodwood Festival, the York Festival in August. (National Hunt) The bank holiday meetings Christmas, Easter, Whitsun, summer Cheltenham Festival, Aintree meeting.

A trainer may have established a good winning record at these meetings, and having discovered the specific requirements for winning a race, is then often able to seasonally reproduce that success. The runners from such a stable at these meetings are therefore always especially well prepared and always give a good account of themselves, even if they fail to win.

The significance of these races to trainers may have arisen due to other than purely racing considerations. Owners who pay the bills may demand to see and be seen watching their horses run at certain meetings and the trainer is therefore forced to accede to their wishes (i.e. H. Cecil and M. V. O'Brien are trainers with horses particularly prepared for Royal Ascot and other major meetings).

The four bank holidays provide a feast of National Hunt races – and without a generally high standard of quality opponents in so many races, allows great opportunity for the well-placed, well-prepared horse. Some trainers who realize the value of having horses 'ready' at these meetings are rewarded with multiple winners on the day – three, four or even five winners. Trainers such as F. Winter, J. Gifford, S. Mellor, M. Dickinson, M. H. Easterby and M. Rimell have good records on these occasions. These may be one of the few occasions when their sporting working owners have the opportunity to watch their horses run and see them win.

Other meetings may be of significance in understanding a trainer's record, not because of the initial success that is obtained but because these meetings serve as preparation races for late successes. These meetings will be essentially before the trainer has his horses completely prepared, but serve as an indicator of the progress still to be made and act as introductory race for 2-year-olds (Flat) and novices (National Hunt).

All the horses of trainers which run at a meeting where he regularly has success should always be seriously considered and their form thoroughly examined. Similar consideration can be given to the runners of a trainer who has a particularly good record in a particular race; whether it is a top-class competitive race like the Derby – where M. V. O'Brien has an enviable record – or the Grand National – where T. F. Rimell reigned supreme – or a particular handicap at a small meeting that one trainer wins regularly.

3. *Significant travelling and jockey engagement.* The significance of a horse being sent a long distance to compete in a race should not be underestimated for there is little point in a trainer going to such time and effort if the horse has not got a winning chance. The strongest indications will be as follows:

(a) When the trainer sends only one horse to the meeting – engaging a top jockey who travels a similar distance for this one ride of the day.

(b) When it is unusual for a top trainer to have a horse or horses travelling such a journey to such a meeting.

When the trainer sends a team of horses it is unlikely they all have an equal chance of winning – one probably has a real chance and the rest may be there to fill up the horse box. This is not always so, but is generally the case. Exceptions to this are leading trainers who send better class horses to a lower grade meeting, often with successful doubles or trebles the outcome of such ventures.

A trainer may also be just sending a horse a long way because the owner wishes to see it run there (i.e. the owner may be a steward at the meeting, live near the course or be on holiday close by). There

161

can be many reasons why a horse is sent a long journey to race; it is a significant factor if it is solely a calculated decision by the trainer to give a horse a positive chance of winning; it assumes less importance if made for other reasons.

Jockey engagement. The engaging of a top jockey to ride a horse will be for two reasons:

1. If the horse has some hint of form that it can win the race, the jockey will be engaged for that purpose.
2. If the horse has no form and/or is inexperienced it is likely the jockey is being engaged to obtain a professional opinion of the horse's racing potential and to give it an education.

It is often a significant move when successful apprentices (Flat) and claimers (National Hunt) are engaged by a trainer especially in handicaps where the reduction of a few pounds of weight gives a horse a winning edge.

The engaging of a top jockey or otherwise cannot alone make a horse win, but coupled with other factors gleaned from a trainer's record and methods is a further indication which may assist in the assessment of a horse's chances. Reference to *Trainers Record* publications will provide this indispensable information.

The successful training of racehorses depends upon a large percentage of work and preparation and a final ingredient of inspiration or intuition, and it is this certain element which separates the great from the merely competent trainers.

OWNERS

To complement the manner and methods employed by trainers in the way they race their horses, it will be enlightening for the selector to have some knowledge and understanding of racehorse owners.

The owner of the horse as understood from the race-card is the person(s) or business officially registered with the Jockey Club as the owner(s). The owner will have bought or leased the horse and be responsible for training fees (that include the additional variables of veterinary bills, entry and jockey fees), but have the privilege of seeing their colours worn on the racetrack.

The owner with such a considerable financial commitment can be seen as the cornerstone of the racing industry, creating and maintaining employment for trainers and their staff by providing the product (i.e. horses) that enable racing to function. Owners may come from any class in society and with the advent of horse syndication (up to 12 partners are allowed to hold shares) even from modest backgrounds, but the high cost required to own and train a horse ensures that principally owners come from the wealthiest echelons. The two different types of racing tend to produce two differing breeds of owners. Flat racing with its ever increasing outlay in new young blood-stock yet with equally its amazingly high potential reward for the most successful, attracts basically the richest and most class-conscious patrons. National Hunt racing, meanwhile, which is less prestigious, without unbounded reward for the most successful and with the prospect of disaster and injury ever looming tends to attract the more sporting enthusiast and die-hard type of owner. This being a most basic classification of the types of owner it will be useful for the selector seeking a greater comprehension of racing to become familiar with the names of leading owners and to recognize their involvement in racing and motives for ownership. Such comprehension will often give the final process of selection confirmation or further indication of a horse's chances that may not be revealed entirely in the bare facts of form.

Owners, whether they be seen as misguided philanthropists ever supporting the horse-racing and betting industry, mere exhibitionists with inflated egos seeking public limelight or perhaps a peculiar mixture of these two extremes, all live with the constant hope and dream of seeing their horse in the winner's enclosure. Having a winner to any owner is vindication of their decision to become owners, it is the reward for their months or maybe years of hope, disappointment and expense. It will serve as the proof to silence the doubters, the mocking critics and act as a rebuff to personal enemies. The racecourse then becomes the place where owners may flaunt their success, respectably exhibiting their possessions and power in the guise of expensive thoroughbred horseflesh. Ownership may become a means of obtaining fame, possibly fortune and self-advancement simply by association, deriving the benefits from the effort, struggle and skills of others (i.e. horse, trainer and jockey).

Ownership with its hands tightly affixed around the purse-strings of racing can be seen to hold the seat of considerable power and influence. In consideration of these observations it will assist the selector to become acquainted with the 'who's who' of racing (reference to the *Directory of the Turf* will be most informative) and acknowledge how trainers will often direct their efforts to produce winners on particular occasions for their most favoured or prestigious patrons, i.e.:

1. An owner who is a racing steward will take particular pleasure from seeing his horse win at the meeting where he is an official.
2. A prospective royal winner(s) will often be indicated by the presence of members of the royal family at the racecourse when they have horses as runners.
3. An owner surrounded by a large party of friends and relatives, all especially invited to the racecourse, is usually expecting or hoping for an occasion to celebrate success.

163

4. A foreign owner in the country on a business or pleasure visit, will without doubt find their stay enhanced at the prospect of witnessing their horse(s) win. Such pleasing memories will in their absence from British racing serve to appease for some time any past or future lack of success that they may encounter.

These examples illustrate (while no owner has the power of guaranteed success) that when trainers focus their efforts on achieving particular aims, the selector who realizes these ambitions is in a most favourable position to recognize what may be the salient factors regarding selection in that instance.

9 THE PRACTICAL APPROACH TO MAKING A SELECTION

The approach to selection must always be in a controlled, reasoned manner, with sufficient time allowed for the unprejudiced examination of the relevant facts of form before considering and forming a selection decision.

THE PRACTICAL STEPS

1. Decide which race(s) are suitable for selection (i.e. choose the more easily discernible ones; these are Flat and National Hunt races where horses carry comparative level weights). They should be non-handicaps and non-selling races with a recommended maximum of 12 runners.
2. Having chosen the race(s) suitable for selection, check the starting time(s), and be sure to allow enough time for thorough, unhurried assessment and analysis. If there is insufficient time do not even begin assessment; if the pressure of time does not allow for the completion of thorough assessment and analysis *do* not become persuaded to make a selection decision.

ASSESSMENT OF THE RACE

1. *Consider the type of race* – Flat or National Hunt – the ease or stiffness of the course and/or fences and what is required for winning, e.g. speed in sprints, stamina in long-distance races and jumping ability in National Hunt racing.
2. *Read the conditions* that apply to the race so as to become acquainted with factors that assert the race's winning requirements.

The conditions will state the following:

(a) The prize-money for winning (the higher the value of prize-money, the better the class of race and often the more competitive).
(b) The distance of the race.
(c) The entry conditions, i.e. mdns at starting, mdns at closing, novices, etc. or other more involved entry qualifications.
(d) The weight conditions, i.e. sex allowances in Flat races, weight-for-age allowances in all-age races (Flat and National Hunt) weight penalties for winners, weight allowances for mdns or horses that have not run before, and other special qualifying conditions of weight.

Note the 'going' – this must always be paid particular attention. Due regard should be given to sudden extreme changes of going (i.e. within a couple of days prevailing ground conditions changing from good to heavy) which can engineer reversals of form. Extremes of going (heavy–hard) often allows certain horses who can only produce their best form under such conditions to reign supreme.

The analysis of the form of each runner in a race

There can be no specific direction given in this area without intrusion upon personal perception, and it must be left to the experience and judgement of each selector to draw their own conclusions (however, always insisting that form analysis be approached without bias and by using the rational power of the reasoning mind).

In practice form analysis consists of:

1. The systematic assessment of the form of each runner in a race;
2. The elimination of the improbables and no-hopers;
3. The formation of a concluding short list of probables.

A GUIDE IN THE USE OF THE SELECTION FORMULA

The selection formula is designed to allow selection to be based upon verifiable factors of reasoned probability. It is therefore necessary during the selection process clearly to identify and evaluate the merits of these factors.

The selection process begins by deciding on the race(s) suitable for selection and then becoming acquainted with the entry and correspondingly the possible winning requirements. This is followed by the most important aspect of selection.

FINAL SELECTION DECISION

If the form analysis should reveal only one probable, the final selection decision can be considered complete – awaiting only final verification from the modifying factors in the formula.

Should form analysis produce more than one probable, a selection is made by comparing the corresponding graded factors of each probable as revealed in the selection formula. The horse(s) with the lowest merit grade rating will be eliminated leaving the remaining probable as the selection choice.

The most desirable situation is for the selection choice to be a probable which has top merit rating in each section of the selection formula.

F *** Proven best from		**F** ***	Proven race fitness within 7 days
C dr Dropped in class		**C** √	Same – going, (G) distance (D)
		+	Getting weight allowance
		√	Ridden by top jockey (J)

In practice this total positive confirmation of all factors occurs only on rare occasions.

N.B. It does occur and the selector who is discriminating and disciplined enough to wait only for these pristine opportunities is likely to be rewarded with an almost 100 per cent success rate. The one failing of such selections is that the odds offered on them tend to be very short, and this makes the betting uneconomic on these alone.

Therefore, it becomes a necessity to be able to balance skilfully all the factors in the formula to provide reliable selections, without having every factor positively confirmed as favourable.

The selection formula must be realized as two parts of distinct degrees of importance.

F – F : C : C

Form is the dominating first part – the *keynote* in importance. Proven form, is the confirmed undeniable proof of what has or has not been achieved in performance.

Fitness/Class/Conditions are the modifying complementary factors of the second part: they can only qualify and/or temper the likelihood of reproducing or improving upon proven form.

The selection formula is based upon the skilful analysis of form with the assessment of the value of form the keynote to selection.

USING THE SELECTION FORMULA TO MAKE A SELECTION DECISION

FORM – THE KEYNOTE

Each section of the formula should be separated, each element divided into its key factors which are graded in an order of merit.

Form can be divided into four categories:

Rating	Abbreviation		
★★★	P	Proven Form	This is of the highest value – it means a horse has proven form better than rivals. It 'holds them' on form.
★★	Prom	Promising Form	This is of the second highest value it means a horse has form of value, but is not emphatically proven as the best (i.e. there may be no means of reliable comparison with other form)
★	Imp	Improving Form	This is of the third highest value – A horse has shown improved form (i.e. has beaten horses that it had previously been beaten by). The true merit of its form is difficult to assess positively, because once a horse improves, it is difficult to judge if or what is its further capacity for improvement.
—	Hti	Has to improve	This is worthy of noting, but not of a merit rating – there are indications of abilities that have still to be realized. It means a horse would have to improve to the maximum degree to have a winning chance – and though yet improbable it would not shock all bounds of reason.

Form is the keynote factor its value cannot be stated too forcibly.

THE MODALITIES: FITNESS, CLASS, CONDITIONS

FITNESS

An element of the fitness factor always has to be taken on trust, but the best proven indication of a horse's race fitness is indicated in a recent racecourse performance.

Fitness can therefore be graded in aspects of its positive and negative elements.

Rating	Days since last race	
★★★	Up to 7 days	The strongest possible indication of a horse being at peak fitness or about to come to peak fitness (a horse without further preparation can hold its peak fitness after a race for about 7 days).
★★	7–14 days	Similar to 7-day fitness – but of a slightly lower order in confirming fitness – a horse can be falling from its peak by this time. *N.B.* It is more common for National Hunt horses to have this slightly longer period between races.
★	14–28 days	After 14 days fitness, confirmed peak fitness is suspect – a horse is likely to be past its peak without careful preparation – it will depend on the trainer's methods.
—	28 days	After a month, or longer absence from racing a horse's fitness has to be taken entirely on trust. The selector will need to be well acquainted with a trainer's methods to have confidence in the horse being race fit. A 28-day+ absence from racing indicates that a horse has met with a training set-back (illness or injury) or has been 'let down' for a rest.

N.B. In the assessment of 2-year-olds, whatever the value of previous form, it is most unwise to consider a 2 y.o. for selection who has had an absence from racing of 42 days (6 weeks) or more because it is likely that due to illness or injury that the horse has suffered a reversal in its training programme. As the season progresses 2 y.o. form becomes subject to constant re-evaluation with more recent form tending to supersede older form, horses begin to improve in response to their physical development aligned often to climatic changes and the increase in distances of races.

CLASS

This means a horse is competing against better, worse or the same quality of opposition.

Abbreviation

dr   Down in class – is the most favourable indication. A horse has less to do.

—   In the same class – requires a horse to repeat its known performances.

Up   Up in class – means a horse must improve upon its best performance to have a winning chance.

CONDITIONS

The final, and the important balancing factors which sometimes hold sway in forming a selection decision.

The first consideration is *weight* (weight is the leveller of ability, the less weight a horse has to carry the faster it should be able to travel). Weight allowance (lb) is positively favourable; weight concession (lb) is a disadvantage. The amount of weight allowed or conceded is the issue. It is always a matter of personal opinion to judge in each instance how much will be the deciding amount. Up to 5 lb in penalties is negligible; 7 lb+ must be given thoughtful consideration. Due regard must be given to 'going' – obviously weight is a greater burden in 'heavy' than 'good' going.

Distance. Change of distance can be of crucial consequences. Most horses are suited to a particular distance and are not so effective over a longer or shorter trip.

Proven/suited   *Unproven and/or untried*

D√   D?   If a horse is untried or unproven at a distance, the indications on whether it will be suited can only be estimated from its breeding and the manner it has been performing over shorter or longer distances (i.e. RO over shorter distances, weakening over longer distances).

N.B. Experienced horses of proven ability will often more readily be successful when reverting to shorter distances than when attempting longer distances where their stamina rather than their speed will be put to the test. Recently MOORSTYLE (1981–7f) successfully reverted to sprint distances, ARDROSS (1981–2½m Gold Cup) won at 1m 5f and ARTAIUS (1977–1¼m Eclipse) won the 1m Sussex Stakes in the same year.

Going. Can the horse act on the ground conditions? Horses have varying actions and confirmations which make it possible for them to produce their best form only on specific ground conditions.

Proven	*Unproven*	
G√	G?	Changes but similar going (i.e. good, good to firm, good to soft, soft) are likely to prove no measurable encumbrance to a horse. It is the extremes of going that produce the ground 'specialists' (heavy, very soft, fast). Breeding and confirmation (action) are the indications to how a horse will adapt to the going.

Further factors that influence conditions

Jockeyship. The subject of jockeyship essentially resolves to opinion. It can be stated that while there are only slight differences in competence and ability among the leading riders, there is a considerable difference in ability between the top-class jockey and the average jockey.

Draw. The draw is only applicable to flat racing. Its significance is dependent on:
1. The racetrack;
2. The distance of the race;
3. The size of the field.

Blinkers. Blinkers are mainly of importance in Flat racing. They become of particular interest when worn by a horse for the first time.

In the context of the formula, merit ratings for the form and fitness sections have been symbolized in degree by stars, a three-star rating representing the highest value and one star the lowest.

The other sections of the formula have been symbolized as positive, negative or passive value for class by dr, up or —; and for conditions by indicating if there is a weight allowance (i.e. 4 lb pen.) and by a tick and question-mark system as proven or unproven values for the following: course (C√, C?), distance (D√, D?), going (G√, G?), jockey (J√, J?), draw (Draw√, Draw?) and blinkers (Bl√, Bl?).

In symbols a six-star rating: *★★★* form + *★★★* fitness + drop in class + weight allowance + (proven) distance + (proven) going would be the top rating, the ideal and desired choice for selection.

As the ideal situation seldom presents itself, an alternative reliable minimum standard must be established which adheres to the principles of the selection formula. It is recommended that a four-star rating, where there are no negative or unproven factors influencing, become the minimum standard for selection. Passive factors will only serve as neutral influences, while positive factors give endorsement to such a selection.

A four-star rating guarantees that a selection is based on reasonable proven elements of form and fitness (not withstanding that any selection not composed of a three-star form rating has a doubt cast to its soundness).

N.B. Less than four-star rating is below the standard necessary for reliable selection, and no selection must ever be considered to be made.

The forming of a selection is made by the comparison of the merits of each probable drawn from form analysis. These merits are more easily identified and evaluated when clearly marked in the visual symbols of the selection formula beside the relative probable. Write out the probables:

Example. Fill in the relative information in the selection formula:

Meeting (course)   **Going**   **Time**

Type of race   **Value**   **Distance**   **Number of runners**

Name of probable   **Trainer**   **Age**   **Weight**   **Jockey**
     (A)

F.   F.   C. C.
P   (5)   —   10 lb pen
★★★   ★★★

Name of probable   **Trainer**   **Age**   **Weight**   **Jockey**
     (B)
F.   F.   C. C.
Imp   (14)   Up 10 lb pen
★   ★★

N.B. (Have a maximum of only three probables. If form analysis has produced more than three, a selection must not be contemplated.)

The formula credentials of each probable can be quickly compared, the one(s) with the lowest merit rating eliminated, leaving the remaining probable as the selection choice.

In the above theoretical example probable (B) would automatically be eliminated with a rating below the minimum standard, and probable (A) which has a rating above minimum standard becomes the selection.

If after evaluation it was found that the final two probables had identical merit ratings for each section of the formula, it must be considered that they are too finely balanced to allow a selection decision to be made. For practical guidance it can be stated that a five-star selection which is not overburdened by negative condition factors is likely consistently to produce winning selections at economic odds.

EVALUATION

SUMMARY OF STAR RATINGS

Rating			Betting odds comment
6 star –	with all the modifying factors favourable	THE IDEAL RATING	Normally odds on
	with a balance of positive and negative factors	MOST DESIRABLE RATING	Normally best – odds–evens
5 star –	with all modifying factors positive	GOOD practical VALUE	Likely to be viable betting odds
	with a balance of modifying factors	GOOD practical VALUE	Viable odds
4 star –	with all modifying factors positive	The MINIMUM requirement. (The most commonly encountered selection rating, lacks absolute quality, but skilful selection will be well served by selection of this merit rating)	Good economic betting

This concludes the practical recommended guide to selection. It has been sought to allow, within a well-constructed framework of the cardinal principles of racing, for each selector to formulate their own judgements and selection decisions by the fine working of the reasoning mind.

10 PRACTICAL EXAMPLES OF THE SELECTION FORMULA AS APPLIED TO ACTUAL RACES

The constant predominating factor and key to successful selection is the correct interpretation of form. So often the factual evidence necessary to assess confidently the value of form is either non-existent, contradictory or incomplete. Therefore, however tightly structured the selection formula is in all other aspects, the analysis and assessment of form resolves to the individual experience and personal judgement of each selector. This aspect allows the selectors to bring their initiative, skill and understanding to bear in laying the foundation-stone of selection while submitting the final decision to the other completely objective uncompromising elements of the whole selection formula.

The races included as examples were all analysed and a final decision concluded on the evidence presented before the races were run and the *result known*. They are a sample taken from many various types of races analysed, and serve to demonstrate how the unchanging principles captured within the selection formula successfully apply despite the constantly changing facets of horse-racing.

The analysis of the majority of races reveal that the most favourable factors stipulated in the selection formula and identified by the star rating system only infrequently exist to the highest desired standard. This means that the selector must either discriminately wait for only the most advantageous selection opportunities or else, to accommodate the needs of the less than discerning 'something must win the race' approach, warily lower the highest standards prescribed in the formula.

In response to these ever present practical realities, races filling both the above categories have been included as examples. Races ranging from the premier in the calendar (i.e. the Classics, their trials, group races and National Hunt equivalent) and having a public familarity, to more obscure races which may be seen to conform more reliably to the highest standard requested in the selection formula.

NATIONAL HUNT SEASON 1980–81

1364 *KEMPTON 26 DEC. 1980 (good)*

1.40—WILLIAM HILL CHRISTMAS HURDLE
£12,500 added (£8,439). 2m. (5)

301	1L13-D1	**BIRDS NEST 20 (C & D D9)** R Turnell 10-11-10 .... A Turnell	● 78
302	4221-31	**HEIGHLIN 13 (D2)** D Elsworth 4-11-10 .... S Jobar	77
304	1D22-22	**CELTIC RYDE 20 (D4)** P Cundell 5-11-6 .... S Smith-Eccles	77
305	11111-6	**FREIGHT FORWARDER 20 (C & D2 D4)** A Pitt 6-11-6 .... I Cox	59
307	L00-	**TOPSIN 308** O Jorgensen 5-11-3 .... R. Rowe	—

Probable S.P.: 5-4 Heighlin, 2 Birds Nest, 4 Celtic Ryde, Freight Forwarder.
FAVOURITES: 1 3 3 2 2.
1979: Birds Nest, 9-11-10 (A. Turnell) 6-4, R. Turnell, 5 ran.

Probables

(1) BIRDS NEST – R. Turnell 10.11.10 A. Turnell
    F.   F.   C. C.
    Prom (20) — C √
    ★★   ★   D √

(2) HEIGHLIN – D. Elsworth 4.11.10 S. Jobar
    F.   F.   C. C.
    Prom (13) — D √
    ★★   ★★   C?
                 10 lb pen

(4) CELTIC RYDE – P. Cundell 5.11.6 J. Francombe, substituted for
    S. Smith–Eccles
    F.   F.   C. C.
    Prom (20) — D √
    ★★   ★

A small field of five runners produced three probables – all of which had raced 20 days earlier with a slightly different arrangement in the weights and with barely one length covering the three runners. Therefore, it would take only a slightly different performance for form to be reversed. Applying the formula, HEIGHLIN had the better credentials with a four-star rating – but was now 3 lb worse off with CELTIC RYDE on a sharp track unlikely to suit its style of running. CELTIC RYDE was 4 lb better off with BIRDS NEST. Although not in strict accord with the formula, CELTIC RYDE was the strongest appearing contender.

Result: 1st CELTIC RYDE (2–1) 2½ lth
        2nd BIRDS NEST (11–4)
        3rd HEIGHLIN (6–5 fav.)

PRACTICAL EXAMPLES OF SELECTION FORMULA APPLIED TO ACTUAL RACES

1365 KEMPTON 26 DEC. 1980 (good)

2.15—KING GEORGE VI 'CHASE.
£25,000 added (£18,358·25). 3m. (8)

401	1118-IL	ANAGLOGS DAUGHTER 13 (BF) A Durkan (Ire) 7-11-10 ..... T Carberry	67
402	131-0P3	BACHELOR'S HALL 20 (C & D) P Cundell 10-11-10 ..... J Francome	56
403	Ddd*-311	CHINRULLAH 6 M O'Toole (Ire) 8-11-10 ..... N Madden	77
404	1/2712-1	NIGHT NURSE 7 M H Easterby 9-11-10 ..... A Brown	77
405	11-111L	SILVER BUCK 13 (C & D D4 BF) M Dickinson 8-11-10 ..... T Carmody	77
406	2LD*7-03	TIED COTTAGE 13 (D2) Mrs J Moore (Ire) 12-11-10 ..... L O'Donnell	67
407	11P-U11	DIAMOND EDGE 21 (D2) F Walwyn 9-11-7 ..... W Smith	• 78
410	34-86L5	TENECOON 36 (D) F A Smith 11-11-3 ..... P Warner	40

Ddd*—disqualifications on technical grounds.

Probable S.P.: 5-2 Diamond Edge, 3 Silver Buck, 5 Night Nurse, 6 Anaglogs Daughter, 7 Chinrullah, 12 Bachelor's Hall, 20 Tied Cottage, 50 Tenecoon.

FAVOURITES: 1 0 0 1 2.
1979: Silver Buck, 7-11-10 (T. Carmody) 3-1. A. Dickson. 11 ran.

Probables
(5) SILVER BUCK – M. Dickinson 8.11.10 T. Carmody
    F.   F.   C.   C.
    Prom (13) — C √
                      D √
    ★★   ★★   3 lb pen.
(7) DIAMOND EDGE – F. Walwyn 9.11.7 W. Smith
    F.   F.   C.   C.
    Prom (21) — D √
    ★★   ★   C?

In a race of quality horses, the two probables revealed by analysis were SILVER BUCK, the winner of the race the previous year, and DIAMOND EDGE – application of the formula favoured SILVER BUCK.

Result: 1st SILVER BUCK (9–4) 5lth

1423 PLUMPTON 29 DEC. 1980 (good to soft)

3.15—HEATHFIELD NOVICES' HURDLE (Div. II).
£700 added (£592·20). 2m. (11)

601	5/P	IRISH BANK 13 A Pratt 6-11-6 ..... Mr C Willett (4)	—
602	6/0U0-96	BOLTINGO 13 E Beeson 5-11-4 ..... R Rowell	51
603	0L6P-	CHINESE TAKEAWAY 244 J Davies 5-11-4 ..... M Perrett (7)	—
605	11	TEA POT 26 (D) M Blanshard 4-11-3 ..... B de Haan (4)	74
606	00-421	BLUE PATROL 25 (D) N Henderson 4-10-10 ..... J Nolan	75
608	F31698	SUMMERCOVE 49 (D) A Moore 4-10-10 ..... G Moore (4)	67
609	04-5707	ALNASR ASHAMALI 7 C Benstead 4-10-3 ..... R Atkins	—
610	F4263-10	BIHAS BOUNTY 27 A Pitt 4-10-3 ..... I Cox	• 78
611	86	CREWE MAJOR 40 Mrs D Oughton 4-10-3 ..... R Rowe	72
612	P80-6B9	FLYING LYNDSAY (B) 27 J Bridger 4-10-3 ..... H Jenkins (4)	58
613	L05-400	ORANGE TOWN MAN 28 D Browning 4-10-3 ..... J Akehurst (7)	—

Probable S.P.: evens Tea Pot, 6-4 Blue Patrol, 6 Summercove, 10 Bihas Bounty, 16 Flying Lyndsay.
FAVOURITES: 3 0 1 — —.

Probables

(5) TEA POT M. Blanshard 4.11.3   B. de Haan (4)
    F.   F.   C. C.
    Prom (26) — D √
    ★★ ★̣   14 lb pen.

(6) BLUE PATROL – N. Henderson 4.10.10   J. Nolan
    F.   F.   C. C.
    Prom (25) dr D √
    ★★   ★   7 lb pen

Analysis revealed only two probables – neither of which unequivocably had the prescribed star rating to warrant selection. Out of the two BLUE PATROL – with a 7 lb weight advantage and a drop in class had the superior credentials.

Result: 1st BLUE PATROL (11–8 fav.) 11th

1425 *FONTWELL 30 DEC. 1980 (good to soft)*

1.15—"SALMON SPRAY" PATTERN HURDLE (4-Y.-O)
£5,000 added (£3,603·00). 2m. 2f. (4)

201	2D46-24 **MOUNT HARVARD 50** (BF) N Henderson 11-4	Bob Davies	● 78
204	210-954 **EGBERT 10** J Gifford 10-10	R Rowe	61
206	4 **GOLDEN RIVER 17** R Turnell 10-10	A Turnell	63
208	43-6489 **PRIVATE AUDIENCE 11** E Beeson 10-10	R Rowell	70

Probable S.P.: Evens Mount Harvard, 2 Golden River, 4 Egbert, 10 Private Audience.
FAVOURITES: 2 0 —

Probables

(1) MOUNT HARVARD – N. Henderson 11.4 B.R. Davies
    F.   F.   C. C.
    P   (50) dr 8 lb pen.
    ★★★ —

(6) GOLDEN RIVER – R. Turnell 10.10 A. Turnell
    F.   F.   C. C.
    Prom (17) up —
    ★★   ★

This small field of four runners resolved to two probables – MOUNT HARVARD a proven, superior hurdler against a good-class Flat performer GOLDEN RIVER who had had only one previous outing in a novice hurdle. Neither fully met the prescribed standard of the formula – of the two MOUNT HARVARD had the proven form and thus superior credentials.

Result: 1st MOUNT HARVARD (4–5 fav.) 8lth

1429 *FONTWELL 30 DEC. 1980 (good to soft)*

3.15— BRIGHTON NOVICES' HURDLE (Div. II) (3-Y.-O.)
£700 added (£679·70). 2m. 2f. (18)

601	IF954 TAMERCO 33 (C & D) K Cunningham-Brown 11-2	C Mann (7)	60
602	1223 WADI ALI 34 (C & D BF2) H Price 11-2	C Gwilliam (4)	75
604	0432 BINEHAM CITY 20 R Hodges 10-9	C Gray (4)	58
605	325 CILIUM 10 F Winter 10-9	J Francome ● 78
607	B COURT GREEN 13 Mrs N Smith 10-9	A Webb	—
609	P FINE RAINS 43 R Voorspuy 10-9	C Kinane	—
610	0 GRIMA 13 I Dudgeon 10-9	R Linley	—
613	2 LAURIUM 35 G P-Gordon 10-9	I Cox (4)	70
615	MY JOHN CHARLOTT J Gifford 10-9	R Rowe	—
617	RP NICE ON THE ICE 8 C Cyzer 10-9	A Curran (4)	—
618	ON WE GO A Moore 10-9	G Hoore (4)	—
621	QUAYSIDE BATTLE T M Jones 10-9	A Webber	—
622	ROYBIRDIE G Balding 10-9	B Reilly	—
623	SALDATORE D Morley 10-9	Bob Davies	—
624	9 SAXON DAWN 35 E Beeson 10-9	R Rowell	—
626	9 THE MIXER 29 J Long 10-9	—	—
627	00 VILLAGE WAY 55 D Greiq 10-9	P Barton	—
628	F YANTLET 8 C Benstead 10-9	D Smith	—

Probable S.P.: 6-4 Cilium, 5-2 Wadi Ali, 4 Laurium, 7 My John Charlott, **10** Roybirdie, 12 Saldatore, 14 Bineham City.

FAVOURITES: — — — 0 —.

Probables

(2) WADI ALI – H. Price 11.2 C. Gwilliam (4)

    F.   F.   C.   C.

    P   (34)   —   C√

    ★★★   —   7 lb pen.

(5) CILLIUM – F. Winter 10.9 J. Francome

    F.   F.   C.   C.

    Prom (10) — —

    ★★   ★★

Analysis produced two probables from a field larger than the desired maximum of 12 runners. CILLIUM was held on a collateral form line through BROADSWORD and HOPEFUL SHOT by WADI ALI. However, CILLIUM's last performance on very heavy going may have been quite misleading, for a reproduction of earlier form againstt BROADSWORD with the present weight allowances placed CILLIUM and WADI ALI on almost equal terms. Applying the formula, CILLIUM was made the Selection choice.

Result:
1st CILLIUM (13–8 fav.) 6lth
2nd WADI ALI

1454 *CHELTENHAM 1 JAN. 1981 (good)*

12.45 — MALVERN NOVICES' HURDLE (DIV. 1).
£1,000 added (£1,007·10). 2m. (17)

1	53-8421 INSULATION 6 L Kennard 7-11-9	Lorna Vincent	67
2	507-421 ROYAL BOWMAN 27 (C) F Rimell 6-11-9	S Morshead	75
6	75 BUSTING 6 R Turnell 7-11-2	Steve Knight	70
8	CRIMSON EMBERS F Walwyn 6-11-2	W Smith	—
9	3 DOCTOR FITZ 138 H Poole 6-11-2	W Morris (7)	—
10	DUKE OF DRESDEN R Head 6-11-2		—
12	2- EASY FELLA 320 N Henderson 7-11-2	J Nolan	• 78
13	8F-0 FLAG LIEUTENANT 17 M Oliver 6-11-2	P Hobbs	—
15	HANSELLS SLAVE C House 6-11-2	C Hawkins	—
16	L0LL-L0 JACK ANTHONY 19 P Kearney 8-11-2	R Mangan	—
19	354/0 PL LEWIS BUILT 30 J Edwards 6-11-2	P Blacker	—
20	0U00-9 LITTLE ROSEBERRY 6 Mrs A Little 6-11-2	P Warner	—
22	08 NICE VALUE 14 R Hollinshead 7-11-2	C Astbury	—
24	32* ROYAL RICHES 84 (BF2) F Winter 6-11-2	J Francome	—
25	SCARLET JUDY G Bishop 6-11-2		—
26	7PP-U TRIPLE SWEET 5 I Maddocks 6-11-2	C Jones	—
28	L CELTIC TUDOR 6 F G Smith 5-11-0	Mr D Smith (4)	—

* N.H. Flat form.

Probable S.P.: 2 Royal Bowman, 4 Insulation, 6 Busting, 8 Easy Fella, Royal Riches, 10 Crimson Embers, Doctor Fitz.

1980: Meeting abandoned—frost.

FAVOURITES: 3 1 2 — —.

Probables

(2) ROYAL BOWMAN – F. Rimell 6.11.9 S. Morshead
   F.   F.   C.   C.
   Prom (24) — C √
   ★★   ★   D √
             7 lb pen.

(6) BUSTING – R. Turnell 7.11.2 S. Knight
   F.   F.   C.   C.
   Imp (6)   — D √
   ★   ★★★

(12) EASY FELLA – N. Henderson 7.11.2 J. Nolan
   F.   F.   C.   C.
   ?   (320) — D √
   —

(24) ROYAL RICHES – F. Winter 6.11.2 J. Francome
   F.   F.   C.   C.
   ?   (84) — —
   —

The inherent dangers of making a selection in a race with above the prescribed maximum of 12 runners was fully revealed in this instance. Analysis produced two probables, ROYAL BOWMAN and BUSTING yet gave a view of two other horses, EASY FELLA and ROYAL RICHES, whose abilities could not be positively assessed.

The formula applied to the list of probables made BUSTING the selection choice.

Result: 1st EASY FELLA (3–1 fav.) 1½lth
2nd BUSTING
3rd DOCTOR FITZ
4th ROYAL BOWMAN

1592 *SANDOWN 10 JAN. 1981 (good to soft)*

1.30— PANAMA CIGAR HURDLE CHAMPIONSHIP QUALIFIER (5-Y.-O.).
£2,000 added (£1,730). 2m. (11)

1	46-1121	**ROLL OF DRUMS 7 (D2)** Mrs J Pitman 11-10	B Smart	77
2	46-3113	**GLAMOUR SHOW 35 (C & D BF)** J Gifford 11-3	R Rowe	66
3	01	**BASSIMOOR 12 (D)** Mrs P Sly 11-10	M Bastard (4)	58
6	42	**GOLDEN RIVER 11** R Turnell 11-0	A Turnell	●78
7	00-4	**HENFOLD LAD 7** A Wates 11-0	J Francome	54
8	432	**HIGH OLD TIME 7** S Mellor 11-0	P Blacker	72
9	F42	**KILBRITTAIN CASTLE 15** F Walwyn 11-0	W Smith	69
12	714	**MISS FURLONG 25 (BF)** P Bailey 11-0	Mr A J Wilson	60
13		**OLD KNOCKER** D Laing 11-0	M Floyd	—
14	P5528P	**SWINGING TRIO 14** R Atkins 11-0	R Atkins	48
16	00	**WALSHFORD LAD 12** D Nicholson 11-0	P Scudamore	—

Probable S.P.: 9-4 Golden River, 4 Roll of Drums, 5 High Old Time, 6 Glamour Show, 7 Kilbrittain Castle, 8 Bassimoor, 16 Miss Furlong.

FAVOURITES: 3 0 2 — 1.

1980: Random Lag, 11-3 (R. Rowe), 4-6 fav. J. Gifford. 11 ran.

Probables

(1) ROLL OF DRUMS – Mrs J. Pitman 11.10 B. Smart
F.   F.   C.   C.
Prom (7)   —   D √
★★   ★★★   10 lb pen.

(6) GOLDEN RIVER – R. Turnell 11.0 A. Turnell
F.   F.   C.   C.
Prom (11)   —   —
★★   ★★★

(8) HIGH OLD TIME – S. Mellor 11.0. P. Blacker
F.   F.   C.   C.
Prom (7)   —   —
★★   ★★★

(9) KILBRITTAIN CASTLE – F. Walwyn 11.0 W. Smith
F.   F.   C.   C.
Prom (15)   —   —
★★   ★

Analysis produced four probables and in accord with the principles of the formula – no selection was attempted.

Result: 1st   KILBRITTAIN CASTLE (3–1) 5lth

        2nd   HIGH OLD TIME

        3rd   MISS FURLONG

1594 *SANDOWN 10 JAN. 1981 (good to soft)*

2.30—TOLWORTH HURDLE.
£4,000 added (£3,194·40). 2m. (8)

2	0346-21	**KNIGHTHOOD 14 (D)** R Turnell 6-11-11	A Turnell	63
3	17	**JONDI 79 (D)** P Mitchell 5-11-9	R G Hughes	63
5	F21	**WESTMINSTER ABBEY 28 (D)** W Holden 5-11-9	Bob Davies	73
6	65-1181	**BICKLEIGH BRIDGE 9 (D2)** R Hodges 7-11-7	S G Knight	68
8	8/FLL47-	**CHRISTMAS VISIT 240** S Wright 7-11-7	P Leach	58
10	9P613	**ARTS AND SPARKS 57 (D)** R Atkins 5-11-5	R Atkins	53
13	12111	**BROADSWORD 21 (C&D, D3)** D Nicholson 4-10-11	P Scudamore	●78
16	10	**GOLLYNO 21 (D)** I Wardle 4-10-4	S Smith-Eccles	52

Probable S.P.: 1-2 Broadsword, 5 Knighthood, 10 Westminister Abbey, 12 Bickleigh Bridge, 20 Gollyno, 25 Jondi.

FAVOURITES: 1 3 1 — 2.

1980: Esparto 5-1-9 (M. O. Sherwood), 9-2, F. Winter, 10 ran.

Probables
(13) BROADSWORD – D. Nicholson 4.10.11 P. Scudamore

    F.   F.   C.   C.

    P   (21)   —   7 lb pen.

    ★★★   ★

Analysis revealed one probable, BROADSWORD, whose form appeared to be superior. The modifying factors, that had to be considered were that BROADSWORD was running against older horses at terms worse than weight for age.

Applying the formula, BROADSWORD was the selection choice. However, in respect of the modifying factors and the expected short odds it was not considered a sound economic betting proposition.

Result: 1st BROADSWORD (4–7 fav.) 4lth

1595 *SANDOWN 10 JAN. 1981 (good to soft)*

3.0—EXPRESS HANDICAP 'CHASE.
£2,500 added (£1,900). 2m. 18yd. (3)

1	522132	**BEACON LIGHT 14 (C & D D 5)** R Turnell 10-11-10	A Turnell	●78
3	L-4F35L	**BREEMOUNT DON 15 (D2)** F Winter 8-11-0	J Francome	76
4	F-15111	**RELDIS 10 (C & D D4)** D Gandolfo 7-10-3	P Barton	75

Probable S.P.: 10-11 Beacon Light, 5-4 Reldis, 8 Breemount Don.

FAVOURITES: — 1 — — 3.

1980: Foreign Legion, 9-10-10 (G. McNally), 4-1. C. James. 5 ran.

Probables
(1) BEACON LIGHT – R. Turnell 10.11.10 A. Turnell
    F.   F.   C. C.
    P   (14) — D √
    ★★★   ★★   C √
                  21 lb (weight concession)?

Analysis revealed the handicap top weight as the only probable with the problematic factor being only the concession of weight. Applying the formula, BEACON LIGHT was the selection choice.

Result: 1st BEACON LIGHT (10/11 fav.) 4lth

1672 *ASCOT 16 JAN. 1981 (good to soft)*

3.40—SILVER DOCTOR NOVICE HURDLE (Div. II).
£2,000 added. (£1,847·60). 2m. (9)

603	FLL47-F **CHRISTMAS VISIT 6** J Wright 7-11-7	P Scudamore	67
605	**GAIE PRETENSE** D Jackson 8-11-7	Steve Knight	—
607	**MORNING MATCH** P Tory 6-11-7	Mr M Felton (7)	—
609	LO **GRECIAN SOVEREIGN 7** A Hide 5-11-5	J Barlow	—
610	432 **HIGH OLD TIME 6 (BF)** S Mellor 5-11-5	P Blacker	76
614	782 **BLACK ROD 20** F Winter 4-10-4	B de Haan (4)	●78
615	LP **DO DASH 37** L Cottrell 4-10-4	S G Knight	—
616	72 **FLEDGE 8** D Elsworth 4-10-4	C Brown	71
617	**INTAKE** G Balding 4-10-4	B Reilly	—

Probable S.P.: 5-2 Fledge, 3 High Old Time, 4 Black Rod, 6 Christmas Visit, Intake

Probables
(10) HIGH OLD TIME – S. Mellor 5.11.5 P. Blacker
     F.   F.   C. C.
     Prom (6)   — —
     ★★   ★★★

(14) BLACK ROD – F. Winter 4.10.4 B. de Haan (4)
     F.   F.   C. C.
     Prom (20) Up D?
     ★★   ★

(16) FLEDGE – D. Elsworth 4.10.4 C. Brown
     F.   F.   C. C.
     Imp (8)   Up —
     ★   ★★

Analysis revealed three probables – HIGH OLD TIME, BLACK ROD, FLEDGE. Applying the principles of the formula, HIGH OLD TIME was the selection choice with credentials of almost the highest standard.

Result: 1st HIGH OLD TIME (5–4 fav.) 6lth
         2nd FLEDGE
         3rd BLACK ROD

1793 *LEICESTER 26 JAN. 1981 (good to soft)*

3.30—CROXTON PARK NOVICES' HURDLE (Div. II).
£1,000 (£690). 2m. (17)

606	F213	WESTMINSTER ABBEY 16 (D) W Holden 5-11-7	S Smith-Eccles	•78
608		CARVEN BOY W Wharton 6-11-2	S J O'Neill	—
613	956-745	INTOXICATED 31 T Nicholls 7-11-2	R F Davies	53
615	OP-0	SCOTTISH MEMORIES 11 M Scudamore 8-11-2	Miss A Sharpe (7)	—
616	B30056-	SENATOR SAM 256 P Bevan 8-11-2	T Wall (7)	57
617	P	TARTAN HEATH 14 M Scudamore 6-11-2	P Scudamore	—
621		CORDUROY D Morley 5-11-0	Bob Davies	—
626	01154	LIR (B) 51 (D2) A Moore 4-11-0	G Moore (4)	66
627	024	NIMBLE DOVE 25 G H Price 5-11-0	R Crank	70
628	07087P	NORTH LONDON (B) 23 K Bridgwater 5-11-0	M O'Halloran	—
631		THRONE OF GRACE T Forster 5-11-0	J Francome	—
633	L4-	VICTOR VALLEY 391 P Felgate 5-11-0	B de Haan (4)	53
635	4210	FEARLESS SEAL 30 (D) R Hollinshead 4-10-7	J Holt (4)	61
638	FL	DOALL 122 R Shelley 4-10-0	Miss Sue Vergette (7)	—
642	2	NORTHERN KING 19 T Kersey 4-10-0	G Kersey (4)	65
643	0440	QUITE LUCKY 30 P M Taylor 4-10-0	S Keightley (7)	64
644	R*	RAVENS TOWER 11 M Pipe 4-10-0	P Leach	—

R*—ran out.

Probable S.P.: 6-4 Westminster Abbey, 3 Lir, 5 Nimble Dove, 6 Corduroy, 7 Throne of Grace, 8 Northern King.

FAVOURITES & 1980: No corresponding race.

Probables

(6) WESTMINSTER ABBEY – W. Holden 5.11.7 S. Smith-Eccles
Γ.   Γ.   C. C.
P   (16) dr D √
★★★   ★   7 lb pen.

Analysis of this race which had above the maximum recommended number of runners revealed only one probable – WESTMINSTER ABBEY. Applying the formula, WESTMINSTER ABBEY was the selection choice.

Result: 1st WESTMINSTER ABBEY (4–5) 1lth

1829 *WOLVERHAMPTON 28 JAN. 1981 (good to soft)*

3.15—HAIG WHISKY NOVICES' HURDLE QUALIFIER.
£1,000 added (£1,149·20). 2m. (20)

403	67-8F14	SEA CARGO 8 (C & D) J Johnson 6-11-5	J Suthern	65
405	01	PRE-EMINENCE 8 D Garraton 5-11-1	P A Charlton	69
406	122	ROADSTER 16 P Bailey 5-11-1	A Webber	•78
407	F	ASDIC 13 D Kent 6-11-0	P Haynes	—
410	3	COSMIC OCCASION 41 M Reid 6-11-0	P Carvill (4)	68
411	FF/P5-	DISHCLOTH 272 Miss S Griffiths 7-11-0	Mr M Oliver (7)	—
413	7U7240	FERNSHAW 25 Miss B Sykes 6-11-0	S Smith-Eccles	77
415		GALLINAZO D Nicholson 6-11-0	P Scudamore	—
419	OF-PPPF	MASTER DEALER 48 C Jackson 7-11-0	R Crank	—
420	642-60F	O'DOWN 30 B Cambridge 7-11-0	Mr J Cambidge (4)	—
425	00	AMBERWELL 44 P Bevan 5-10-10	DOUBTFUL	—
429		CARA BID E Barlow 5-10-10	Mr R Wooley	—

430	7F46	CASHED IN 30 A Jarvis 5-10-10	Bob Davies	62
432	907	CONEY GLEN 16 V Bishop 5-10-10	Mr C Crozier	—
434		FAIR ARTHUR W Jenks 5-10-10	R F Davies	—
435		FEODORA Miss B Sykes 5-10-10	N Breeze (7)	—
442	800	MISANFIELD 19 M Oliver 5-10-10	P Hobbs	—
444	7-880	OXFORD LANE 44 P Bailey 5-10-10	Mr P Webber	—
445		RUGBY ROYAL J Czerpak 5-10-10	M Worthington (7)	—
446	L09	THE WOMPER 30 F Rimell 5-10-10	Mr W Woods	—

Probable S.P.: 5-2 Roadster, 3 Pre-Eminence, 4 Cosmic Occasion, 9-2 Sea Cargo, 10 Asdic, 12 The Womper, Gallinazo.

FAVOURITES: No corresponding race.

Probables

(6) ROADSTER – P. Bailey 5.11.1 A. Webber

F. F. C. C.

Prom (16) — D ∨

★★ ★ 5 lb pen

The problems of day-to-day selection can be seen to be highlighted in this inconsequential midweek race. Analysis revealed only one probable, ROADSTER in a field larger than the recommended 12 runners.

Applying the formula, no selection could be made as ROADSTER had only a three star rating with a negative 5 lb weight penalty. ROADSTER did in fact win, although only narrowly from a horse that had fallen in its only previous race, clearly demonstrating the balancing factors responsible for producing results which in practice just favoured ROADSTER.

Result: 1st ROADSTER (7–4 fav.) ½lth

2073 *FAKENHAM 20 FEB. 1981 (good to soft)*

2.30—WALTER WALES MEMORIAL CUP HUNTERS' 'CHASE
(Amateur riders).
£800 added (£784·80). 2m. 5f. 180yd. (9)

2	211112-	MR MELLORS 265 (C&D C2 D) Mrs A Villar 8-12-6	Miss Lucy King (4)	●78
4	11125-2	TILSTON 13 (D) Mrs P Shields 9-12-2	Miss S. Williamson (7)	72
7		GENERAL MEAD J Bridger 7-11-10		—
8	9P60/0	GREY TARQUIN 9 S Mellor 9-11-10	P Gee (7)	—
10	OOP4/F6-	LIGHTNING BRIGADE 270 O V-Jones 8-11-10	O Vaughan-Jones (7)	—
12	P341-5	QUIMILT 8 (D) B Ward 9-11-10	M Heaton-Ellis (7)	47
14	41222P-	ST TORBAY 381 Mrs G Bateson 8-11-10	M Ley (7)	64
15	439952/	THUMPER 628 D Wales 10-11-10	W. Wales (7)	—
17	22/L3U5-	VULBAY RULER 379 M Bates 13-11-10	W Tolhuist (7)	46

Probable S.P.: 5-4 Mr Mellors, 7-2 Tilston, 6 Quimilt, 8 Grey Tarquin, 10 St. Torbay, 12 Vulbay Ruler.

FAVOURITES: 3 2 — — 1.

1980: Mr Mellors, 7-11-9 (Miss L. King), 8-11 fav., Mrs. A. Villar, 15 ran.

Probables

(2) MR. MELLORS – Mrs A Villar 8.12.6 Miss Lucy King (4)

F.	F.	C.	C.
P	(265) —	C	√
★★★	—	D	√
		J	√

10 lb pen.

(4) TILSTON – Mrs P. Shields 9.12.2 Miss S. Williamson (7)

F.	F.	C.	C.
Prom	(13) —	C?	
★★	★★	D	√
		J	√

6 lb pen.

Analysis revealed two probables in this hunter chase MR. MELLORS and TILSTON. It raised the issue of comparing recent promising form with older proven form, focusing the dilemma often encountered in seleection. In this instance there were two evenly balanced probables – MR. MELLORS with the proven form yet without the benefit of a recent race as proof of fitness, and TILSTON with recent race fitness and promising form. MR. MELLORS was a C/D (2) winner and had won the same race the previous season, but carried a 10 lb penalty. TILSTON was a distance winner, but unproven over this tight course and carried a 6 lb penalty. Both had relatively inexperienced jockeys with TILSTON's jockey the least experienced.

Applying the formula strictly on star ratings TILSTON was the selection choice. This decision was shown by the race result to be incorrect – and the judicial decision with hindsight was to refrain from selection in such a finely balanced case.

Result: 1st MR. MELLORS (8–11 fav.) 3lth
2nd TILSTON

2083 *NEWCASTLE 21 FEB. 1981 (heavy).*

1.45—BREAM NOVICE HURDLE (Div. I).
£1,000 added (£898·60). 2m. 120 yd. (7)

1	222211	LEADING LADY 14 (C & D D) R Hobson 6-11-13...............................D Shaw (7)	75
2	222433	BIRSBY 70 (D) R McDonald 7-11-8...D Goulding	•78
6	053315	HIS REVERENCE 22 Denys Smith 5-11-7 ....A Stringer (7)	77
7	40-6330	LYNE MILL 66 D Swindlehurst 7-11-3..........................Mr D Swindlehurst (7)	71
8	0	MOLE CATCHER 29 N Crump 6-11-3...C Hawkins	—
13	9	DARTH VADER 15 K Oliver 5-11-2 ....T V O'Connell (4)	—
18		PATH OF PEACE C Thornton 5-11-2...D Atkins	—

Probable S.P.: 6-4 Path of Peace, 5-2 Leading Lady, 5 His Reverence, 6 Birsby, 10 Lyne Mill.

FAVOURITES: 1 2 — — —.

1980: Abandoned – waterlogged course

185

Probables

(1) LEADING LADY – R. Hobson 6.11.13 D. Shaw (7)

    F.   F.   C.   C.

    Prom (14) — C √

    ★★   ★★   D √

               10 lb pen.

(18) PATH OF PEACE – C. Thornton 5.11.2 D. Atkins

Analysis of form revealed only one probable – LEADING LADY. However, further investigation showed hurdle-racing débutant PATH OF PEACE to be a good-class Flat race handicapper whose ability had to be respected.

Applying the formula, LEADING LADY, with a four-star rating but a 10 lb weight penalty, failed to meet the prescribed standard, therefore no selection decision was made as PATH OF PEACE could not be confidently selected without proof of hurdle race form.

Result: 1st PATH OF PEACE (8–11 fav.) 15lth

       2nd LEADING LADY

2088 *NEWCASTLE 21 FEB. 1981 (heavy)*

4.30—BREAM NOVICE HURDLE (Div. II).
£1,000 added (£928). 2m. 120y (13)

601	741613 HIGH HILLS 8 (D2) (B) T Craig 7-11-13	R Lamb	•78
603	94381 FINAL ARGUMENT 11 G Richards 5-11-7	R Barry	60
604	F712 TORREON 22 (D) M H Easterby 5-11-7	Mr T Easterby	71
606	F4P BELLAPORT 14 R Hobson 6-11-3	D Shaw (7)	—
609	009063 HISTORIC HOUSE 11 E Carter 6-11-3	P Charlton	60
611	9U LOCH SPARTAN 14 W A Stephenson 7-11-3	Mr A Fowler (4)	—
613	RENNIS BAR G Fairbairn 9-11-3	C Pimlott	—
615	SILVER WAY P Calver 6-11-3	C Tinkler	—
616	205707 SPANISH HANDFUL 33 R Stubbs 6-11-3	M Maith (7)	63
617	L-00UL0 SUPER HARD 12 W Storey 8-11-3	Miss F Storey (7)	—
620	2 MY UNCLE SAM 12 C Thornton 5-11-2	D Atkins	56
623	O-L RICH DISCOVERY 18 E Heseltine 5-11-2	G W Gray (7)	—
624	RIKKI TIKKI TAVI W A Stephenson 5-11-2	T G Davies (7)	—

Probable S.P.: 5-4 Torreon, 5-2 My Uncle Sam, 9-2 High Hills, 7 Final Argument, 10 Historic House.
FAVOURITES: — — — — — .

Probables

(1) HIGH HILLS – T. Craig 7.11.13 R. Lamb

    F.   F.   C.   C.

    Prom (8) dr D √

    ★★   ★★   10 lb pen.

               BL √

(20) MY UNCLE SAM – C. Thornton 5.11.2 D. Atkins

    F.   F.   C.   C.

    Prom (12) — D √

    ★★   ★★

Analysis revealed two probables – HIGH HILLS and MY UNCLE SAM – of which HIGH HILLS had form that appeared to be improving having performed very respectably in handicap class carrying almost top weight in a £1,727 race. HIGH HILLS, now reverting to novice company, could be considered dropped in class, likely to defy a 10 lb weight penalty. Applying the formula to the probables with considerations, plus the two-race-winning experience of HIGH HILLS against MY UNCLE SAM'S one race, HIGH HILLS was the selection choice.

Result: 1st HIGH HILLS (3–1) 5lth

2103 *NOTTINGHAM 21 FEB. 1981 (good)*

1.30—NOTTINGHAMSHIRE NOVICE 'CHASE.
£6,000 added (£4,487·40). 2m. (7)

1	11L31L	ALICK 35 (D2) M H Easterby 6-11-11	A Brown	●78
3	322114	MILLIONDOLLARMAN 28 (D2) W Jenks 7-11-11	R F Davies	52
4	31L7/4-L	FLYING DIPLOMAT 21 A Smith 10-11-1	K Whyte	—
6	401/2-13	STACCATO 19 (C & D) D Morley 8-11-1	Bob Davies	61
7	0-4L31L	THE ROUE 42 (D) J Webber 6-11-1	Mr P Webber	45
8	L90013	FOOLISH HERO 14 (D) K Bailey 5-10-7	A Webber	60
9	042422	PALACE DAN 10 Γ Rimell 5-10-7	S Morshead	73

Probable S.P.: 6-4 Alick, 3 Staccato, 4 Palace Dan, 7 Foolish Hero, 12 The Roue, 16 Milliondollarman, 20 Flying Diplomat.

FAVOURITES: 0 — — — 2.

1980: Beacon Light, 9-11-11 (A. Turnell), 4-9 fav. R. Turnell. 5 ran.

Probables

(1) ALICK – M. H. Easterby 6.11.11 A. Brown
    F.   F.   C. C.
    Prom (35) — D √
    ★★ — 10 lb pen
(9) PALACE DAN – F. Rimell 5.10.7 S. Morshead
    F.   F.   C. C.
    Prom (10) dr —
    ★★ ★★

Analysis revealed two probables, ALICK and PALACE DAN – ALICK had good earlier season form but had not raced for some weeks and appeared to no longer be quite at peak form. PALACE DAN meanwhile, especially in its races against PRAYUKTA could be seen to be improving and against this opposition appeared to be dropped in class.

Applying the formula, PALACE DAN was the selection choice.

Result: 1st PALACE DAN (2–1 fav.) 2lth

2200 *DONCASTER 2 MARCH 1981 (good to soft)*

4.0—FEVERSHAM NOVICES' 'CHASE.
£1,700 added (£1,492·30). 2m. 150yd. (9)

501	213F52	LITTLE BAY (B) 9 G Richards 6-11-10 .... R Barry	●78
507	644523	ARTIMARVAL 37 (BF) J Blundell 8-11-0.................... A Brown	52
512	30-LF89	COLE PORTER 40 M Banks 6-11-0.................... G McCourt	—
515	IL7/4-L4	FLYING DIPLOMAT 9 A Smith 10-11-0.................... K Whyte	74
516	07206	FRENCH FEEVAGH 51 N Crump 6-11-0.................... P Craggs	—
517	63L7BL	HANDYCUFF 10 A Scott 9-11-0.................... R. Lamb	40
520	FOP-596	MISTER KETCHUP 34 P Calver 6-11-0.................... C. Tinkler	—
521	23363U	PRINCESS TOKEN 23 J Gill 9-11-0.................... Mr H J Gill (4)	62
526	L5	WELTON GAMESUN 10 J Webber 7-11-0.................... A Webber	—

Probable S.P.: 9-4 Little Bay, 4 Flying Diplomat, 8 Princess Token, 10 Artimarval, 12 Handycuff.
FAVOURITES: 0 — 1 — 0.

Probables

(1) LITTLE BAY – G. Richards 6.11.10 R. Barry

    F.   F.   C. C.

    P   (9) dr D √

    ★★★ ★★   10 lb pen.

                BL?

Analysis revealed only one probable, LITTLE BAY, whose credentials were almost of the highest standard. LITTLE BAY had the proven form, was fit, dropped in class, likely to cope with the distance and posing only the question of how the blinkers would affect its jumping and performance.

Applying the formula, LITTLE BAY was the selection choice.

Result: 1st LITTLE BAY (4–5 fav.) 4lth

2288 *MARKET RASEN 7 MARCH 1981 (soft)*

2.30—NEWARK STORAGE JUVENILE HURDLE
(4-Y.-O.). £2,000 added (£1,744). 2m. (5)

2	710321	B AND K EMPEROR 22 (D2) M W Easterby 11-5...................... P Tuck	72
7	76110	OUR BARRA BOY 8 (C & D D) M Ryan 11-5 .... G McCourt	●78
15	040	MI DAD 33 P Brookshaw 10-10.................... A Brown	54
17	0324	ROANDER 59 W Marshall 10-10.................... M Harrington (7))	68
18	P3	WELSH DISPLAY 42 P Brookshaw 10-10 .... M Murphy	74

Probable S.P.: 4-7 Our Barra Boy, 5-2 B and K Emperor, 12 Welsh Display, 15 Roander, 20 Mi Dad.
FAVOURITES: & 1980: No corresponding race.

Probables

(7) OUR BARRA BOY – M. Ryan 11.15 G. McCourt

F.	F.	C.	C.
P	(8)	dr	C √
★★★	★★		D √
			10 lb pen.

Analysis revealed one probable, OUR BARRA BOY, who had credentials of almost the highest standard. Applying the formula, OUR BARRA BOY was the selection choice.

Result: 1st OUR BARRA BOY (ev. fav.) 8lth

2278 *NEWBURY 7 MAR. 1981 (good to soft)*

4.0—SOAPEY SPONGE HUNTER CHASE (Amateur Riders). £1,200 added (£1,082·10). 3m. 2f. 82yd. (9)

602	215UL-P	COOLISHALL 33 B Munro-Wilson 12-12-6 .... B Munro-Wilson (4)	59
603	31-3122	DANCING BRIG 8 (D) T Clay 10-12-6 .... T Clay (7)	77
605	8L1/LP4-	KITE 402 (D) W Jenks 9-12-6 .... T Bowen (7)	—
609	P/151RF-	ROYAL FROLIC 311 (D) F Rimell 12-12-6 .... E Woods	71
611	12U1P/5	FLEXABILITY 8 (C) J Bosley 9-11-10 .... M Bosley (7)	—
612	0/U3U1-3	ROYAL RUSSE 14 G Yardley 8-11-10 .... J Weston (4)	62
613	11F23-0	SUN LION 29 N Henderson 11-11-10 .... C Bealby (7)	•78
616		BONUM OMEN F Walwyn 7-11-5 .... P Webber	—
619		TED'S LAD E Griffith 12-11-5 .... J Griffiths (7)	—

Probable S.P.: 5-4 Dancing Brig, 4 Sun Lion, 11-2 Royal Russe, 7 Royal Frolic, 12 Flexability, , 14 Bonum Omen.

FAVOURITES: 2 2 — 2 1.

1980: Ten Up, 13-11-13 (Capt. J. Hodges), 8-13 fav., T. Forster. 6 ran.

Probables

(3) DANCING BRIG – T. Clay 10.12.6 Mr T. Clay (7)

F.	F.	C.	C.
Prom	(8)	—	D √
★★	★★		8 lb pen.

Analysis revealed one probable, DANCING BRIG, who had excellent recent hunter chase form, running in its fifth race of the hunter chase season while most of its rivals where competing after an absence, some making their seasonal debut.

Applying the formula, DANCING BRIG with 8 lb penalty, yet proven fitness and ability to get the distance of the race was the selection choice.

Result: 1st DANCING BRIG (5–4 fav.) nk

2304 *BANGOR 11 MARCH 1981 (soft)*

3.30—WREXHAM NOV' 'CHASE (5-Y.-O.).
£1,000 (£640). 2m. 160yd. (6)

1	900135	**FOOLISH HERO** 18 K Bailey 11-3	A Webber	75
3	P-00	**KINGS FORT** 90 D McCain 10-10	W Beardwood (7)	—
6	9PL	**RUEBECIA** 32 R Whitaker 10-10	A Bowker	—
7	082323	**SAINT TAFFY (B)** 11 (BF) J Webber 10-10	Mr P Webber	●78
8	PFLO-OF	**SPARTAN CLOWN** 46 D Nicholson 10-10	P Scudamore	—
10	7-L7080	**THE SAMPSON BOYS** 15 R Fisher 10-10	C Brownless	—

Probable S.P.: 7-4 Saint Taffy, 2 Foolish Hero, 8 Spartan Clown, Kings Fort, 10 Ruebecia, 12 The Sampson Boys.

FAVOURITES: — — — — 1.

1980: Limit Up, 10-10 (B. R. Davies), 4-5 fav., D. Morley. 9 ran.

Probables

(1) FOOLISH HERO – K. Bailey 11.3 A. Webber
  F.   F.   C.   C.
  Prom (18) — 7 lb pen.
  ★★   ★

(7) SAINT TAFFY – J. Webber 10.10 Mr P. Webber
  F.   F.   C.   C.
  Prom (11) — G?
  ★★   ★★   BL?

Analysis revealed two probables – FOOLISH HERO and SAINT TAFFY – who on form were evenly matched. FOOLISH HERO having beaten SAINT TAFFY 11th over 2 m (level weights) 31 January. Each horse had raced since this encounter.

Applying the formula, and with due regard to the concession of 7 lb FOOLISH HERO now had to make, SAINT TAFFY was the selection choice.

Result: 1st   SAINT TAFFY (11-10 fav.) 2½lth
       2nd   FOOLISH HERO

2359 *CHELTENHAM 17 MARCH 1981 (heavy)*

3.30—WATERFORD CRYSTAL CHAMPION
HURDLE CHALLENGE TROPHY.
£45,000 added (£32,260·00). 2m. (14)

302	132121	**BADSWORTH BOY** 24 (D7) M Dickinson 6-12-0	T Carmody	67
303	3-D1223	**BIRDS NEST** 22 (C & D C2 D12 BF2) R Turnell 11-12-0	A Turnell	76
304	2-22111	**CELTIC RYDE** 38 (C & D D8) P Cundell 6-12-0	H Davies	74
306	21-1611	**DARING RUN** 31 (D3) T McCreery (Ire) 6-12-0	M T Walsh	72
308	001P31	**GOING STRAIGHT** 10 (D5) J Maxwell (Ire) 6-12-0	J P Byrne	60
309	21-3133	**HEIGHLIN** 19 (C & DD BF2) D Elsworth 5-12-0	S Jobar	76
310	1211d0	**IVAN KING** 10 (D3) J Kiely (Ire) 6-12-0	F Berry	60
311	235	**MARTIE'S ANGER** 19 T Forster 6-12-0	Bob Davies	40
312	140540	**MELADON** 24 (C D5) S Mellor 8-12-0	A Carroll	64

313	46-2412 **MOUNT HARVARD 22 (D3)** N Henderson 5-12-0 .... S Smith-Eccles	58
314	12-3122 **POLLARDSTOWN (B) 31 (C D5)** S Mellor 6-12-0 .... P Blacker	75
315	2113-11 **SEA PIGEON 122 (C & D C D16)** M H Easterby 11-12-0 .... J Francome	●78
316	151-3L6 **SLANEY IDOL 31 (C & D D)** L Browne (Ire) 6-12-0 .... P Scudamore	56
317	F1-24F1 **STARFEN 52 (D4)** M H Easterby 5-12-0 .... Mr T Easterby	63

d—disqualified from 2nd place.

Probable S.P.: 5-2 Sea Pigeon, 4 Heighlin, Celtic Ryde, 6 Daring Run, 12 Pollardstown, Slaney Idol, 16 Birds Nest.

FAVOURITES: 1 0 0 1 3.

1980: Sea Pigeon (USA), 10-12-0 (J. J. O'Neill), 13-2. M. H. Easterby. 9 ran.

Probables

(4) CELTIC RYDE — P. Cundell 6.12.0 H. Davies

F.	F.	C.	C.
Prom	(38)	—	C √
★★	—		D √

(9) HEIGHLIN — D. Elsworth 5.12.0 S. Jobar

F.	F.	C.	C.
Prom	(19)	—	C √
★★	★		D √

(15) SEA PIGEON — M. H. Easterby 11.12.0 J. Francombe

F.	F.	C.	C.
P	(122)	—	C √
★★★	—		D √

A fiercely competitive race such as the Champion Hurdle with 14 runners is not the kind of race recommended for selection. It has been included to demonstrate how the formula may be applied to even the most testing race analysis.

In a race as public as the Champion Hurdle a list of probables must always raise some contention. The race analysed produced form probables — CELTIC RYDE, HEIGHLIN, SEA PIGEON, STARFEN. This could be said to be headed by the reigning champion SEA PIGEON opposed by the contenders for the champion's crown. CELTIC RYDE and HEIGHLIN raced against each other with CELTIC RYDE finishing in front of HEIGHLIN on two occasions, while STARFEN with an impressive victory over BIRDS NEST was obviously improving.

Applying strictly the principles of the formula, no selection could be made with the advent of four probables. In such a quality race fitness of each runner is an almost guaranteed criteria, so in this instance the second principle of the formula is made redundant. Selection, therefore, resolves to form and the only runner to fulfil this standard was the reigning champion SEA PIGEON.

Result: 1st SEA PIGEON (7—4 fav.)
2nd POLLARDSTOWN
3rd DARING RUN
4th STARFEN

2353 *SEDGEFIELD 17 MARCH 1981 (good to soft)*

3.0—SOUTH DURHAM OPEN HUNT PERPETUAL
CHALLENGE CUP HUNTER 'CHASE. (Amateur
Riders). (£445·80) £500 added. 3m. 2f. 160yd. (6)

1	1L8/L7-1	**BRIEF BAY 18** (C) Mrs L Fraser 12-12-8	J Walton	68
2	5/3351-P	**CLONMELLON 43** Mrs E Lees 14-12-8	Miss L King (4)	70
3	125-222	**TILSTON 14** (C2) Mrs P Shields 9-12-8	J Peckitt (7)	●78
6	FU6-P33	**MASTER MARMADUKE (B) 3** (BF) C Bell 8-12-5	R Shields (7)	71
8	OU6/2-33	**DRYBURN 18** W Walton 10-12-0	Mrs A Hamilton (7)	71
10	21P-03F	**PRINCE KEEL 14** J Wade 10-12-0	J Wade (7)	55

Probable S.P.: 2 Tilston, 3 Brief Bay, 5 Clonmellon, Dryburn, 8 Master Marmaduke, 10 Prince Keel.

FAVOURITES: 1 — 0 2 3.

1980: Master Brutus, 8-11-10 (A. Fowler), 5-1, Miss C. Mason. 14 ran.

Probable

(3) TILSTON – Mrs P. Shields 9.12.8 J. Peckitt (7)

F.	F.	C.	C.
Prom	(14)	—	C√
★★	★★		D?
			J?

Analysis revealed one probable, TILSTON. Applying the Formula, TILSTON became the selection choice.

Result: 1st TILSTON (ev. fav.) 7lth

2355 *SEDGEFIELD 17 MARCH 1981 (good to soft)*

4.15—SEAHAM NOVICE 'CHASE.
£800 added (£655). 2m. (11)

1	000PP-P	**ADRO ADYL 26** J Gilbert 7-11-0	S J O'Neill	—
2	4UFULL	**AUTOMATON 18** W A Stephenson 7-11-0	R Lamb	—
3	234125	**BENOWEN 45** (BF) R Fisher 6-11-0	D Goulding	—
5		**EASTER POEM** R Jeffrey 8-11-0	K Whyte	—
6	211F00	**HAPPY WORKER 38** M W Easterby 6-11-0	P Tuck	—
8	PP8566	**IMP (B) 18** R Robinson 6-11-0	C Pimlott	—
9	9236P4	**KING TUD (B) 18** N Chamberlain 7-11-0	C Charlton	●78
10	L-7LOPO	**LINATEA 26** P Curtis 6-11-0	D Wilkinson (4)	—
11	6638P5	**MERRY MISSUS 3** D Moorhead 7-11-0	D McCaskill (4)	—
12	74U2L3	**MYSTIC MATCH 39** J Brockbank 7-11-0	M Barnes	77
13	PU5/U3P	**REFORMINA 10** V Thompson 8-11-0	Mr M Thompson (7)	—

Probable S.P.: 5-2 Benowen, 3 Happy Worker, 5 King Tud, 6 Mystic Match, 8 Automation, 10 Merry Missus, 16 Imp.

FAVOURITES: 0 — 1 1 2.

1980: Gay Invader 6-10-7 (E. Burns), 3-1. W. A. Stephenson 8 ran.

Probable

(3) BENOWEN – R. Fisher 6.11.0 D. Goulding

F.	F.	C.	C.
P	(45)	dr	
★★★	—		

Analysis revealed a field of very poor novice chasers, with the exception of BENOWEN a reasonable handicap hurdler making its début at chasing. BENOWEN had an absence of 45 days from racing which may be interpreted as part preparation for its chasing début. It was considered that BENOWEN only had to jump the course to win.

Applying the formula considering hurdle form as proof of ability and accepting 45 days as preparation rather than denial of fitness, BENOWEN was the selection choice.

Result: 1st BENOWEN (11–10 fav.) 11th

2371 *CHELTENHAM 19 MARCH 1981 (soft)*

3.30—TOTE CHELTENHAM GOLD CUP CHASE.
£60,000 added (£44,258·75). 3m. 2f. (15)

302	4F-4642	APPROACHING 34 (D BF) J Gifford 10-12-0	R Champion	56
304	114370	CHINRULLAH 1 (C) M O'Toole (Ireland) 9-12-0	P Scudamore	68
305	U11345	DIAMOND EDGE 40 (C BF2) F Walwyn 10-12-0	W Smith	73
306	33/4U63	FAIR VIEW 12 (C) G Fairbairn 11-12-0	R Barry	46
307	20B-223	JACK OF TRUMPS 15 E O'Grady (Ireland) 8-12-0	N Madden	72
310	1F-1111	LITTLE OWL 12 (C) M H Easterby 7-12-0	Mr A J Wilson	71
312	35-1P3F	MIDNIGHT COURT 12 (C & D) F Winter 10-12-0	J Francome	64
313	2-1U332	NIGHT NURSE 40 M H Easterby 10-12-0	A Brown	•78
314	111L-3P	RAFFI NELSON 47 (C D) N Henderson 8-12-0	S Smith-Eccles	50
315	1F1114	ROYAL BOND 33 A Moore (Ireland) 8-12-0	T McGivern	60
316	1F1132	ROYAL JUDGEMENT 19 (BF) J Gifford 8-12-0	J Rowe	60
317	111L11	SILVER BUCK 21 M Dickinson 9-12-0	T Carmody	77
318	01002F	SO SO 98 Y Porzier (France) 12-12-0	Mr D Gray	50
319	21-D1F1	SPARTAN MISSILE 5 (C & D, D) M Thorne 9-12-0	Mr J Thorne	50
320	7-035F4	TIED COTTAGE 26 (C) Mrs J Moore (Ireland) 13-12-0	L O'Donnell	65

Probable S.P.: 9-2 Silver Buck, 5 Little Owl, 11-2 Jack of Trumps, 13-2 Tied Cottage, 7 Royal Bond, 10 Night Nurse, Diamond Edge.

FAVOURITES: 0 0 2 1 0

1980: Master Smudge 8-12-0 (R. Hoare), 14-1, A. Barrow. 15 ran.

Probables

(10) LITTLE OWL – M. H. Easterby 7.12.0 Mr A. J. Wilson
F.   F.   C. C.
Prom (12) — C√
★★   ★★   D√

(12) MIDNIGHT COURT – F. Winter 10.12.0 J. Francome
F.   F.   C. C.
?   (12) — C√
★★   D√

(13) NIGHT NURSE – M. H. Easterby 10.12.0 A. Brown
F.   F.   C. C.
Prom (40) — C√
★★   —   D?

(17) SILVER BUCK – M. Dickenson 9.12.0 T. Carmody

F.	F.	C.	C.
P	(21)	—	D?
★★★	★		G?

This race, the highlight of the Cheltenham Festival, is again not a race ideally suited to confident selection prediction.

Analysis revealed four probables – LITTLE OWL, a rising star, NIGHT NURSE, the ex-champion hurdler seeking a unique big race double, MIDNIGHT COURT an ex-Gold Cup winner who since injury had still to recapture past form and SILVER BUCK whose form throughout the season was arguably superior to any other horse, but who was not guaranteed to act on the ground or stay the distance of the race on such ground.

Applying the formula strictly according to the principles there would be no selection with four probables. However, deciding that the recent form of MIDNIGHT COURT did not entitle it to be one of the probables, a selection decision was taken applying it to the other three probables. SILVER BUCK was the choice.

Result: 1st LITTLE OWL (6–1) 1½lth
2nd NIGHT NURSE (6–1)
3rd SILVER BUCK (7 – 2 fav).

2491 *SANDOWN 31 MARCH 1981 (heavy)*

5.10—A NOVICE 'CHASE (Div. II).
£2,000 added (£1,584·20). 2m. 4f. 68yd. (9).

7	144UFL **BUJOJI 57** R Ledger 8-11-5 .... Mrs N Ledger (4)	56
12	621325 **TILTHAMMER MILL 25** F Rimell 7-11-5 .... E Woods	77
18	**CAMEO SHIP** R Blakeney 9-11-0 .... P Leach	—
21	BL25P4 **CREGG 8** Mrs J French 8-11-0 .... Mrs S French	54
23	35751P **GLISSANDO 36** B Wise 8-11-0 .... J Akehurst (7)	61
28	6-5POF6 **PARDON 38 (B)** F Winter 7-11-0 .... J Francome	55
31	546/06-3 **TANTALIZA 199** G Maundrell 6-11-0 .... Mr G Maundrell	51
35	232315 **SAINT TAFFY (B) 12** J Webber 5-10-10 .... Mr P Webber	●78
36	00F76F **COMMANDER CHRISTY 36** H O'Neill 5-10-5 .... G Gracey (4)	—

Probable S.P.: 2 Tilthammer Mill, Saint Taffy, 6 Glissando, 10 Bujoji, Tantaliza, 14 Pardon

FAVOURITES: 2 1 1 1 1.

1980: Royal Judgement, 7-12-1 (R. Rowe), 100-30 jit.-fav. J. Gifford. 17 ran.

Probable

(12) TILTHAMMER MILL – F. Rimell 7.11.5 E. Woods

F.	F.	C.	C.
Prom	(25)	—	D?
★★	★		5 lb pen.

(35) SAINT TAFFY – J. Webber 5.10.10 Mr P. Webber

F.	F.	C.	C.
Prom	(12)	—	D√
★★	★★		5 lb pen.

Analysis revealed two probables – TILTHAMMER MILL and SAINT TAFFY. Both were first season novice chasers. On recent form SAINT TAFFY seemed to be improving, especially after its last race at the Cheltenham Festival.

Applying the formula, SAINT TAFFY was the Selection choice.

Result: 1st SAINT TAFFY (11–4) 3lth

2501 *LIVERPOOL 2 APRIL 1981 (good to soft)*

3.10—SIEMATIC KITCHENS NOVICE 'CHASE.
£6,000 added (£4,900·80). 3m. 1f
(Mildmay Course, Flag Start). (8)

302	21U1F	**BREGAWN** 14 (D2) M Dickinson 7-11-8	R Earnshaw	●78
305	PL/3-221	**THE DRUNKEN DUCK** 20 (D) B Munro-Wilson 8 11 8		
			Mr B Munro-Wilson	58
306	50/4P-48	**CRESTINO** 44 O O'Neil 10-11-5	J Suthern	41
311	2F2P11	**MEADSGROVE** 14 (D) I Usher /-11-5	D Atkins	53
312	L5FP43	**MOONLIGHT EXPRESS** 40 J Gifford 8-11-5	R Champion	53
313	1F161L	**PILOT OFFICER** 15 F Rimell 6-11-5	Mr E Woods	71
315	042	**SPARTAN PRINCE** 40 C Kinane (Ireland) 7-11-5	M J Byrne	46
317	53-P3L4	**THE HEENAN KID** 86 W A Stephenson 8-11-5	P Scudamore	41

Probable S.P.: 11-4 Bregawn, 5 Pilot Officer, 8 Meadsgrove, 10 Spartan Prince, 12 Moonlight Express.
FAVOURITES & 1980: No corresponding race.

Probable

(2) BREGAWN – M. Dickenson 7.11.8 R. Earnshaw

F.	F.	C.	C.
Prom	(14)	dr	D√
★★	★★		3 lb pen.

Analysis originally revealed two probables, but RUNNING WILD was withdrawn leaving only BREGAWN. Back to novice class, BREGAWN appeared to have a comparatively easy task provided it had recovered from the fall in its last race at Cheltenham. Applying the formula, BREGAWN was the selection choice.

Result: 1st BREGAWN (7–4 fav.)

2508 *LIVERPOOL 3 APRIL 1981* (*good to soft*)

3.45 — SEAN GRAHAM HURDLE (4-Y.-O.).
£12,000 added (£11,731·50). 2m. (10)

401	27111	**BARON BLAKENEY** 15 (D3) M Pipe 11-7	P Leach	75
403	12111B	**APPLE WINE** 15 (D) M W Easterby 11-3	P Tuck	57
404	111112	**BROADSWORD** 15 (D6 BF) D Nicholson 11-3	P Scudamore	77
406	11180	**THE VERY THING** 15 (D3) W Treacy (Ire) 11-3	G Newman	68
407	1123	**TIE ANCHOR** 15 (D2) P Prendergast jun (Ire) 11-3	T McGivern	75
411	915020	**HILL'S NORTHERN** 6 (D) R Turnell 11-0	Steve Knight	51
414	115129	**KOLME** 15 (D3) A Geraghty. (Ire) 11-0	F Berry	•78
415	043	**LUTANIST** 30 (BF) P Makin 11-0	J Francome	40
416	135215	**MANSKY** 15 (D2) E O'Grady (Ire) 11-0	T J Ryan	73
419	F31581	**ROYAL CASINO** 35 (D2) I Warde 11-0	S Smith-Eccles	50

Probable S.P.: 6-4 Broadsword, 5 Baron Blakeney, 6 Tie Anchor, 7 Mansky, 8 Kolme, 10 Apple Wine, 14 The Very Thing.

FAVOURITES: 2 2 0 1 2.

1980; (Kennedy Asphalt Hurdle) Starfen 11-0 (J J O'Neill), 3-1. M H Easterby, 20 ran.

Probables

(1) BARON BLAKENEY – M. Pipe 11.7 P. Leach

F.	F.	C.	C.
P	(15)	—	D√
★★★	★		7 lb pen.

(4) BROADSWORD – D. Nicholson 11.3 P. Scudamore

F.	F.	C.	C.
P	(15)	—	D√
★★★	★		4 lb pen.

Analysis produced two probables, BARON BLAKENEY and BROADSWORD, the two resuming rivalry after the Triumph Hurdle in which BARON BLAKENEY won by ¾lth at level weights. With a concession of 3 lb to BROADSWORD it seemed likely form would be reversed.

Applying the formula, BROADSWORD was the selection choice.

Result: 1st BROADSWORD (6–5 fav.) 5lth

FLAT RACE SEASON 1981

51 *DONCASTER 26 MARCH 1981 (soft)*

3.35—DONCASTER MILE
£10,000 added (£7,167), 1m. (str.). (9) STALLS

401	(9)	523856- CRACAVAL 159 B Hills 5-9-4...	S Cauthen
402	(8)	01/114- BONOL 345 (C) M H Easterby 4-8-13	M Birch
403	(1)	0L62L1- BRAUGHING 156 (D) C Brittain 4-8-13..	E Johnson
405	(6)	563830- DAVIDGALAXY AFFAIR 149 F Yardley 4-8-13	Pat Eddery
406	(2)	02L151- JONDALE 139 (C & D D2) W Elsey 4-8-13......................................	E Hide
407	(7)	01/1- JUBILEE LIGHTS 338 (C) R Turnell 4-8-13..	W Carson
409	(3)	33/2376- PENSCYNOR 281 J Bingham 5-8-13..	C Dwyer
410	(4)	135263- SON FILS 222 (C) M Pipe 6-8-13	L Piggot
411	(5)	9879L0- TOPSIN 156 (D) O Jorgensen 6-8-13	J Reid

Probable S.P.: 11-4 Bonol, 100-30 Cracaval, 4 Son Fils, 8 Braughing, 10 Jondale, 12 Jubilee Lights, 14 Penscynor.

FAVOURITES: & 1980: No corresponding race

Probables
(1) CRACAVAL – B. Hills 5.9.4 S. Cauthen (9)

F.	F.	C.	C.
P	(159)	dr	D?
★★★	—	5 lb pen.	
		Draw√	

(2) BONAL – M. H. Easterby 4.8.13 M. Birch (8)

F.	F.	C.	C.
P	(345)	—	C√
★★★	—	D?	

This race in the opening week of the 1981 Flat race season posed the major problem facing all selection decisions in the early part of a season – would form be defeated by fitness'. Analysis produced two probables CRACAVAL and BONAL – CRACAVAL who ran throughout the 1980 Flat season in group races and BONAL winner of the 1980 Northern Free Handicap, but who had been off the racecourse for almost one year. It appeared that CRACAVAL had clearly the better and proven form with doubts only as to his preparation for this race and the suitability of the distance which was shorter than his best.

Applying the formula strictly, neither horse met the minimum required standard in accord with the star rating system for neither horse's fitness could be confirmed. However, considering this factor was equal for each runner in the race (none had raced in the current campaign), a selection decision was made using the other factors. CRACAVAL was the selection choice.

Result: 1st CRACAVAL (3–1) 2lth
       2nd BONOL (4–5 fav.)

294 *EPSOM 21 APRIL 1981 (good)*

3.5—LADBROKE BLUE RIBAND TRIAL STAKES (3-Y.-O).
£16,000 added (£13,180). 1m. 110yd. (6) STALLS

301	(6)	121116-	**ROBELLINO 178** I Balding 9-0 .... J Matthias	77
303	(2)	8137-7	**BLACKFOOT 17** R Sheather 8-9 .... R Cochrane	65
305	(4)	21L-	**CENTURIUS 186** M Stoute 8-9 .... W R Swinburn	•78
306	(1)	L713L6-	**McCARTHY 223** A Bailey 8-9 .... P Eddery	74
308	(5)	13-243	**RASA PENANG 24** R Armstrong 8-9 .... L Piggott	72
309	(3)	0	**DHANTERAS 10** G Lewis 8-6 .... P Waldron	—

Probable S.P.: 5-4 Centurius, 15-8 Robellino, 8 McCarthy, 10 Blackfoot, 12 Rasa Penang, 20 Dhanteras.

FAVOURITES: 0 2 0 1 2 2 0 3.

1980: Last Fandango 8-9 (S. Cauthen), 9-2 B, Hills, 8 ran.

Probables
(1) ROBELLINO – I. Balding 9.0 J. Matthias

    F.   F.   C. C.

    P   (178) — D√

    ★★★   —   5 lb pen.

(5) CENTURIUS – M. Stoute 8.9 W. Swinburn

    F.   F.   C. C.

    Prom (186) — D?

    ★★   —

This race was one of the seasons recognized Classic trials. Analysis revealed two probables – ROBELLINO and CENTURIUS. The fitness of both having to be accepted on trust together with the skilful preparation of their respective trainers.

Applying the principles of the formula, neither horse met the required standard, and as three other runners in the race had already made their début it was considered unwise to make a selection decision using the other factors.

Result: 1st CENTURIUS (11–8)
           2nd ROBELLINO (5–4 fav.)

409 *ASCOT 29 APRIL 1981 (good to soft)*

2.30—SAGARO STAKES
£10,400 added (£7,375). 2m. (5) STALLS

201	(1)	11462-6 **NICHOLAS BILL 18 (C&DD)** H Candy 6-9-5	P Waldron	●78
203	(4)	2743-31 **RUSSIAN GEORGE 11 (D)** G Hunter 5-9-5	P Cook	62
204	(5)	4450-21 **DONEGAL PRINCE (B) 11 (D)** P Kelleway 5-9-0	P Robinson	63
205	(3)	5263-84 **SON FILS 18** M Pipe 6-9-0	G Starkey	71
207	(2)	5294L-0 **KARLINSKY 11** Miss S Morris 4-8-7	S Cauthen	59

Probable S.P.: 4-6 Nicholas Bill, 11-4 Russian George, 8 Sons Fils, Donegal Prince, 33 Karlinsky.

FAVOURITES:1 3 0 0 0 0 2 2.

1980: Pragmatic, 5-9-5 (J. Reid), 9-2, R. Houghton, 5 ran.

Probables

(1) NICHOLAS BILL – H. Candy 6.9.5 P. Waldron

F.	F.	C.	C.
P	(18)	—	C√
★★★	★		D√

(3) RUSSIAN GEORGE – G. Hunter 5.9.5. P. Cook

F.	F.	C.	C.
Prom	(11)	up	D√
★★	★★		

Analysis produced two probables NICHOLAS BILL and RUSSIAN GEORGE – both well suited to the distance of 2m. The race also had the renewed rivalry between SON FILS and NICHOLAS BILL who was now considered likely to reverse the form of their previous meeting (1m 4f John Porter Stakes, Newbury) since he was now racing at his most appropriate distance.

Applying the formula NICHOLAS BILL was the selection choice.

Result: 1st NICHOLAS BILL (ev. fav.) 2½lth

411 *ASCOT 29 APRIL 1981 (good to soft)*

3.40—WHITE ROSE STAKES
(3-Y.-O). £14,000 added (£10,292·80). 1m. 2f.
(9) STALLS

402	(9)	076-1 **MOUHANNED 23** C Brittain 9-4	L Piggott	74
403	(2)	7-12 **RIDGEFIELD 9 (D BF)** G Harwood 9-4	G Starkey	73
405	(3)	52- **BEDFORD 193** I Balding 9-0	J Matthias	75
406	(7)	80-8 **BRIGADIER HAWK 19** C Brittain 9-0	S Cauthen	—
407	(8)	32- **CUT ABOVE 188** W Hern 9-0	W Carson	●78
408	(5)	9 **HARD TO SAY 5** W Hern 9-0	B Rouse	—
410	(4)	09- **SETTIMINO 222** R Houghton 9-0	J Reid	—
411	(1)	**DRAGON STEED** M Jarvis 8-9	B Raymond	—
412	(6)	**JOHN BRUSH** P Walwyn 8-9	J Mercer	—

Probable S.P.: 4-7 Cut Above, 6 Ridgefield, 7 Mouhanned, 8 Settimino, Bedford.

FAVOURITES: 3 1 0 3 0 1 1 0.

1980: Dukedom, 9-0 (L. Piggott), 11-I, I. Balding 11 ran.

Probable

(7) CUT ABOVE – W. Hern 9.0 W. Carson

F.	F.	C.	C.
P	(188)	—	D?
★★★	—		W√

Analysis of the race produced one probable – CUT ABOVE whose 2 y.o form was considerably superior to that of any of his opponents, and likely to be equally better than those with 3 y.o. form. The only doubts posed were in consideration of the distance and current fitness.

Applying the formula strictly, CUT ABOVE failed to reach the minimum standard in respect of the star rating system. However, with due regard to its superior form and W. Hern's record in producing horses fit on their racecourse reappearance, CUT ABOVE was accepted as the selection choice.

Result: 1st CUT ABOVE (10–11 fav.) 3lth

429 NEWMARKET 30 APRIL 1981 (good)

3.5—1,000 GUINEAS STAKES. Group 1. (3-Y.-O. fillies).
£50,000 added (£52,180). 1m. (14) STALLS

301 (5)	AUCTION BRIDGE B Hills 9-0	S Cauthen	—
	b f Auction Ring-Brig O'Doon		
	Emerald green, royal blue sleeves, white cap, green spots		
302 (1)	4- BELLEAIR DREAM 335 F Durr 9-0	Pat Eddery	66
	b f Tower Walk-Dowerless		
	Yellow, green hoop, hooped sleeves, white and green check cap		
303 (13)	421-1 FAIRY FOOTSTEPS 14 (C) H Cecil 9-0	L Piggott	●78
	b f Mill Reef-Glass Slipper Black, scarlet body		
304 (9)	89811-1 GO-LEASING 26 (C) G Harwood 9-0	G Starkey	70
	ch f Star Appeal-Grand Velvet Royal blue and white hoops, red sleeves, orange cap		
305 (10)	314- GRECIAN SEA 242 W Hern 9-0	J Mercer	69
	ch f Homeric -Sea Venture Pale blue, yellow and blue check cap		
306 (3)	421- KITTYHAWK 253 W Hern 9-0	W Carson	73
	b f Bustino-Sky Fever Eton blue, black hooped cap		
307 (8)	672-3 MADAM GAY 7 P Kelleway 9-0	A Murray	69
	b f Star Appeal-Saucy Flirt Yellow, emerald green star, hooped cap		
308 (6)	11111-1 MARWELL 20 (C) M Stoute 9-0	W R Swinburn	77
	b f Habitat-Lady Seymour Yellow, dark blue sleeves, black cap		
309 (2)	4211-2 SHARK SONG 14 (C) J Hindley 9-0	B Taylor	67
	gr f Song-Sylvanecte Leon, dark blue diamond and sleeves		
310 (11)	41424-3 SWEDISH RHAPSODY 16 G P-Gordon 9-0	G Duffield	66
	br f Targowice-Tuola Brown and Yellow check, brown sleeves, quartered cap		
311 (7)	11- TOLMI 278 H Hobbs 9-0	E Hide	77
	b f Great Nephew-Stilvi Black, white spots on body and sleeves		
312 (14)	9112-0 VOCALIST 15 F Durr 9-0	P Robinson	69
	b f Crooner-Rhythm Yellow, white cross-belts, green cap		
313 (12)	12222-2 WELSHWYN 26 C Benstead 9-0	B Rouse	74
	b f Welsh Saint-Takawin Black, white sash, quartered cap		
314 (4)	4534-8 WHAT HEAVEN 15 P Kelleway 9-0	P Young	67
	b f So Blessed-Stolen Love Yellow, emerald green star, hooped cap.		

Probable S.P.: 4-5 Fairy Footsteps, 6 Marwell, Tolmi, 12 Kittyhawk, 20 Go Leasing, 33 Madam Gay, 40 Grecian Sea, 50 Auction Bridge, Shark Song, Welshwyn.

FAVOURITES:0 0 0 1 0 0 1 0.

1980: Quick as Lightning 9-0 (B. Rouse), 12-1, J. Dunlop. 23 ran.

Probables
(3) FAIRY FOOTSTEPS – H. Cecil 9.0 L. Piggott
F.   F.   C. C.
Prom (14) — C√
★★   ★★   D?
(4) GO LEASING – G. Harwood – 9.0 G. Starkey
F.   F.   C. C.
Prom (26) — C√
★★   ★
(11) TOLMI – H. Hobbs 9.0 E. Hide
F.   F.   C. C.
Prom (278) — D?
★★   —

This race, the first Classic of the season, has often produced unexpected winners with fillies who were champions as 2-year-olds failing to maintain that standard as 3 year-olds.

The 1981 1,000 Guineas on analysis appeared to resolve to three probables – FAIRY FOOTSTEPS, GO LEASING and TOLMI. FAIRY FOOTSTEPS who was lightly raced but ever improving as a 2y.o. came out to win her seasonal début as a 3y.o. most impressively with a performance that suggested even greater promise for the future. GO LEASING also improved as a 2y.o. but was raced in a lower class, yet reappeared as a 3y.o. to win comprehensively Salisbury's 1,000 Guineas trial and now could be seen as a strong challenger for the full champion's crown. TOLMI meanwhile, was the hardest probable to assess as she was unbeaten in her two 2y.o. races but yet to make her reappearance as a 3y.o.

Applying the formula, FAIRY FOOTSTEPS was made the selection choice.

Result: 1st FAIRY FOOTSTEPS (6–4 fav.) nk
2nd TOLMI (11–2)
3rd GO LEASING (13–1)

442 *NEWMARKET 2 MAY 1981*

3.0——THE 2,000 GUINEAS STAKES (3-Y.-O., Group (1).
£55,000 added (£64,136). 1m. (19) STALLS

301	(4)	3-IL2 **ACCESSION 7 (D)** M O'Toole (Ireland) 9-0	B Raymond	69
		b c Crowned Prince-Saphire Spray		
		Cerise, white spots, cerise sleeves, cerise cap white spots		
303	(12)	41315-1 **ANOTHER REALM 21 (C)** F Durr 9-0	J Mercer	73
		gr c Realm Tiara III *Purple, pink sleeves, pink and yellow check cap*		
304	(19)	31212-4 **BEL BOLIDE 17** J Tree 9-0	Pat Eddery	74
		ch c Bold Bidder-Lady Graustark *Green, pink sash and cap, white sleeves*		
305	(3)	41141-3 **BELDALE FLUTTER 21 (D BF)** M Jarvis 9-0	Y Saint-Martin	72
		b c Accipiter-Flitter Flutter		
		Yellow, black sleeves, yellow and light blue quartered cap		

306 (9) 113- **CHURCH PARADE (B) 234** W Hern 9-0... **W Carson** 70
b c Queen's Hussar-Christchurch
Purple, gold braid, scarlet sleeves, black velvet cap, gold fringe

307 (6) 11116-1 **COOLINEY PRINCE 14** P Prendergast jun (Ireland) 9-0 .... **G McGrath** 73
gr c Tumble Wind-Aquaria
Maroon, white Cross of Lorraine, maroon cap, white spots

308 (17) 10121-5 **CUT THROAT 21** H Candy 9-0.. **P Waldron** 70
br c Sharpen Up-Zanterdeschia *Orange, black and green striped cap*

309 (14) 1111-33 **DALBY MUSTANG 18** T Dahl (Norway) 9-0 .... **B Taylor** 68
b c Welsh Saint-Princess Tam *Brown, red horseshoe and collar, red cap*

311 (16) L-1 **KIND OF HUSH 18 (C & D)** B Hills 9-0.. **L Piggott** 77
b c Welsh Pageant-Sauceboat *Light green and black stripes, green sleeves*

312 (8) 2321-68 **MATTABOY 6 (C)** R Armstrong 9-0 .... **J Reid** 67
ch c Music Boy-Green Chartreuse *Lemon, dark blue diamond and sleeves*

313 (7) 21214-1 **MOTAVATO 17 (C)** B Hills 9-0.. **S Cauthen** 76
br c Apalachee-Lovelight
Emerald green, royal blue sleeves, while cap, green spots

314 (11) 14124-1 **NOALTO 14 (D)** F Durr 9-0.. **P Robinson** 72
ch c Nonoalio-Lyrical *Pink, lime green sleeves, check cap*

315 (15) 6122-1 **PRINCE ECHO 28** L Browne (Ireland) 9-0 .... **P Cook** 70
ch c Crowned Prince-Dawn Echo *Black, red white and black hooped sleeves*

316 (13) 13-2433 **RASA PENANG 11** R Armstrong 9-0 .... **P Tulk** 66
ch c Gay Fandango-Lancette *Yellow, red cross-belts, quartered cap*

317 (5) 47131-5 **SCINTILLATING AIR 18** B Hobbs 9-0 .... **G Baxter** 69
b c Sparkler-Chantal *Saxe blue, black collar, check cap*

318 (18) 16-2 **SPOLETO 25** F Boutin (Rance) 9-0 .... **P Paquet** 68
b c Nonoalco-Antrona *Chocolate and white hoops, white cap*

319 (10) 5L5-2 **STAR FLEET 14** P Kelleway 9-0 .... **M Miller** 64
ch c Record Token-New Way *Yellow, emeral green star, hooped cap*

320 (2) 11332-2 **THE QUIET BIDDER 17** R Hollinshead 9-0 .... **S Perks** 66
b c Auction Ring-Capule *Royal blue, grey epaulets*

321 (1) 21112-2 **TO-AGORI-MOU 18 (BF)** G Harwood 9-0 .... **G Starkey** •78
br c Tudor Music-Sarah Van Fleet *Yellow, green diamond on body and cap*

Probable S.P.: 7-4 To-Agori-Mou, 5 Motavato, 7 Kind of Hush, 8 Beldale Flutter, 10 Another Realm, 12 Church Parade, 14 Prince Echo, 16 Bel Bolide, 25 Cut Throat, 33 Noalto.

FAVOURITES: 0 3 0 1 0 0 0 0.

1980: Known Fact (U.S.), 9-0 (W. Carson), 14-1. J. Tree. 14 ran.

Probables

(3) ANOTHER REALM – F. Durr 9.0 J. Mercer
F.   F.   C. C.
Prom (21)   — C√
★★   ★   D?

(4) BEL BOLIDE – J. Tree 9.0 P. Eddery
F.   F.   C. C.
Prom (17)   — C√
★★   ★   D√

(11) KIND OF HUSH – B. Hills 9.0 L. Piggott
F.   F.   C. C.
Prom (18)   — C√
★★   ★   D√

(21) TO-AGORI-MOU – G. Harwood 9.0 G. Starkey
F.   F.   C. C.
Prom (18)   — D√
★★   ★

202

The 2,000 Guineas is the first of the 3y.o colts Classics, and as previous recent records display it has not been a race whose result favoured the most fancied horses.

Analysis of the 1981 2,000 Guineas field proved no easy task with some enigmatic lines of form that were difficult to assess, but were resolved to produce four probables – ANOTHER REALM, BEL BOLIDE, KIND OF HUSH and TO-AGORI-MOU.

ANOTHER REALM was the winner of the (Group 3) Greenham stakes at Newbury in April, appearing to have improved on his 2 y.o. form which was consistent but just below that of the very best horses.

BEL BOLIDE, on the same Free Handicap mark as ANOTHER REALM, had run very well in the actual Free Handicap finishing third, beaten just over 1½lth in attempting to give the winner 7 lb.

KIND OF HUSH's form was the most difficult to interpret, having as a maiden at level weights defeated by ¾lth the erstwhile Guineas favourite TO-AGORI-MOU on both horses seasonal reappearance as 3 year-olds. Excuses had been made publicly as to TO-AGORI-MOU's lack of condition on the day, but objectively the result could not be disputed.

Applying the formula strictly in accord with principle, a selection should not be attempted when there are four or more probables. However, because of the public familiarity with the race a selection was made. A further reduction of the initial number of probables was undertaken with elimination of ANOTHER REALM because of the doubts as to whether a horse with its breeding would be able to stay the unrelenting straight mile at Newmarket in such a competitive race. BEL BOLIDE was also eliminated because it seemed unlikely that 3rd place in the Free Handicap even carrying 9 st 7 lb represented form good enough to win a 2,000 Guineas.

The selection decision then resolved to choose between KIND OF HUSH and TO-AGORI-MOU – and as the inexperienced KIND-OF-HUSH had already won a race there was no reason not to expect it to improve even on that form.

KIND-OF-HUSH was the selection choice for the 2,000 Guineas.

Result: 1st TO-AGORI-MOU (5–2 fav.)
2nd MATTABOY (50–1)
3rd BELBOLIDE (14–1)

519 *CHESTER 7 MAY 1981 (good)*

2.45 —ORMONDE STAKES. (Group 3).
£20,000 added (£12,656·00). 1m. 5f. 88yd. (5)

201	(6)	14694-1 PELERIN 26 H Wragg 4-9-4 .... B Taylor	77
202	(3)	1/11114- SEA CHIMES 306 J Dunlop 5-9-4 .... L Piggott	●78
203	(5)	12114-5 SHAFTESBURY 26 M Stoute 5-8-10 .... W R Swinburn	77
204	(1)	40/4457- BILLBROKER 313 R Simpson 5-8-10 .... B Crossley	67
205	(2)	35/411L- NATIONAL IMAGE 194 M Tate 4-8-10 .... W Carson	48

Probable S.P.: 5-4 Pelerin, 2 Sea Chimes, 8 Shaftesbury, 20 Billbroker, National Image.

FAVOURITES: 2 3 2 1 1 1 1 1.

1980: Niniski (USA), 4-9-4 (W. Carson), 4-7 fav. W. Hern. 10 ran.

Probables
(1) PELERIN – H. Wragg 4.9.4 B. Taylor

F.	F.	C.	C.
P	(26)	—	C?
★★★	★		D√
			8 lb pen.

(2) SEA CHIMES – J. Dunlop 5.9.4 L. Piggott

F.	F.	C.	C.
Prom	(36)	Up	C?
★★	—		D√
			8 lb pen.

Analysis reveals two probables PELERIN and SEA CHIMES. Applying the formula PELERIN became the Selection choice.

Result: PELERIN (11–8 fav.) 1½lth

521 *CHESTER 7 MAY 1981 (good)*

3.45 —DEE STAKES.
£14,000 added (£9,441·00). (3-Y.-O. Group 3).
1m. 2f. 85yds. (7) STALLS

402	(3)	211-4 EUCLID 19 (BF) M O'Brien (IRE) 8-12 .... Pat Eddery	77
404	(1)	221-3 JUNTA 19 I Balding 8-12 .... J Matthias	68
405	(7)	13-3 KING'S GENERAL 12 G Harwood 8-12 .... G Starkey	74
406	(5)	2144-3 KIRTLING 12 H Wragg 8-12 .... L Piggott	71
407	(2)	1L-4 NORMAN STYLE 19 J W Watts 8-12 .... E Hide	65
410	(4)	122111- SULA BULA 180 M H Easterby 8-12 .... M Birch	●78
413	(6)	6-4 HERBIE QUAYLE 42 B Hills 8-8 .... S Cauthen	43

Probable S.P.: 3 King's General, 4 Kirtling, Euclid, 8 Sula Bula, 10 Junta, 12 Herbie Quayle, 14 Norman Style.

FAVOURITES: 3 0 0 0 0 3 3 0.

1980: Playboy Jubilee, 8-8 (P. Robinson), 16-1, F. Durr. 9 ran.

Probables

(6) KIRTLING – H. Wragg 8.12 L. Piggott

F.	F.	C.	C.
P	(12)	—	C?
★★★	★★		D✓

(5) KINGS GENERAL – G. Harwood 8.12 G. Starkey

F.	F.	C.	C.
Prom	(12)	—	C?
★★	★★		D✓

Analysis of the prestigious Group 3 race resolved to two probables – KINGS GENERAL and KIRTLING who had beaten KINGS GENERAL by 1½lth when they had both finished second and third behind SHERGAR at Sandown. KIRTLING, having already made a winning season reappearance, had an obvious fitness advantage over KINGS GENERAL on that occasion.

Applying the Formula with the understanding that KINGS GENERAL still had to improve to beat KIRTLING, KIRTLING was accepted as the Selection choice.

Result: KIRTLING (3–1) 6lth

548 *LINGFIELD 8 MAY 1981 (good to soft)*

3.0—JOHNNIE WALKER OAKS TRIAL STAKES.
(Group 3, 3-Y.-O. f). £16,000 added (£13,189).
1m. 4f. (7) STALLS

301	(5)	112- ALLEGRETTA 189 M Stoute 9-0	G Starkey	69
302	(4)	21513-1 CONDESSA 22 (D) J Bolger (Ire) 9-0	D Gillespie	74
303	(1)	21412-5 EXCLUSIVELY RAISED 24 M Stoute 9-0	W R Swinburn	●78
305	(7)	5511-5 LEAP LIVELY 15 I Balding 9-0	J Matthias	77
306	(2)	15117-4 STATS EMMAR 20 H Price 9-0	B Rouse	75
308	(6)	4-7 FRUITION 20 P Kelleway 8-9	P Young	—
309	(3)	0009- XENIA 221 W Wightman 8-9	S Woolley	—

Probable S.P.: 13-8 Leap Lively, 3 Exclusively Raised, 5 Stats Emmar, 6 Allegretta, 12 Condessa, 16 Fruition, 33 Xenia.

FAVOURITES: 2 0 1 3 1 2 2 1.

1980: Gift Wrapped 9-0 (P Robinson), 11-8 fav. F Durr. 7 ran.

Probables

(3) EXCLUSIVELY RAISED – M. Stoute 9.0 W. Swinburn

F.	F.	C.	C.
Prom	(24)	—	D?
★★	★		

(5) LEAP LIVELY – I. Balding 9.0 J. Matthias

F.	F.	C.	C.
Prom	(24)	—	D?
★★	★		

Analysis showed there to be two probables – EXCLUSIVELY RAISED and LEAP LIVELY – rated within 1 lb of each other in the Free Handicap. Each one had one race in the current season, EXCLUSIVELY RAISED finishing 5th beaten approx. 3½lth FAIRY FOOTSTEPS over 7f at Newmarket, while LEAP LIVELY had been beaten 10½lth (approx.) by PETROLEUSE (1m at Epsom).

Applying the formula strictly, neither reached the minimum standard in the star rating system to warrant selection. However, with due regard to the manner in which trainers race their horses and the consideration of breeding to see who would be most suited to the distance of 1½m, LEAP LIVELY was made the selection choice.

Result: 1st LEAP LIVELY (2–1 jt. fav.) 3lth

550 *LINGFIELD 8 MAY 1981 (good to soft)*

4.0—SLEEPING PARTNER MAIDEN STAKES (3.Y.-O.).
£1,500 added (£1,324·80). 7f. (18) STALLS

501	(14)	4430-87	ZACCIO (B) 22 J Bethell 9-4	I Johnson	68
503	(8)	23	CARVED OPAL 28 (BF) B Hills 9-1	S Cauthen	64
504	(16)	937008-	STREGGA 205 M Masson 9-1	Pat Eddery	61
505	(10)		SUZY'S PAL S Mellor 9-1	J Rowe (5)	—
506	(17)	2202-32	MINMAX (B) 6 Pat Mitchell 8-12	W Carson	77
507	(4)	02552-	MRS LEADBETTER 200 G P-Gordon 8-12	D Brockbank (7)	70
509	(5)		ROUGH SKETCH I Balding 8-12	J Matthias	—
510	(6)	L-	SHALL WE TELL 251 D Kent 8-12	B Raymond	—
512	(13)	00557-0	SPANNERLEE (B) 20 G Balding 8-12	R Weaver	69
513	(15)	30-627L	SITEX 14 M Bolton 8-9	W Newnes (3)	64
515	(2)	9	CYPRUS GARDEN 18 D Elsworth 8-6	R Fox	—
516	(9)	20	DUSTY ISLES 17 M McCormack 8-6	W R Swinburn	66
517	(3)	408L0-	FRIENDLY ECHO 211 Mrs C Reavey 8-6	A Clark (5)	61
518	(1)	60200-	GAYTHORN 205 A Davison 8-6	M Saunders (7)	56
519	(18)	L00-	GRYLOS 182 O Jorgenson 8-6	J Reid	—
520	(11)	00-0	MERCIFUL SUN 17 M Haynes 8-6	G Ramshaw	—
521	(7)	353-984	SEA MISS 9 P Kelleway 8-6	P Young	●78
522	(12)		TUDOR IMP P Butler 8-6	W Higgins	— .

Probable S.P.: 5-2 Minmax, 7-2 Sea Miss, 9-2 Rough Sketch, 5 Carved Opal, 8 Mrs Leadbetter, 12 Zaccio, 16 Stregga, Spannerlee.

FAVOURITES: 0 1 3 2 2 0 0.

1980: Protectress, 8-12 (J. Reid), 9-1, G. P-Gordon. 20 ran.

Probables

(6) (17) MINMAX – Pat Mitchell 8.12 W. Carson
F.   F.   C. C.
Prom (6) — D√
★★   ★★★   BL?
Draw√

(21) (7) SEA MISS – P. Kelleway 8.6 P. Young
F.   F.   C. C.
Prom (9) dr D√
★★   ★★

Analysis of a race with above the recommended 12 runners revealed two probables – MINMAX and SEA MISS. MINMAX who had been running consistently in maiden races at Newmarket and Kempton was being fitted with blinkers to see if they could galvanize his performance into a winning one, while SEA MIST was dropped in class after races in a fillies classic trial, and good-class fillies mdn races at Sandown and Ascot.

Applying the formula, with star rating system, MINMAX was the selection choice, but with doubts as to his adaptability to blinkers for the first time on a racecourse.

In practice the author went against the principles laid down and instead made for SEA MIST, the selection choice because the drop in class was considered to represent better form.

Result: 1st MINMAX (7–4 fav.) 4lth

610 *YORK 12 MAY 1981 (good to soft)*

3.0—MUSIDORA STAKES Group 3 (3-Y.-O. f.).
£25,000 added (£24,770). 1m. 2f. 110yds. (5)
STALLS

301	(1)	1513-13	CONDESSA 4 J Bolger (Ire) 9-0	D Gillespie	69
303	(2)	421-11	FAIRY FOOTSTEPS 12 H Cecil 9-0	L Piggott	•78
304	(5)	672-35	MADAM GAY 12 P Kelleway 9-0	G Starkey	75
305	(4)	3	MISS MARKEY 26 B Hills 9-0	S Cauthen	72
307	(3)	190-365	PATCHINIA 8 S Norton 9-0	J Lowe	40

Probable S.P.: 4-5 Fairy Footsteps, 3 Madam Gay, 5 Miss Markey, 8 Condessa, 50 Patchinia.

FAVOURITES:0 1 0 1 3 0 2 3.

1980: Bireme 9-0 (W. Carson) 5-1. W. Hern. 9 ran.

Probables

(3) FAIRY FOOTSTEPS – H. Cecil 9.0 L. Piggott

F.	F.	C.	C.
P	(12)	dr	D?
★★★	★★		G?

(4) MADAM GAY – P. Kelleway 9.0 G. Starkey

F.	F.	C.	C.
Prom	(12)	—	D?
★★	★★		G?

(5) MISS MARKEY – B. Hills 9.0 S. Cauthen

F.	F.	C.	C.
Prom	(26)	Up	D?
★★	★		G?

This example has been included to demonstrate how even the best laid plans can almost inexplicably fail in the ever turbulent world of horse-racing. Analysis of this small field revealed three probables – FAIRY

FOOTSTEPS, MADAM GAY, MISS MARKEY with MISS MARKEY the least probable, FAIRY FOOTSTEPS had already defeated MADAM GAY by approximately 1 length at level weights in the 1,000 Guineas. They were meeting on the same terms over a distance 2f further on going described as good to soft, but which was in fact extremely testing.

Applying the formula, the selection choice would be FAIRY FOOTSTEPS with doubts only to her unproven ability over the extended distance and the going. As a betting proposition FAIRY FOOTSTEPS at 4−9 was considered utterly uneconomic. The result of the race was a shock 16−1 winner CONDESSA who 4 days previously was comprehensively beaten by LEAP LIVELY. FAIRY FOOTSTEPS never raced again and was retired to stud.

Result: 1st CONDESSA (16−1) 41th
2nd MADAM GAY (9−2)
3rd FAIRY FOOTSTEPS (4−9 fav.) 11th

617 *YORK 13 MAY 1981 (good to soft)*

3.0—MECCA-DANTE STAKES GROUP 3 (3-Y.-O.).
£40,000 added (£43,172). 1m. 2f. 110yd. (6) STALLS

301	(5)	1141-30	BELDALE FLUTTER 11 M Jarvis 9-0	Pat Eddery	74
302	(3)	211-1	CENTURIUS 22 M Stoute 9-0	W R Swinburn	75
303	(6)	11111-1	KALAGLOW 27 G Harwood 9-0	G Starkey	77
305	(2)	21116-2	ROBELLINO 22 (BF) I Balding 9-0	J Matthias	●78
306	(1)	7131-56	SCINTILLATING AIR 11 (C) B Hobbs 9-0	G Baxter	67
308	(4)	311-1	SHOTGUN 13 (C) C Thornton 9-0	J Bleasdale	65

Probable S.P.: 11-8 Kalaglow, 7-2 Centurius, 4 Robellino, 8 Beldale Flutter, 10 Shotgun, 12 Scintillating Air.

FAVOURITES: 1 3 2 0 0 0 2 3
1980: Hello Gorgeous 9.0 (J. Mercer) 4-1 H. Cecil 8 ran

Probables

(1) BELDALE FLUTTER − M. Jarvis 9.0 P. Eddery
F.   F.   C. C.
Prom   (11)   — D?
★★   ★★

(3) KALAGLOW − G. Harwood 9.0 G. Starkey
F.   F.   C. C.
Prom   (27)   — D?
★★   ★

(5) ROBELLINO − I. Balding 9.0 J. Matthias
F.   F.   C. C.
Prom   (22)   — D?
★★   ★

The Dante Stakes which serves as a trial for the premier Classic, the Derby, has like a number of Classic trials proven a disappointing race for the most favoured runners. The 1981 Dante with its compactly sized field of six runners, all with exposed public form, provided a good test for selection.

Analysis revealed three probables – BELDALE FLUTTER, KALAGLOW and ROBELLINO. KALAGLOW as the unbeaten highly fancied contender for the Derby, with ROBELLINO having his racing programme similarly focused in that direction.

In the 2y.o. Free Handicap ratings ROBELLINO was 4 lb ahead of BELDALE FLUTTER who was 4 lb ahead of KALAGLOW. So on 2y.o. form there was little to separate these three, while on 3y.o. form they had no factor to make a positive comparison. BELDALE FLUTTER, winner of the prestigious William Hill Futurity 2y.o. was the only horse to have defeated the emerging potential champion horse SHERGAR.

Applying the formula to the three probables, on the star rating system BELDALE FLUTTER was made the selection choice.

Result: 1st BELDALE FLUTTER (11 – 1) $\frac{3}{4}$lth

---

620 *YORK 13 MAY 1982 (good to soft)*

4.30—GLASGOW STAKES (3y.o.)
£4,051 1m 2f 110y (10) STALLS

1	-12 **AMYNDAS 11** B Hobbs 9-3	G Baxter
2	0 11 **BRAVE HUSSAR 9** H. Cecil	L Piggott
3	63-1 **RIGHTS OF MAN 32** G. Pritard-Gordan 9.0	G. Duffield
4	050- **BOTTISHAM 204** W. Wragg 8.10	P. Eddery
5	80-83 **BRIGADIER HAWK 14** C. Brittain 8.10	E. Johnson
7	-4 **DRAGON STEED 14** M. Jarvis 8.10	B. Raymond
8	3- **GHADEER 215** H Thomson Jones 8.10	P. Cook
9	23-3 **HOT FIRE 9** J. Fitzgerald 8.10	M. Birch
12	00- **PETRUS 300** D. Morley 8-10	B. Rouse
15	**BELL RAMMER** B Hills 8-7	S. Cauthen

Probable S.P.: 2-1 Brave Hussar 3-1 Amyndas 4-1 Ghadeer 6-1 Dragon Steed 10-1 Rights of Mars 14-1 Bar.

1980: Pelerin 8.10 (PEddery) 16-1 H. Wragg 8 ran

Probables

(1) AMYNDAS – B. Hobbs 9.3 G. Baxter
F.   F.   C. C.
P   (11)   — D√
★★★   ★★   7 lb pen.

(5) BRIGADIER HAWK – C. Brittain 8.10 E. Johnson
F.   F.   C. C.
Prom   (14)   — D√
★★   ★★

(7) DRAGON STEED – M. Jarvis 8.10 B. Raymond
F.   F.   C. C.
Prom   (14)   — D√
★★   ★★

Analysis revealed three probables with what might be considered as an obvious choice, BRAVE HUSSAR, not included because on a collateral form line through BLARE, AMYNDAS comfortably held BRAVE HUSSAR by a very wide margin. The probables resolved to a choice between AMYNDAS and the pair who had raced against each other BRIGADIER HAWK and DRAGON STEED of whom BRIGADIER HAWK seemed the superior; meanwhile BRIGADIER HAWK had earlier been held comfortably by BRAVE HUSSAR who was considered inferior to AMYNDAS.

Applying the formula there was little to choose on the star rating system between the three probables – AMYNDAS with a five-star rating and a 7 lb penalty acting as a negative aspect became the selection choice.

Result: 1st AMYNDAS (7–2) 8lth
2nd BRIGADIER HAWK (14–1)

728 *GOODWOOD 21 MAY 1981 (heavy)*

4.30—SEABEACH MAIDEN FILLIES STAKES (3Y.O)
£2,918 7f. (9)

1	(6)		ARDMAY H. R. Price 8-11	B. Rouse
2	(5)	099L-7 0	BALAINE (GER) 15 S. Woodman 8-11	J. Blanks
5	(4)	96-3	COPT HALL PRINCESS 15 J. Winter 8-11	S Cauthen
7	(8)	0-00	ELITE PETITE 17 M. Haynes 8-11	M. Hills (5)
11	(10)	0-00	LADY GREENE 19 A. Pitt 8-11	I. Jenkinson
12	(1)	08-0	L'OUVERTURE 30 J. Sutcliffe 8-11	B. Raymond
16	(2)		PEARL OF WISDOM B Swift 8-11	D. McFeeter (7)
17	(7)		QUALITY OF MERCY G. Harwood 8-11	G. Starkey
20	(9)	477-72	SINGWARA 6 G Benstead 8-11	W. Swinburn

Probable S.P.: 2-1 Singwara 9-4 Copt Hall Princess 5 Quality of mercy 12 Ardmay 16-1 Others
1980: (Div 1) Cracking Form 9.0 (PEddery) 6-1 PWalwyn 16 ran
(Div II) Cardinal Flower 9.0 (GDuffield) 9-2 G Pritchard-Gordon 16 ran

Probables
(5) (4) COPT HALL PRINCESS – J. Winter 8.11 S. Cauthen
F.   F.   C.   C.
Prom   (15)   —   D✓
★★   ★   G?
(20) (9) SINGWARA – G. Benstead 8.11 W. R. Swinburn
F.   F.   C.   C.
Prom   (6)   —   D?
★★   ★★★   G?

Analysis of the race resolved to two probables – COPT HALL PRINCESS and SINGWARA. Applying the selection formula, SINGWARA was the selection choice.

Result: 1st SINGWARA (7–4 fav.) sh. hd

730 *GOODWOOD 21 MAY 1981 (heavy)*

3.30—LUPE STAKES (3-Y.-O. fillies).
£8,000 added (£5,631·40). 1m. 4f. (4) STALLS

401	(4)	32134-1 **HUNSTON 15 (D)** B Hobbs 8-11	G Baxter	70
402	(3)	5211-52 **GOLDEN BOWL 15 (BF)** I Balding 8-8	J Matthias	77
403	(1)	4-74 **FRUITION 13** P Kelleway 8-3	W Carson	●78
404	(2)	LL-52 **SUSANNA 33 (BF)** H Wragg 8-3	Pat Eddery	71

Probable S.P.: 4-5 Golden Bowl, 11-4 Fruition, 4 Hunston, 8 Susanna.

FAVOURITES & 1980: No corresponding race.

Probables
(1) (4) HUNSTON – B. Hobbs 8.11 G. Baxter

    F.   F.   C.   C.

    Prom   (15)   — D√

    ★★   ★   G√

                   3 lb pen.

(2) (3) GOLDEN BOWL – I. Balding 8.8 J. Matthias

    F.   F.   C.   C.

    Prom   (15)   — D√

    ★★   ★

Analysis revealed two probables – HUNSTON and GOLDEN BOWL – who met previously a couple of weeks previously with only a head separating them.

Applying the formula strictly neither probable had the minimum star rating system that qualified as a selection choice. However, in a race such as this with only four runners that appeared to be between two horses then it was decided to make a choice between the two. GOLDEN BOWL was the selection choice as she was 7 lb better off for a head defeat.

Result: 1st GOLDEN BOWL (11–10 fav.) 3lth

950 *EPSOM 3 JUNE 1981 (good to soft)*

3.35—THE DERBY, for three-year-old entire colts and fillies only (no fillies run this year). All carry nine stone. One mile and a half. With £100,000 added to stakes. First prize approximately £149,000, which will include a golden trophy worth £3,000. (19) STALLS

301	(15)	1-11 **AL NASR (Fr)** 10 (M Dabaghi) A Fabre (France) 9-0	A Gibert	70
303	(10)	113-0 **CHURCH PARADE** 32 (The Queen) W Hern 9-0	W Carson	68
305	(3)	121-11 **GLINT OF GOLD** 24 (C&D D) (P Mellon) I Balding 9-0	J Matthias	61
306	(12)	16-1262 **GOLDEN BRIGADIER** 18 (W Gredley) C Brittain 9-0	P Bradwell	51
307	(9)	1111-15 **KALAGLOW** 21 (BF) (J Vanner) G Harwood 9-0	G Starkey	76
308	(2)	L-10 **KIND OF HUSH** 32 (A Shead) B Hills 9-0	S Cauthen	67
309	(14)	13-36 **KING'S GENERAL** 27 (BF) (J Bodie) G Harwood 9-0	B Taylor	61
310	(8)	01-64 **KRUG** 25 (V Raibin) M Jarvis 9-0	B Raymond	53

211

311	(18)	031-21	**LYDIAN 44** (Ecurie Aland) Mme C Head (France) 9-9	F Head	68
313	(11)	61L-1	**RIBERETTO 25 (D)** (D McIntyre) R Boss 9-0	Pat Eddery	61
314	(19)	1116-24	**ROBELLINO 21** (Mrs J McDougald) I Balding 9-0	P Cook	72
315	(13)	08-L27	**SASS 25** (M Fine) P Kelleway 9-0	J Reid	53
316	(7)	131-563	**SCINTILLATING AIR 21** (K Dodson) B Hobbs 9-0	G Baxter	62
317	(4)	113-L42	**SHEER GRIT 25** (Capt M Lemos) C Brittain 9-0	J Mercer	66
318	(6)	12-11	**SHERGAR 29 (D)** (H H Aga Khan) M Stoute 9-0	W R Swinburn	•78
319	(5)	311-12	**SHOTGUN 21** (G Reed) C Thornton 9-0	L Piggott	68
320	(17)	64-4D11	**SILVER SEASON 11** (M Hassan) C Brittain 9-0	E Johnson	60
321	(1)	0115-42	**SUNLEY BUILDS 29** (B Sunley & Sons Ltd) G Hunter 9-0	P Waldron	56
322	(16)	0	**WAVERLEY HALL 49** (G Zandona) R Simpson 9-0	B Crossley	—

FAVOURITES: 1 1 2 2 2 2 2 2.

1980: Henbit 9-0 (W Carson) 7-1 W Hern. 24 ran.

BETTING FORECAST

10-11 Shergar	20 Riberetto	66 Krug
	Robellino	Silver Season
6 Shotgun	25 Church Parade	100 Sunley Builds
10 Glint of Gold	Kind of Hush	200 Golden Brigadier
	Lydian	Kings General
12 Kalaglow	Sheer Grit	Sass
14 Al Nasr	50 Scintillating Air	500 Waverley Hall

Probables

(5) (3) GLINT OF GOLD – I. Balding 9.0 J. Matthias

     F.   F.   C. C.

. Prom (24) — D√
  ★★   ★   J?

(13) (11) RIBERETTO – R. Boss 9.0 P. Eddery

     F.   F.   C. C.

  Prom (25) — C√
  ★★   ★   D√
                  G√
                  J√

(18) (6) SHERGAR – M. Stoute 9.0 W. R. Swinburn

     F.   F.   C. C.

  P   (29) — C?
  ★★★   —   D√
                  G√
                  J?

(19) (5) SHOTGUN – C. Thornton 9.0 L. Piggott

     F.   F.   C. C.

  Prom (21) — D?
  ★★   ★   G√
                  J√

The Derby is the most prestigious race in the racing calendar and therefore always fiercely competitive and difficult to win. It is not a race normally recommended as suitable for selection. However, has been included as an example because of public familiarity. The 1981 Derby provided a very fair test of selection skills and on analysis produced four probables – GLINT OF GOLD, RIBERETTO, SHERGAR, SHOTGUN.

GLINT OF GOLD was a course and distance winner, therefore proven to stay the distance and act on the track, his most recent performance had been to win the Italian Derby and was therefore improving and a horse with ability that was not easy to assess positively.

RIBERETTO's only race of the season was to comprehensively win the Lingfield Derby Trial, it was such an improved performance on his 2y.o. form that it posed the question as to how much further improvement was possible. SHERGAR was the form horse of the race, having trounced by wide margins all opposition in two races which in the past have served as notable Derby trials.

SHOTGUN, with the Derby specialist L. Piggott booked as its jockey, was the fourth probable. Having shown marked improvement on its 2y.o. form to win on its seasonal debut at Newmarket SHOTGUN progressed to run a close second in the Dante Stakes which is considered a useful Derby trial.

In a race such as the Derby it is not possible to apply formula in its strictest sense because the element of fitness can usually be reliably guaranteed. The issue therefore resolved to form and the modifying affect the conditions element may have upon it.

Applying the formula without regard to the fitness element, SHERGAR was the obvious selection choice. This view was upheld by the result as the easiest Derby win in living memory was witnessed.

Result: 1st SHERGAR (10–11 fav) 10lth
2nd GLINT OF GOLD (13–1)
3rd SCINTILLATING AIR (50–1)
4th SHOTGUN (7–1)

951 *EPSOM 3 JUNE 1981 (good to soft)*

4.20—WOODCOTE STAKES (2-Y.-O.).
£6,000 added (£4,854). 6f. (10) STALLS

401	(8)	2211 CHRIS'S LAD 18 A Goodwill 9-0	J Mercer	73
402	(6)	221D CRIMSON COURT 28 R Hannon 9-0	L Piggott	•78
405	(10)	118 PRAIRIE DUNES 21 (C) G Hunter 9-0	P Cook	69
406	(5)	461 WINDMILLS 9 C Brittain 9-0	W Carson	71
407	(4)	31410 BROADWAY LODGE 18 C Wildman 8-11	T Rogers	58
408	(9)	303 CASHEL BAY 28 E Beeson 8-9	I Johnson	—
410	(2)	8 KASAROSE 40 H O'Neill 8-9	R Cochrane	—
413	(1)	7 TIDWORTH TATTOO 19 D Elsworth 8-9	R Fox	—
415	(3)	AIRSPIN H Price 8-6	B Rouse	—
416	(7)	ALWAYS ALERT R Simpson 8-3	B Crossley	—

Probable S.P.: 9-4 Crimson Court, 5-2 Chris's Lad, 3 Windmills, 8 Prairie Dunes, 12 Broadway Lodge, 14 Tidworth Tattoo.

FAVOURITES: 2 3 0 1 2 2 1 1.

1980: Redden, 8-9 (J. Lynch), 5-2, fav. B. Swift. 8 ran.

213

Probables

(1) (8) CHRIS'S LAD – A. Goodwill 9.0 J. Mercer

      F.   F.   C. C.

      Prom (18)   — D?

      ★★   ★

(2) (6) CRIMSON COURT – R. Hannon 9.0 L. Piggott

      F.   F.   C. C.

      Prom (28)   — D?

      ★★   ★

This 2y.o. race was programmed at a time in the season when 2y.o. form is just becoming reliably established. It is one of the first 6f races in the calendar, and had entry conditions which gives concessions to mdn horses and horses running for the first time. Analysis revealed two probables, CHRIS'S LAD and CRIMSON COURT.

Applying the selection formula neither probable qualified to the lowest standards required for selection. The correct selection choice in such circumstances is to make no selection choice for the factors presenting themselves are so evenly balanced.

Result: 1st CHRIS'S LAD (5–2) ¾1th

         2nd CRIMSON COURT (2–1 fav.)

965 *EPSOM 5 JUNE 1981 (good)*

4.50—ALBERTA ROSE MAIDEN FILLIES STAKES (3-Y.-O.).
£3,000 added (£2,586·60). 1m. 110 yd. (12) STALLS

602 (11)	6	GOLDYKE 51 L Cumani 8-11	R Guest	—
604 (2)	7	HAUGHTY MANNER 55 H Candy 8-11	P Waldron	—
605 (7)	800-	LA BORIE 304 P Mitchell 8-11	R Fox	—
606 (4)	0-007	LADY GREENE 15 A Pitt 8-11	I Jenkinson	—
608 (5)		NEEDS SUPPORTING B Hills 8-11	S Cauthen	—
609 (3)	4-75	OCH AYE 25 J Bethell 8-11	I Johnson	—
610 (8)	8-22	ROUND DANCE 14 J Winter 8-11	W Carson	77
611 (1)	3-98452	SEA MISS 8 P Kelleway 8-11	L Piggott	●78
612 (6)	2	SHADEMAH 21 M Stoute 8-11	W R Swinburn	76
613 (9)	6240-78	SISTER KITTY 32 R J Williams 8-11	J Mercer	—
614 (12)	L	SPEED THE PLOUGH 37 P Makin 8-11	G Baxter	—
615 (10)	0	TORY JAYNE 30 M Haynes 8-11	J Matthias	—

Probable S.P.: 13-8 Shademah, 5 Sea Miss, 6 Goldyke, 7 Round Dance, 10 Och Aye, 12 Needs Supporting

FAVOURITES: — — — — — — 2.

1980: Orange Leaf, 8-11 (S. Cauthen), 15-8, B. Hills, 11 ran.

Probables

(10) (8) ROUND DANCE – J. Winter 8.11 W. Carson

F.	F.	C.	C.
Prom	(14)	—	C?
★★	★★		D√

(11) (1) SEA MISS – P. Kelleway 8.11 G. Starkey (subst.)

F.	F.	C.	C.
Prom	(8)	—	C√
★★	★★		D√

(12) (6) SHADEMAH – M. Stoute 8.11 W. R. Swinburn

F.	F.	C.	C.
Prom	(21)	—	D?
★★	★		G?

Analysis revealed three probables – ROUND DANCE, SEA MISS, SHADEMAH. There was no collateral form line between these three probables and so it was not possible to state positively that one horse's form was superior to the others. As with inexperienced mdn horses it is judicial to consider the most recent form of the utmost importance.

Applying the formula, SHADEMAH was eliminated and the issue resolved between ROUND DANCE and SEA MISS with equal star rating. SEA MISS was made the Selection choice as her most recent form was considered to be improving and the balancing factors such as course and distance seemed to favour her.

Result: 1st SEA MISS (13–2) ¾lth

1178 *ROYAL ASCOT 16 JUNE 1981 (firm)*

2.30—QUEEN ANNE STAKES (Gp 3).
£18,000 (£12,909·60) 1m. (10) STALLS

101	(8)	160-111 **BELMONT BAY 31 (C D4)** H Cecil 4-9-11	L Piggott	77
102	(6)	1907-31 **CURRENT CHARGE 24** C Grassick (Ireland) 4-9-8	G McGrath	50
103	(3)	1123L-1 **LAST FANDANGO 10** M V O'Brien (Ireland) 4-9-8	Pat Eddery	74
104	(10)	126L-3L **PLAYBOY JUBILEE 31** F Durr 4-9-8	G Starkey	60
105	(1)	3-12531 **SAHER 13 (D4)** R Sheather 5-9-8	R Cochrane	75
106	(9)	21/14-13 **DALSAAN 31** M Stoute 4-9-5	W R Swinburn	•78
108	(7)	12/351-2 **MORAYSHIRE 62 (D2)** B Hobbs 4-9-5	G Baxter	74
109	(2)	653*-5 **SLENDERHAGEN 10 (D2)** M Stoute 5-9-5	Wally Swinburn	—
110	(4)	222-341 **BUFFAVENTO 17 (D)** G P-Gordon 3-8-5	G Duffield	61
111	(5)	2-32111 **MINMAX (B) 10** P Mitchell 3-8-5	W Carson	54

* Winner of 8 races in Germany.

Probable S.P.: 2 Belmont Bay, 3 Last Fandango, 4 Dalsaan, 8 Morayshire, 12 Saher, Current Charge, 16 Buffavento.

FAVOURITES: 2 0 1 0 1 0 3 0.

1980: Blue Refrain, 4-9-8 (B. Rouse), 8-1, C. Benstead. 11 ran.

Probables

(1) (8) BELMONT BAY – H. Cecil 4.9.11 L. Piggott
      F.   F.   C. C.
      P   (31)   — C√
      ★★★   —   D√
                    6 lb pen.

(3) (3) LAST FANDANGO – M. O'Brien 4.9.8 P. Eddery
      F.   F.   C. C.
      Prom (10) — D?
      ★★   ★★   3 lb pen.

(6) (9) DALSAAN – M. Stoute 4.9.5 W. Swinburn
      F.   F.   C. C.
      Prom (31) — D?
      ★★   —

The Royal Ascot 4-day meeting in June is one of the highlights of the racing season where top-class horses compete over varying distances in fiercely fought races. Usually they are not races to recommend for the purposes of selection/betting because of their fiercely competitive nature.

The Queen Anne Stakes which opened the meeting was a typical example of the type of race encountered. Analysis revealed three probables – BELMONT BAY, LAST FANDANGO, DALSAAN – with balancing factors such as distance and weight giving each horse almost an even chance.

BELMONT BAY was the proven form choice, but had not raced for some time and was burdened with 9 st 11 lb. LAST FANDANGO had promising form but was not proven over the stamina-sapping straight mile as Ascot. DALSAAN beaten hd, 2lth by BELMONT BAY at Newbury was now 6 lb better off at the weights, but equally was not guaranteed to get the distance of the race at Ascot.

Applying the formula strictly, LAST FANDANGO was the selection choice.

Result: 1st BELMONT BAY (4–1) hd
         2nd LAST FANDANGO (5–2 fav.)

216

1180 *ROYAL ASCOT 16 JUNE 1981 (firm)*

3.45—ST. JAMES'S PALACE STAKES (3-Y.-O.).
£30,000 added (£26,196·00). 1m. (8) STALLS

301	(3)	1315-15 **ANOTHER REALM** 45 F Durr 9-0 .... J Reid	65
302	(9)	212-435 **BEL BOLIDE** 31 J Tree 9-0 .... W Carson	72
304	(4)	15-46 **GREAT SUBSTENCE** 30 (D) M Saliba (France) 9-0 .... A Gibert	66
305	(2)	211-31 **KINGS LAKE** 31 (D) M O'Brien (Ireland) 9-0 .... Pat Eddery	77
308	(6)	22-103D **PRINCE ECHO** 15 L Browne (Ireland) 9-0 .... A Murray	74
309	(5)	116-240 **ROBELLINO** 13 (C&D) I Balding 9-0 .... J Matthias	71
310	(1)	113-012 **SHASAVAAN** 13 (C D BF) M Stoute 9-0 .... W R Swinburn	69
311	(7)	112-212 **TO-AGORI-MOU** 31 (D BF) G Harwood 9-0 .... G Starkey	•78

Probable S.P. 6-4 Kings Lake, To-Agori-Mou, 12 Prince Echo, 14 Another Realm, Bel Bolide, 20 Robellino.

FAVOURITES: 2 2 1 0 0 2 2 3.

1980: Posse, 9-0 (P. Eddery), 11-2. J. Dunlop, 8 ran.

Probables

(5) (2) KINGS LAKE – M. O'Brien 9.0 P. Eddery

    F.   F.   C.   C.

    Prom   (31)   —   C?

    ★★   —   D√

(11) (7) TO-AGORI-MOU – G. Harwood 9.0 G. Starkey

    F.   F.   C.   C.

    Prom   (31)   —   C?

    ★★   —   D√

Analysis of this famous Group 2 race resolved simply to two probables, KINGS LAKE and TO-AGORI-MOU who resumed rivalry after their controversial encounter in the Irish 2,000 guineas in which KINGS LAKE won the race by a neck only to lose the race on an objection yet later to be reinstated as the winner after a further legal enquiry. Applying the formula could reveal nothing not already known and would therefore not produce a clear decision. It demonstrated how racing knowledge and insight can be the vital factor in arriving at a selection decision.

The author, disregarding the principles of selection which were to not attempt selection in such a finely balanced situation, made TO-AGORI-MOU the selection choice, because it was considered the race this time with a stiff uphill finish would be run better to suit it.

Result: 1st TO-AGORI-MOU (2–1) nk

          2nd KINGS LAKE (6–4fav.)

(The result capably demonstrated the wisdom of the formula in refraining from selection.)

1232 *ASCOT 20 JUNE 1981 (firm)*

2.30—FENWOLF STAKES (2-Y.-O)
£5,000 added (£4,097). 6f. (9) STALLS

201 (4)	411	**NORWICK 8 (D2)** G Harwood 9-3 .... G Starkey	•78
202 (5)	421	**SWANSEA BAY 21** M Kauntze (Ireland) 9-3 .... M J Kinane	70
203 (1)	14L714	**WINDY LAD 21** S Matthews 9-3 .... S Salmon	71
204 (8)	0	**BRIGHT WIRE 15** A Jarvis 8-11.. W Carson	—
205 (9)	2	**CAUSE FOR APPLAUSE 19** G Huffer 8-11........................... L Piggott	66
206 (2)	6	**READING (B) 49** J Tree 8-11... Pat Eddery	68
209 (7)		**FAVOLOSO** R Boss 8-6... —	—
210 (6)		**HAZIM** Thomson Jones 8-6... P Cook	—
215 (3)		**SIGN DANCER** G Hunter 8-6.. B Raymond	—

Probable S.P.: 100-30 Cause For Applause, 7-2 Swansea Bay, 4 Norwick, 5 Hazim, 8 Reading, 10 Sign Dancer, 16 Bright Wire.

FAVOURITES: 0 1 2 3 3 3 1 2

1980: Pellegrini (USA), 8-11 (L. Piggott), 9-4. H. R. Price. 7 ran.

Probables
(1) (4) NORWICK — G. Harwood 9.3 G. Starkey
  F.F.C.C. C.
  Prom (8) — D√ D√
  ★★ ★★ 6 lb pen. 6 lb pen.

N.B. Newcomers
(10) (6) HAZIM — H. Thomson Jones 8.6 P. Cook
(15) (3) SIGN DANCER — G. Hunter 8.6 B. Raymond

Form analysis revealed one probable — NORWICK — with two previously unraced 2-year-olds whose breeding and trainers record could be the only indication of how they may perform in their racecourse début.

Applying the formula, NORWICK was made the selection choice.

Result: 1st NORWICK (7–2) 11th

1234 *ASCOT 20 JUNE 1981 (firm)*

3.35—CHURCHILL STAKES (3.-Y.-O.)
£5,000 added (£4,164). 1m. 4f. (3) STALLS

402 (2)	13-L426	**SHEER GRIT 17** C Brittain 8-13 .... L Piggott	•78
408 (3)	791361	**REGAL STEEL 9** R Hollinshead 8-9................................... S Perks	64
409 (1)	11-5336	**SIX MILE BOTTOM 27** H Wragg 8-9................................. Pat Eddery	75

Probable S.P.: 4-9 Sheer Grit, 7-2 Six Mile Bottom, 6 Regal Steel.

FAVOURITES: 1 1 1 3 1 1 3 1.

1980: Fingals Cave, 8-9 (W. Carson) 15-8 fav. J. Dunlop. 7 ran.

Probables
(2) SHEER GRIT — C. Britton 8.13 L. Piggott
  F. F. C. C.
  Prom (17) dr D√
  ★★ ★★ 4 lb pen.

218

(9) SIX MILE BOTTOM – H. Wragg 8.9 P. Eddery

F.	F.	C.	C.
P	(27)	dr	D√
★★★	★		

Analysis of this three-horse race revealed two probables. A collateral form line through SHERGAR (a most reliable example) with the adjustment in weight gave SIX MILE BOTTOM the beating of SHEER GRIT on form. Applying the selection formula, SIX MILE BOTTOM was the selection choice.

This was a good example of making use of top-class form strictly factually.

Result: 1st SIX MILE BOTTOM (5–2) ¾th comfortably
2nd SHEER GRIT (4–6 fav.)

1540 *NEWMARKET 7 JULY 1981 (good)*

3.35—PRINCESS OF WALES STAKES (Group 2)
£20,966 1m 4F (8) STALLS

1	1321 72 **LIGHT CAVALRY 18** H. Cecil 4-9-9	L. Piggott
3	1111-54 **CASTLE KEEP 18** J. Dunlop 4-8-11	E. Hide
4	1136-52 **ROYAL FOUNTAIN 49** P. Walwyn 4-8-11	J. Mercer
5	263-842 **SON FILS 69** M. Pipe 6-8-11	S. Cauthen
6	004153- **WORLD LEADER (FR)** L. Cumani 4-8-11	R. Guest
8	21L-1Ld **CENTURIUS 19** M. Stoute 3-8-2	W. Swinburn
11	31-5633 **SCINTILLATING AIR 34** B. Hobbs 3-7-13	G. Baxter
12	**CAPSTAN 73** W. Hern 3-7 11	W. Carson

Probable S.P.: 2-1 Light Cavalry 4-1 Castle Keep, Scintilating Air 6-1 Royal
Fountain 12 Bar
1980: Nicholas Blu 5-9.2 P. Waldron 12-1 H. Candy 9 ran

Probables

(1) (2) LIGHT CAVALRY – H. Cecil 4.9.9. L. Piggott

F.	F.	C.	C.
P	(18)	—	D√
★★★	★		G√
			J√
			12 lb pen.

(11) (1) SCINTILLATING AIR – B. Hobbs 3.7.11 G. Baxter

F.	F.	C.	C.
Prom	(34)	—	C√
★★	—		D?
			W√
			G?

Analysis revealed two probables – LIGHT CAVALRY and SCINTILLATING AIR. This race provided the meeting and comparison of two generations of Classic horses, LIGHT CAVALRY the winner of the 1980 St Leger and SCINTILLATING AIR who was third in the 1981 Derby. On last seasons form LIGHT CAVALRY seemed superior and appeared to be returning to that peak on the evidence of his most recent race performance at Royal Ascot.

SCINTILLATING AIR was obviously improving, especially on the evidence of his performance in the Derby and so in receiving 12 lb more that weight for age was a strong contender.

Applying the formula, LIGHT CAVALRY was the selection choice, but with the negative factor of 12 lb weight concession likely to be an extremely important balancing factor. The author, with due regard to this element, at his peril ignored the principal of the star rating system of the formula and made SCINTILLATING AIR with the weight allowance his selection choice.

Result: 1st LIGHT CAVALRY (11–4) nk

1573 *AYR 10 JULY 1981 (good to firm)*

4.45—DUNOON MAIDEN STAKES (3 y.o.)
£909 1m 2f (9) STALLS

2	4-80 DARK PROPOSAL (U.S.A) (B) 13 B. Hanbury 9-0	P. Young
3	0-00922 DUSTY PATH 7 W. Bentley 9-0	O. Gray
4	007641 GRANPARK 21 J. Wilson 9-0	Richard Hutchinson
6	5670-45 POINT NORTH 48 W. H. Willims 9.0	K. Darley
7	454-234 ROMOS 13 H. Rohan 9.0	C. Dwyer
9	-000L VOORTREKKER 1 J. Leigh 9.0	J. Mercer
10	-8 YANKEE DOODLE DANDY 8 C. Thornton 9-0	S. Webster
13	-536 JILL BUCK (B) 18 M. Stoute 8-11	R. Cochrane
18	0 RHEEDIA (FR) 18 J. W. Watts 8-11	E. Hide

Probable S.P.: 2-1 Romoss 7-2 Rheedia 4-1 Jill Buck 6-1 Dusty Path 10-1 Bar

1980: Nawaf 9-0 (A. Kimberley) 2-1F M. Stoute 11 ran

Probable

(7) (5) ROMOSS – P. Rohan 9.0 C. Dwyer
　F.　　F.　　C. C.
　Prom　(13)　— D√
　★★　　★★

Analysis revealed one probable, ROMOSS – applying the formula ROMOSS was the selection choice.

Result: 1st ROMOSS (5–4 fav.) 8lth

1574 *AYR 11 JULY 1981 (good)*

1.45—ROMAN WARRIOR SHIELD (2y.o.)
£1903 7f (14) STALLS

1	(4)	66896	**ALLAN WELLS** T. Craig 9-0		S. Webster
2	(5)	232	**BELDALE BID** M. Jarvis 9-0		P. Eddery
3	(9)	25877	**BOY SANDFORS** C. Bell 9-0		T. Tues
6	(13)	5	**ISOM DAN** B. Hills 9-0		E. Hide
10	(14)	87	**PENSEUR (FR)** B. Hanbury 9-0		P. Young
11	(8)	05	**PERPLEX (B)** Denys M. Smith 9-0		P. Kellher
12	(6)	09L	**RHY-YAN-TUDOR** T. Fairhurst 9-0		M. Beecroft (7)
13	(7)		**RUFFORD LINE** R. Hobson 9-0		J. Higgins
15	(1)		**TOP MATCH** C. Bell 9-0		Richard Hutchinson
18	(10)	008L	**COLUMBOOLA** T. Craig 8-11		B. Graham (7)
19	(3)	0	**DIJLA** H. Thomson Jones 8-11		R. Hills (5)
23	(11)	854	**LINPAC BELLE** W. Elsey 8-11		J. Mercer
24	(12)	353	**LUXURY** E. Carr 8-11		L. Charnock
25	(2)	80	**MISS GALLANT** T. Barnes 8-11		N. Connorton (3)

SP. Forecast 5.4 Beldale Bin 4-1 Isom Dart 6-1 Dijla, Luxury 10- Limpac Belle 15 Ban.

1980: Sausolito 9-0 (M. Birch) Evens F M. H. Easterby 8 ran

Probables
(2) (5) BELDALE BID – M. Jarvis 9.0 P. Eddery

F.   F.   C.   C.

Prom   (7)   —   D✓

★★   ★★★   G✓

Analysis of a race with the above recommended number of runners, revealed one probable, BELDALE BID.

Applying the formula, BELDALE BID was the selection choice.

Result: 1st   BELDALE BID (10–11 fav.) hd

1794 *FOLKESTONE 21 JULY 1981 (firm)*

4.15—HAM STREET MAIDEN STAKES (3-Y.-O.).
£800 (£552). 1m. 4f. (8) STALLS

4	(3)	00	**MARCOM BOY** 15 P Mitchell 9-0		B Jago	—
5	(6)	70500	**RARE SCOTCH (B)** 18 N Vigors 9-0		R Curant	62
7	(4)	80-0634	**THAUMATURGE (B)** 12 R Smyth 9-0		Pat Eddery	58
9	(5)	L-25	**ALL SUMMER** 20 (BF) M Jarvis 8-11		B Raymond	60
11	(8)	07	**BUSTELLA** 15 J Dunlop 8-11		B Rouse	—
13	(7)	083-070	**JET ROMANCE** 20 F Durr 8-11		P Robinson	●78
14	(2)	02-722	**ON HER OWN** 12 G Harwood 8-11		G Starkey	76
15	(1)	70-0694	**SUBRIQUETTE** 25 R Smyly 8-11		P Waldron	77

Probable S.P.: 5-4 On Her Own, 4 All Summer, 9-2 Bustella, 15-2 Thaumaturge, 10 Jet Romance.

FAVOURITES: — 2 1 1 2 1 3 1.

1980: Welsh Display 9-0 (P. Eddery), 10-11 fav. P. Walwyn, 18 ran.

Probables

9 (5) ALL SUMMER – M. Jarvis 8.11 B. Raymond

F.	F.	C.	C.
Prom	(20)	—	D√
★★	★		G√

14 (2) ON HER OWN – G. Harwood 8.11 G. Starkey

F.	F.	C.	C.
Prom	(12)	—	D√
★★	★★		G√

15 (1) SUBRIQUETTE – R. Smyly 8.11 P. Waldron

F.	F.	C.	C.
Imp	(25)	—	D√
★	★		

Analysis revealed three probables – ALL SUMMER, ON HER OWN, SUBRI-QUETTE. Applying the Formula, ON HER OWN was the selection choice.

Result: 1st   ON HER OWN (4–5 fav.) ½lth

1868 *ASCOT 25 JULY 1981 (good to firm)*

2.0—REGENT DIAMOND STAKES (Ladies Race).
£3,000 added (£2,805). 1m. (16) STALLS

103	(15)	13-23L2	CRACKING FORM 7 (C&DDBF) P Walwyn 4-10-3	Franca Vitadini	*78
105	(1)	808380-	CHRYSIPPOS 273 J Priday 4-10-0	Sally Maloney (3)	76
106	(7)	0L0-906	DRED SCOTT (B) 14 Mrs A Finch 9-10-0	Margaret Fraser-Stuart (3)	—
107	(12)	7070-L0	HOME WIN (B) 24 M James 7-10-0	Lynn Wallace (3)	—
108	(2)	74-0514	IRISH EMPEROR 52 R Sheather 4-10-0	Elin Guest	71
110	(2)	590-085	MARKIE 7 (D) R Peacock 5-10-0	Carmen Peacock (3)	51
111	(16)	341-380	RED SEED 38 P Haslam 7-10-0	Sue Vergette	70
112	(8)	125237	TOWN SKY (B) 24 J S Norton 5-10-0	Sandy Brook (3)	62
113	(6)	8	ENSIGNS KIT 14 M James 6-9-11	Sharron James (3)	—
115	(5)	20326	DUSTY ISLES 42 M McCormack 3-9-3	Celia Radband (3)	48
116	(9)	9510L1	ILLINI 8 (D2) B Hanbury 3-9-3	Moira Hanburry (3)	63
117	(14)	2-5535	MADISON STYLE 11 (BF) R Houghton 3-9-3	Gale Johnson Houghton	66
119	(3)	6-22111	RAMANNOLIE 21 (D3) H Thomson Jones 3-9-3	Elain Mellor	68
120	(13)	L-34124	SHARP STAR 25 (D) G Blum 3-9-3	Jane Barlow (3)	50
122	(10)	1-93069	SWINGING RHYTHM 21 L Holt 3-9-3	Ann Holt	70
123	(11)	0-70	FLYING SISTER 64 G Fletcher 3-9-0	Jenny Brown (3)	—

Probable S.P.: 7-4 Cracking Form, 7-2 Ramannolie, 5 Irish Emperor, 7 Red Seed, 8 Madison Style, 12 Swinging Rhythm.

FAVOURITES: 0 3 1 2 2 1 0 1.

1980: Cracking Form (F. Vittadini), 6-5 fav., P. Walwyn, 17 ran.

Probables

(3) (15) CRACKING FORM – P. Walwyn 4.10.3 Franca Vittadini

F.	F.	C.	C.
Prom	(7)	—	C√
★★	★★★		D√
			J√
			3 lb pen.

222

(11) (16) RED SEED – P. Haslam 7.10.0 Sue Vergette
   F.   F.   C. C.
   Prom (38)   — D√
   ★★   —

(19) (3) RAMANNOLIE – H. Thomson Jones 3.9.3 Elaine Mellor
   F.   F.   C. C.
   Prom (21)   — D√
   ★★   ★   J√

Analysis of this prestigious ladies' race resolved to three probables –
CRACKING FORM, RED SEED, RAMANNOLIE. CRACKING FORM was the winner
of the corresponding race in 1980 and was ridden then as now by the
experienced Franca Vittadini. Applying the formula, CRACKING FORM
was the clear selection choice.

Result: 1st CRACKING FORM (15–8 fav.) 1½lth

1870 *ASCOT 25 JULY 1981 (good to firm)*

3.20—KING GEORGE VI AND QUEEN ELIZABETH DIAMOND STAKES (Group 1, Entire Colts & Fillies). £143,000 added (£119,206). 1m. 4f. (7) STALLS

301	(3)	6-12344 **CRACAVAL 21 (D)** B Hills 5-9-7	S Cauthen	56
		ch h Mount Hagen-Priddy Main *(Brown and green stripes, brown sleeves and cap)*		
302	(5)	2231L-3 **FINGAL'S CAVE 21 (C & D2)** J Dunlop 4-9-7	Pat Eddery	57
		b c Ragstone-Blue Echoes *(White, Robertson tartan sash and cap)*		
303	(4)	321-721 **LIGHT CAVALRY 18 (C & D D2)** H Cecil 4-9-7	L Piggott	68
		b c Brigadier Gerard-Glass Slipper *(Black, scarlet cap)*		
304	(1)	122-111 **MASTER WILLIE 21 (D2)** H Candy 4-9-7	P Waldron	65
		ch c High Line-Fair Winter *(Cherry, black sash, primrose and white quartered cap)*		
305	(7)	694-111 **PELERIN 36 (C & D D)** H Wragg 4-9-7	B Taylor	71
		b or br c Sir Gaylord-Padrona *(Black and white halved, sleeves reversed, red cap)*		
307	(6)	12-1111 **SHERGAR 28 (D3)** M Stoute 3-8-8	W R Swinburn	•78
		b c Great Nephew-Sharmeen *(Green, red epaulets)*		
308	(2)	352214 **MADAM GAY 21** P Kelleway 3-8-5	G Starkey	61
		b f Star Appeal-Saucy Flirt *(Yellow, emerald green star, hooped cap)*		

Probable S.P.: 4-11 Shergar, 7 Master Willie, 8 Pelerin, 10 Light Cavalry, 25 Fingal's Cave, 33 Madam Gay. 66 Cracaval.

FAVOURITES: 3 1 1 2 1 0 1 2

1980: Ela-Mana-Mou, 4-9-7 (W. Carson). 11-4. W. Hern. 10 ran.

Probables

4 (1) MASTER WILLIE – H. Candy 4.9.7. P. Waldron
   F.   F.   C. C.
   Prom (21)   — D√
   ★★   ★

7 (6) SHERGAR – M. Stoute 3.8.8. W. Swinburn
   F.   F.   C. C.
   Prom (28)   — D√
   ★★   ★

Analysis revealed two probables MASTER WILLIE representing the 1980 Classic generation and SHERGAR the current Classic generation.

MASTER WILLIE unbeaten in three races in 1981 and the winner of the Eclipse in his previous race seemed to provide a searching test for the obvious selection choice SHERGAR, who was heralded the horse of the century after his two facile Derby successes.

A race of this magnitude seldom accurately conforms to the designs of any formula – fitness is likely to be guaranteed, the issue resolves as always to the assessment of form.

Applying the formula in strict accord with the star rating system no selection could be made. SHERGAR was the obvious choice, but as 2–5 fav., a completely uneconomic betting proposition. The author having witnessed the poor showing of the current generation of 3-year-olds made MASTER WILLIE the selection choice especially at the odds of (7–1) appeared to belie his real chances.

Result: 1st SHERGAR (2–5 fav) 4lth

1987 *NEWMARKET 1 AUGUST 1981 (good)*

1.30—BROOKE BOND COFFEE CUP (Amateur Riders).
£2,000 added (£1,842). 1m. 4f. (14)   STALLS

1	(12)	20-4452 ASCOT AGAIN 11 R Mason 5-11-1	Ray Hutchinson	54
2	(13)	239/00-3 COOL DECISION 14 M Stoute 4-11-1	Corinne Hamer (5)	75
3	(11)	0U-0000 GWYNFI NI 10 K Bridgwater 5-11-1	K Bridgwater (5)	—
4	(7)	300-000 MERLANE 10 G Balding 6-11-1	Elin Guest	—
6	(8)	L/80-048 RAGAFAN 10 R Smyth 4-11-1	C Wood (5)	—
7	(14)	00/0890- TIP TOOL 408 W. Marshall 4-11-1	Amanda Marshall (5)	—
8	(9)	38LL-L7 WINDSOR WARRIOR 14 Peter Taylor 4-11-1	A Shenston (5)	56
10	(2)	LU957 BLUE EROTICA 9 D A Wilson 3-10-4	Brooke Sanders	—
13	(11)	9038-06 HATTAN 10 K Brassey 3-10-4	W Muir (5)	61
14	(10)	56-2 MORE OATS 14 (BF) G Harwood 3-10-4	A J Wilson	69
16	(3)	270228 SASS 12 P Kelleway 3-10-4	Gay Kelleway	•78
17	(4)	9-00000 SMITHY LANE 10 C Wildman 3-10-4	Margaret Fraser-Stuart (5)	—
18	(6)	347-LLO SOVEREIGN MUSTAPHA (B) 18 M Haynes 3-10-4	Yvonne Haynes (5)	61
19	(5)	54-8033 CAVORT 21 G P-Gordon 3-10-1	Elain Mellor	68

Probable S.P.: 7-4 Saas, 5-2 More Oats, 5 Cavort, 6 Ascot Again, 7 Cool Decision.

FAVOURITES: — — — — — — 3.

1980: Lone Raider, 3-10-11 (Miss F. Vittadini), 5-1, R. Boss, 14 ran.

Probables

14 (10) MORE OATS – G. Harwood 3.10.4 A. J. Wilson

     F.   F.   C. C.

     Prom   (14)   — D√

     ★★   ★★   J√

16 (3) SASS – P. Kelleway 3.10.4 Gay Kelleway

     F.   F.   C. C.

     P   (12)   — P?

     ★★★   ★★   J?

Analysis revealed two probables, MORE OATS and SASS. MORE OATS beaten in a mdn racing on his seasonal reappearance appeared to be the main rival to SASS who earlier in the season had run in the Derby but was yet to lose his maiden badge.

Applying the formula, SASS was made the selection choice.

Result: 1st SASS (11−4.) 4lth

2228 *SALISBURY 13 AUGUST 1981 (good)*

4.30—AMESBURY MAIDEN STAKES (3-Y.-O).
(Div. 1). £1,400 added (£1,189·30). 1m. (13) STALLS

1	(4)	9 ALDINGTON BOY 50 Mrs J Reavey 9-0	T Rogers	—
5	(3)	0-0205 AVENTURA 61 H Candy 9-0	P Waldron	61
11	(8)	99-700 FROGTOWN 5 G Harwood 9-0	G Starkey	—
15	(7)	43-2422 ICEN 14 M Smyly 9-0	R Curant	72
17	(13)	46-5080 MASQUERADER (B) 45 P Makin 9-0	Pat Eddery	62
24	(9)	747L57 ROCKETONE 26 C Benstead 9-0	B Rouse	—
25	(12)	623-4D2 RUSHMOOR 12 (BF2) W Hern 9-0	W Carson	●78
29	(11)	008-00 THE FLOORLAYER 17 D Elsworth 9-0	R Fox	—
32	(10)	00 BURFORD BELLE 49 W Wightman 8-11	B Raymond	—
40	(1)	700 MISS STREAKY 61 R Houghton 8-11	J Reid	56
41	(6)	34 PALATARA (B) 42 B Hills, 8-11	S Cauthen	56
42	(2)	754443 PATAS BLANCAS 8 G Lewis 8-11	G Sexton	64
47	(5)	680-LO SOVEREIGN SHOT 31 L Blanshard 8-11	R Cochrane	60

Probable S.P.: 8-13 Rushmoor, 7-2 Icen, Palatara, 10 Patas Blancas, 12 Frogtown, 16 Aventura.

1980: Mar del Plata, 8-11 (E. Johnson), 9-1, C. Brittain. 17 ran.

Probables

(25) (12) RUSHMOOR − W. Hern 9.0 W. Carson

F. F. C. C.

P (12) dr C√

★★★ ★★ D√

G√

J√

Analysis revealed one probable − RUSHMOOR − and this served as a perfect example of the rare pristine opportunities that befall the selector. RUSHMOOR had the proven form, was in fact a winner that had been disqualified, was therefore proven over the course and distance, now dropped in class after a recent race in higher class.

Applying the formula, RUSHMOOR had a five-star rating with all other factors positive.

Result: 1st RUSHMOOR (4−6 fav.)

These examples show how the formula was applied in practice to actual races. They demonstrate how a selection decision may be

225

reached by applying the criteria of the formula's star rating system to a list of probables or one probable. These examples illustrate the successes, failures and sometimes practical difficulties encountered as selection decisions were subjected to the scrutiny of the formula's objective assessment.

11 CONCLUSION

The conclusion to the selection is the race result. This is the inevitable moment of truth when the opinion of selection is tested against and forced to face the practical reality of the actual outcome of the race. It is an encounter that by its confirmation or denial will provide indisputable proof of a selector's ability successfully to apply the selection formula and gives rise to the post-race questions: 'How' and 'Why' did the horse win the race?

The question 'How' may be quickly answered; it is always because on the day at the time of the race the horse was the first to reach the winning post. The question 'Why', however, requires a fuller explanation, demanding a satisfactory and more detailed answer, especially when selection is formulated on the understanding that all events are the subject of cause and effect. The reasons why a horse may have won the race vary and can range from the almost inexplicable through to causes less incomprehensible but extremely rare (i.e. the freak occurrences which border the edges of possibility). In the majority of instances, the reasons for a horse winning will be found contained within the bounds of reasoned probability. This, therefore, allows a developing understanding to be achieved by closely referring race results to the factors that constitute the selection formula. The elements of the selection formula consistently can be identified, combined or singly, as the salient factors responsible for affecting the results of races. The power of reasoning probability is therefore seen to play a commanding role in the successful prediction of race results, and such realization sweeps aside the bafflement and mystery which can surround the outcome of events. The selector is then placed in the favourable position of being able, by using the selection formula, to assess objectively the issues pertaining to past and future races.

Although there are numerous ways of making a selection it is only by the constant use of a truly objective method that the backer can hope to remain detached when partaking in the act of betting. It is essential in the understanding of success and failure for the backer to retain an unemotional detatchment which will allow the selection betting process to be observed from a viewpoint of balance and calm. Intuitive powers and inspiration can undoubtedly play a part (sometimes to a good, devastating effect) in the acts of selection and betting, but they can never reliably replace the solid power of logical reasoning. The qualities of intuitive prediction (selection) should not be disregarded lightly or scorned, but their value realized for what it is – the spontaneous response to situations.

This cannot easily be resolved with the suggested approach which recommends that selection/betting always be a calculated act of limited emotion. Intuitive powers must be considered cautiously as they will not serve as a dependable basis for selection and therefore can be no substitute for the power of reasoning. Intuition as a finely developed faculty dispassionately assumes the role of another sense, but soon loses its pristine edge if it becomes regarded as an asset constantly to be exploited for profit. (This is why even the most inspired clairvoyant cannot or does not make fortunes from their predictions; once the idea of material gain enters and intrudes upon their consciousness, their mental energies will quickly become dissipated in the desire and pursuit of such ends.)

The initial clear intuitive insight quickly becomes clouded in confusion and self-delusion until the higher faculty of understanding is permanently or temporarily lost in the mundane chase for financial reward.

Successful betting, the profit-motivated exploitation of selection, has then always to be approached in a cool calculated objective fashion and its aims are best achieved by the use of the objective selection method provided in the selection formula.

The selection formula, although containing and packaged to display only the cold abstracted facts of the situation, can with imaginative translation swiftly transform to be the embodiment of the living events and acts it has represented. The selection formula therefore, ensures that, while retaining its qualities for objective assessment, it never loses contact with the flesh and blood issues it has encapsulated in names, numbers and symbols.

REFERENCES

Daily Mail: daily – national newspaper recommended by the author for racing coverage. (Associated Newspapers Group, Carmelite House, London EC4Y OJA. Tel. 01 353 6000.)

Directory of the Turf: bi-annual – biographical backgrounds of trainers, jockeys, owners, etc. (Pacemaker Publications Limited, P.O. Box 90, 642 Kings Road, London SW6 2DF. Tel. 01 731 4404; Postal subscriptions and orders to 20 Oxford Road, Newbury, Berks RG13 1PA.)

Raceform Up-to-Date: weekly – official form book; Flat-racing edition and National Hunt edition. (Raceform Limited, 55 Curzon Street, London W1. Tel: 01 499 4391; Postal subscriptions and orders to 2 York Road, Battersea, London SW11.)

Raceform Up-to-Date Flat Annual: annually, August. (Published by Raceform Limited – see above.)

The Sporting Life: daily – national daily racing paper. (Mirror Group Newspapers Limited, Orbit House, 9 New Fetter Lane, London EC4A 1AR. Tel. 01 353 0246.)

Timeform ('Black book'): weekly. (Timeform Publications, Timeform House, Northgate, Halifax, West Yorks HX1 1XE. Tel. 0422 63322.)

Timeform Racecards (Flat and National Hunt meetings): daily. (Published by Timeform Limited – see above.)

Racehorses of 19– (Flat): annually, March. (Published by Timeform Limited – see above.)

Chasers and Hurdlers (National Hunt): annually, October. (Published by Timeform Limited – see above.)

Trainers Record: annually – annual analysis of trainers' records, Flat and National Hunt edition. (Trainers Record, Melplash Farmhouse, Melplash, Bridport, Dorset DT6 3UH. Tel. 030888 383.)

Trainers Record Two-year Olds of 19–: annually – form-supplement analysis of each seasons 2 y.o. horses in training. (Published by Trainers Record – see above.)

FURTHER READING

Pacemaker: monthly racing magazine. (Pacemaker Publications Limited, P.O. Box 90, 642 Kings Road, London SW6 2DF. Tel. 01 731 4404; Postal subscriptions and orders to 20 Oxford Road, Newbury, Berks RG13 1PA.)

Racing Calendar: weekly – official Jockey Club record of entries; Stewards report; horses' official handicap rating, etc. (Weatherbys, Sanders Road, Wellingborough, Northants NN8 4BX. Tel. 0933 76241.)

Statistical Record: annual – details of sires' and dams' performances. (Published by Weatherbys – see above.)

The European Racehorse: quarterly racing publication. (Raceform Limited, 55 Curzon Street, London W1. Tel. 01 499 4391.)

INDEX

The numerals in **bold** type refer to the illustrations